ecpr PRESS

I0091177

Judicial Politics and International Cooperation
From Disputes to Deal-Making at the World Trade Organization

Arlo Poletti
Dirk De Bièvre

ecpr PRESS

© Arlo Poletti and Dirk De Bièvre 2016

First published by the ECPR Press in 2016

The ECPR Press is the publishing imprint of the European Consortium for Political Research (ECPR), a scholarly association, which supports and encourages the training, research and cross-national co-operation of political scientists in institutions throughout Europe and beyond.

ECPR Press
Harbour House
Hythe Quay
Colchester
CO2 8JF
United Kingdom

Typeset by Lapiz Digital Services

Printed and bound by Lightning Source

British Library Cataloguing in Publication Data

A catalogue record for this book is available from the British Library

HARDBACK ISBN: 978-1-785521-50-8
PAPERBACK ISBN: 978-1-785522-55-0
PDF ISBN: 978-1-785521-90-4
EPUB ISBN: 978-1-785521-91-1
KINDLE ISBN: 978-1-785521-92-8

www.ecpr.eu/ecprpress

ECPR Press Series Editors
Peter Kennealy (European University Institute)
Ian O'Flynn (Newcastle University)
Alexandra Segerberg (Stockholm University)
Laura Sudulich (University of Kent)

If you are interested in Judicial Politics you may like

Visions of Judicial Review: A Comparative Examination of Courts and Policy in Democracies
Benjamin Bricker
This book establishes a framework to consider the value of judicial review in modern democracy, grouping answers to this question into one of three main arguments, or 'visions' for judicial review: legalist; rights-protecting; and majoritarian.
Paperback ISBN 9781785521478

More in the ECPR Press Monographs series

Europeanised or European?
(ISBN: 9781785522321)
Sandra Kröger

Situating Governance
(ISBN: 9781907301681)
Antonino Palumbo

Democratic Reform and Consolidation: The Cases of Mexico and Turkey
(ISBN: 9781907301674)
Evren Celik Wiltse

Please visit http://www.ecpr.eu/ecprpress for information about new publications.

Table of Contents

List of Figures and Tables

Figures

Tables

Abbreviations

AB	Appellate body
AMS	Aggregate measurement of support
CAP	Common agricultural policy
CBD	Convention on biological diversity
CEFIC	European Chemical Industry Council
COPA-COGECA	European Farmers and Agro-Cooperatives Organisation
DG	Directorate general
DS	Dispute settlement
DSM	Dispute settlement mechanism
EFPIA	European Federation of Pharmaceutical Industries and Associations
ESF	European Services Forum
EU	European Union
EUROFER	European Confederation of Iron and Steel Industries
FAO	UN Food and Agriculture Organization
FTA	Foreign Trade Association
GATS	General Agreement on Trade in Services
GATT	General Agreement on Tariffs and Trade
GM	Genetically modified
GMO	Genetically modified organism
GVC	Global value chain
IPR	Intellectual property rights
ISIC	International standard industrial classification of all economic activities
MC	Ministerial conference
MFN	Most favoured nation
NCPI	New commercial policy instrument
NGO	Non-governmental organisation
PTA	Preferential trade agreement
SCM	Subsidies and countervailing measures
TBR	Trade barriers regulation
TRIPS	Agreement on trade-related aspects of intellectual property rights
UNAIDS	Joint UN programme on HIV/AIDS
UNICE	Union of Industrial and Employers' Confederations of Europe

UPOV	International Union for the Protection of New Varieties of Plants
URAA	Uruguay Round Agreement on Agriculture
US	United States
WHO	World Health Organization
WIPO	World Intellectual Property Organization
WTO	World Trade Organization

Preface

This book originates from our common research activities on judicial politics in the World Trade Organization (WTO). Throughout the last few years, we have worked together and individually on different aspects of the political economy of WTO judicial politics. In this book, we discuss one particular aspect of this interesting research agenda: the relationship between judicial politics and multilateral trade negotiations. Scholars in political science have devoted a great deal of attention to the political economy of WTO disputes. This is a growing and important research agenda and we have ourselves sought to contribute to it in different ways. A less studied, and yet in our view perhaps more important, issue concerns the systemic effects of the centrality acquired by judicial politics in the multilateral trading system. Has judicial politics made cooperation in the form of negotiated comprehensive multilateral trade deals more or less likely in the WTO? While judicial politics are crucial to determine whether and under which conditions WTO members comply with existing commonly agreed rules, it is at least equally important to ask ourselves whether judicial politics have acted as a motor or as an impediment for further trade liberalisation commitments in the WTO. In short, given the emergence of judicial politics as a central feature of the multilateral trading system and the steep decline in the WTO's ability to deliver negotiated trade liberalisation, this book advances innovative arguments and presents original evidence to shed light on the important, and surprisingly under-researched, question of whether, and if so how, judicial politics has affected the prospects for cooperation in the WTO through multilateral trade rounds.

Our analysis covers both cooperation on the elimination of traditional, at-the-border barriers to trade, as well as on newer, behind-the-border regulation, showing how these interact very differently with the strong judicial institutions of the organisation. We furthermore explore how strong enforcement of rules in the WTO affects international forum choices in a fundamental way, and how international judicial politics trigger specialisation in domestic interest mobilisation. Whereas we have consistently pursued research on these issues, driven by our curiosity and scientific explanatory take on them, we also believe that insight into the interactions between the legislative and the judicial arm of this important international organisation can also inform actual policymaking, as well as its limits.

Our fruitful and intense research collaboration started at the Lisbon Joint Sessions of Workshops of the European Consortium for Political Research (ECPR) in 2009, where we both contributed to a workshop convened by Andreas Dür and Manfred Elsig. Shortly afterwards, we applied for and obtained an international cooperation grant to work on the political–economic implications of judicial politics in the WTO. This grant from the Antwerp University Research Council enabled Arlo Poletti to join the Department of Political Science of the University of Antwerp as a post-doctoral researcher in the research group Antwerp Centre for Institutions and Multilevel Politics. Dirk De Bièvre had started a research agenda on this broad topic a few years earlier, first at the Max Planck Institute for Research on Collective Goods in Bonn, obtaining a Volkswagen Foundation grant taken up at the University of Mannheim. Arlo Poletti had just obtained his PhD through a comprehensive study of the trade politics in multilateral trade negotiations at the University of Bologna and, as a next step in his research, he was keen to explore the causal links connecting the institutional design features of the WTO and the politics of multilateral trade negotiations. Joining forces seemed like an excellent idea, and, after a further series of grant applications, we were able to push this research agenda forward, providing the basis for a research collaboration that is still very much alive and that continued even as Arlo Poletti moved to the LUISS Guido Carli University in 2013. This book brings together in a comprehensive and systematic fashion both a number of arguments we have explored in the past and some entirely new ones.

During all these years, much of the theoretical and empirical contents of this book has been discussed at various conferences, workshops, and seminars. We are grateful to all the colleagues who offered their input on these various occasions. While it is impossible to provide a detailed list of all these colleagues, we would like to thank here those among them who read and commented on earlier drafts of the manuscript or earlier research drafts on which the manuscript builds: Leonardo Baccini, Andreas Dür, Jappe Eckhardt, Manfred Elsig, Bart Kerremans, Soo Yeon Kim, Petros Mavroidis, Jean-Frédéric Morin, and Alasdair Young. Special thanks also to Jan Willem Burgers for his English-language check.

We would like to gratefully acknowledge the financial support of the Research Council of the University of Antwerp, provided for the post-doctoral research project *Cooperating in the shadow of the law: judicialization and the expansion of WTO reach* and the post-doctoral research project jointly financed with the National Bank of Belgium *When litigation turns into trade liberalization: judicialization in the World Trade Organization and trade liberalization by the European Union.* We are also grateful to the Research Foundation Flanders (FWO) for funding for Arlo Poletti's post-doctoral fellowship for the research project *Investigating how latent and actual disputes can remove barriers to trade.* Furthermore, the FWO and the Antwerp Research Council jointly funded a research sabbatical and leave of absence for research and writing for Dirk De Bièvre during the academic year 2014–15.

Arlo Poletti would also like to thank the Department of Political Science and the School of Government of the LUISS Guido Carli for the support provided to his research since he joined this academic institution in 2013, in particular Professor Sergio Fabbrini, the Director of the School of Government of the LUISS Guido Carli, for his critical support and intellectual stimulus.

We would also like to acknowledge that some of the arguments and empirical evidence we present in the book have appeared in the following journal articles: De Bièvre, Dirk, Arlo Poletti, Marcel Hanegraaff, and Jan Beyers (2016) 'International institutions and interest mobilization: the WTO and lobbying in

EU and US trade policy', *Journal of World Trade*; Poletti, Arlo, Dirk De Bièvre, and Marcel Hanegraaff (2016), 'WTO judicial politics and European Union trade policy: business associations as vessels of special interests?', *British Journal of Politics and International Relations*; Poletti, Arlo, Dirk De Bièvre, and Tyson Chatagnier (2015), 'Cooperation in the shadow of WTO law: why litigate when you can negotiate', *World Trade Review*, 14(Supplement1): 33–58; De Bièvre, Dirk, Arlo Poletti, and Lars Thomann (2014), 'To enforce or not to enforce? WTO judicialization, forum shopping and global regulatory harmonization', *Regulation & Governance,* Vol. 8 (3), pp. 269–86. We are grateful to our co-authors in these articles for authorising us to use some of the material we produced together in this book.

On a more personal note, Arlo Poletti would like to thank his wife Silvia for her continuous and patient support, and he would like to dedicate this research endeavour to his three daughters: Amelia, Lucia, and Daria. Dirk De Bièvre in turn gives his thanks to his wife Ingeborg for accompanying him through all the highs and lows of intellectual and academic life, and for joining in the intellectual and personal friendship with Arlo that has made writing this book together such a wonderful experience.

Rome and Antwerp

December 2015

Chapter One

Introduction

This book aims to assess whether, and if so how, judicial politics in the World Trade Organization (WTO) affect the dynamics of lawmaking through multilateral trade rounds. The institutional structure of the international trade regime performs both a legislative function in the form of recurrent multilateral trade negotiations and an adjudicative function through the dispute settlement mechanism (DSM). With regards to the former role, the WTO provides a forum for bargaining and agreeing upon new rules and commitments for the multilateral liberalisation of international trade. With regards to the latter role, the WTO possesses the necessary enforcement mechanisms to foster compliance with any rules that have been agreed. While the WTO increasingly seems unable to steer a way towards broad multilateral trade deals to bring down tariff and non-tariff barriers to trade, the DSM is widely regarded as a well-functioning mechanism, one that largely fosters compliance with existing multilateral trade rules and acts as a buffer against protectionist policies. The multilateral trade regime has, thus, evolved in two distinct ways over the last two decades: legislative trade liberalisation has weakened, while judicial trade liberalisation has strengthened.

The remarkable decline in the WTO's ability to deliver negotiated trade liberalisation has certainly contributed to making judicial trade liberalisation more central to the multilateral trading system. As the members of the multilateral trade regime have found it more and more difficult to find common ground in the setting up of new multilateral commitments for the liberalisation of international trade, the judicial arm of the WTO has gradually become more prominent in advancing trade liberalisation. While this 'conventional' explanation for the rise in judicial trade liberalisation is plausible and has merit, we believe that understanding the current WTO's inability to perform its legislative functions also requires a systematic investigation of the reverse causal pathways between a stronger enforcement of rules and the politics of lawmaking through multilateral trade deals.

While arguments belonging to the 'conventional' camp abound, such reverse causal pathways have surprisingly received only scant attention. Since the creation of the WTO in 1995, the so-called politics of WTO dispute settlement have been the subject of a rich and growing body of scholarly literature. However, we believe our knowledge of judicial politics in the WTO remains far from comprehensive. More specifically, while we seem to know a lot about how the WTO dispute settlement mechanism works, the existing literature has overlooked the less visible, but perhaps more important, question of whether, and if so how, the creation of strong enforcement mechanisms has influenced cooperation among the members of the multilateral trade regime. Has the strengthening of the enforcement mechanisms of the WTO decreased the likelihood that the members of the multilateral trade regime will reach multilateral trade agreements?

In this book, we address this question starting from the core assumption that policy can be understood as the result of calculated choices made by political and economic actors. When considering the impact of judicial politics on the WTO's ability to perform its legislative functions, we thus believe in the necessity of looking into how judicial politics interact with the trade-related interests of domestic actors, by affecting their preferences, resources, and incentives to mobilise politically and demand that governments act on their behalf. Hence, this book investigates three broad and interrelated issues: (1) the impact of judicial politics on the preferences of the WTO members' trade-related domestic actors in relation to agreements for the reduction of tariff barriers to trade; (2) the impact of judicial politics on the preferences of the WTO members' trade-related domestic actors in relation to agreements for the harmonisation of regulatory barriers to trade; and (3) the impact of judicial politics on the organisational format of the representation of domestic trade-related interests. The central claim of this book is that the judicialisation of the WTO has influenced the domestic politics of WTO members in systematic ways and ultimately has affected their willingness and ability to further pursue multilateral trade liberalisation in the form of broadly negotiated multilateral trade deals.

The legislation – adjudication nexus in the WTO

Our analysis starts with the simple empirical observation that a fundamental tension currently characterises the multilateral trade regime. In 2009, on the eve of the fifteenth anniversary of the creation of the WTO, the Director General of the WTO Pascal Lamy declared,

> [T]he WTO earlier this month reached the milestone of having the 400th trade dispute brought to the body's dispute settlement mechanism. ... This is surely a vote of confidence in a system which many consider to be a role model for the peaceful resolution of disputes in other areas of international political or economic relations. ... The dispute settlement system is widely considered to be the jewel in the crown of the WTO. ... Members agree that, as the bedrock of the multilateral trading system, the dispute settlement system will not be subject to any seismic shift in its fundamental structure as a result of the Members' deliberations (WTO 2009).

As this quote nicely summarises, with the establishment of the WTO in 1995, members of the trade regime created a quasi-judicial mechanism for the enforcement of rules that, by any standard, can be considered highly successful. Of course, this system has not been impermeable to problems and critique. As the famous disputes on the European Union (EU)'s bans on imports of genetically modified crops and hormone-treated beef, or the dispute on United States (US) cotton subsidies, have shown, a few WTO disputes have proven particularly intractable; these are highly politicised and the source of both heated domestic political debates and diplomatic tensions. Yet, despite these notable exceptions, the DSM of the WTO has been remarkably successful as an enforcement mechanism of existing multilateral trade rules.

For all these successes, however, the emergence of judicial politics as a central feature of the multilateral trading system has gone hand in hand with a steep decline in the WTO's ability to deliver negotiated trade liberalisation. As Goldstein and Steinberg (2009: 218) nicely put it, 'for those favouring rapid and deeper liberalization, the WTO's biggest contemporary problem is an inability to gain consensus on a negotiated outcome. Stalemate in multilateral trade negotiations is the order of the day.' Despite the absence of strong enforcement mechanisms for rules, the General Agreement on Tariffs and Trade (GATT) system was very successful in fostering bargaining processes for the elimination and/or reduction of barriers to trade among the members of the multilateral trade regime. In the period spanning the adoption of the GATT in 1947 to the conclusion of the Uruguay Round in 1994, the members of the trade regime were able to successfully conclude eight rounds of multilateral trade negotiations, which contributed to bringing down tariff barriers on manufactured goods from an average of 40 per cent in 1947 to an average of 4 per cent in 1995, brought the particularly difficult issue of trade in agricultural goods into the realm of multilateral trade rules, and expanded the WTO's scope to include a wide array of regulatory issues traditionally confined within the boundaries of domestic governance.

With the successful conclusion of the Uruguay Round, however, the capacity of the multilateral trade regime to perform its legislative function seems to have come to a halt. In November 2001, the Doha Development Round was launched with great fanfare. It promised to bring about a broad legislated trade deal that would significantly deepen existing commitments for the reduction of barriers to trade in service, agricultural, and manufactured goods, and the protection of intellectual property rights (IPRs), as well as to further expand the WTO's regulatory reach on issues such as government procurement, trade facilitation, competition, and environmental protection. Despite these ambitions, the Bali 2013 agreement's narrow focus on trade facilitation illustrates that the Doha Round failed to produce a significant move forward in multilateral trade liberalisation. As a result of the WTO's inability in this regard, members of the multilateral trade regime have largely shifted to bilateral and regional deal making in trade diplomacy.

In short, the developments that have characterised the multilateral trade regime in the last two decades suggest that WTO lawmaking has moved out of the legislative venue of the member states and into the courtroom (Goldstein and Steinberg 2009). That is, concomitantly with judicial politics gaining centre stage in multilateral trade governance, legislative trade liberalisation in the form of negotiated multilateral trade deals has gone out of business.

Are these two processes connected in some way? The conventional wisdom posits that the causal arrow goes from the crisis of legislative lawmaking to the strengthening of judicial lawmaking. According to this view, judicial politics have become a central feature of the multilateral trade regime *because* of the failure of multilateral trade negotiations. The increased heterogeneity of WTO members' preferences due to the rising number of member states, the politicisation of trade policymaking brought about by the inclusion of regulatory issues in the WTO's agenda, and the ability of rising economic powers, such as China, India and Brazil, to sustain a common and unified position in the Doha Round have all been considered key factors to explain the stalemate of multilateral trade deal making (De Bièvre and Poletti 2014).

While these factors have certainly been important in making bargaining in the Doha Round a more complicated business than in previous trade rounds, it is worth investigating whether, and if so to what extent, the WTO has become unable to perform its legislative function *precisely* because it has equipped itself with stronger enforcement mechanisms. In fact, the argument about the existence of systematic causal links between the creation of strengthened enforcement mechanisms and multilateral deal making in the WTO is not new. In a seminal article published a year before the Doha Round was even launched, Goldstein and Martin (2000) warned us about the potential downsides of judicial politics. They suggested that, while strengthening enforcement mechanisms could enhance the WTO's ability to bring about compliance with existing rules, it could also bring about unintended effects that interfere with the pursuit of progressive liberalisation through multilateral trade agreements.

Have the predictions of these authors been correct? Have the members of the WTO gone too far in putting in place a quasi-judicial system of rule enforcement? Addressing these questions is not only key to advancing the scholarly debate on how international institutions can foster cooperation in an anarchical system that lacks centralised enforcement; it is also crucial from a real-world perspective, particularly for the stakeholders involved in the policy debate about how global trade governance should look in the time to come. Should we expect a permanent demise in negotiated trade liberalisation at the WTO? If judicial politics indeed work as a systematic impediment on the path towards broad multilateral trade deal making, we might as well say goodbye to the system that so successfully liberalised global trade for more than half a century. In that case, we should get ready to deal with a world in which the WTO merely serves as a system that can at best incentivise compliance with existing global trade rules and accept that lawmaking will take place primarily in other fora. Most likely, then, we should come to terms with the fact that Preferential Trade Agreements (PTAs) will be the only hothouse in which tomorrow's negotiated trade liberalisation is going to take place (Mavroidis 2015). On the other hand, if one were to find that judicial politics do not necessarily make WTO members shy away from negotiated trade liberalisation, future global trade governance may turn out to be one in which new forms of negotiated trade liberalisation, such as through PTAs, can coexist with multilateral trade deals constructed under the auspices of the WTO.

This book addresses the important, and surprisingly under-researched, question of whether, and if so how, judicial politics have affected the prospects for cooperation in the WTO. Has judicialisation made WTO members more or less prone to further cooperation, either by deepening existing commitments or by expanding the WTO's reach to a host of new issue areas? Ultimately, has the strengthening of the WTO's enforcement mechanisms increased or decreased the likelihood that it will remain the central international institutional venue for negotiated multilateral trade liberalisation?

Research question(s)

International institutions are often equipped with enforcement mechanisms. Of course, there is wide variation in the design of international institutions when it comes to this particular dimension. Some institutions completely lack any form of enforcement mechanism and have to rely on voluntary cooperation from their members, while others can rely on sophisticated and effective enforcement mechanisms. Theories tend to account for this particular design feature of international institutions by tracing it back to the need to put in place mechanisms to reduce incentives to renege on agreed rules and to reduce uncertainty about compliance (Keohane 1984; Martin 1992). In line with the classical portrayal in the cooperation literature of international trade policy as a prisoner's dilemma, the establishment of the DSM in the international trade regime should be considered as crucial to fostering compliance by decreasing the incentives to cheat and to revert to protectionist trade strategies.

However, international cooperation theory has long noted that the effects of credible enforcement mechanisms for the rules of international institutions are not just limited to making compliance with existing rules more likely. The existence of a strong enforcement mechanism also casts a shadow on the processes of cooperation. The prospect of credible and rigid enforcement of rules can actually make agreements more difficult to reach (Fearon 1998) or it can lead to shallow commitments (Downs et al. 1996), particularly when uncertainty about the future preferences of the actors involved in the bargaining process is high (Koremenos et al. 2001). This is so because, under conditions of uncertainty, cooperators value institutional flexibility to make sure that, if needed, they will be able to renege on agreed commitments without paying a cost.

These insights are particularly relevant for the analysis of an institutional context such as the multilateral trade regime in which mechanisms of enforcement cast a constant shadow on processes of lawmaking in the form of negotiated trade deals. The reform of the dispute settlement mechanism that came with the creation of the WTO should be expected to have significantly changed the context within which members of the trade regime decide upon new commitments and, thus, to have affected the likelihood that existing cooperation can be deepened and/or expanded.

Building on the fundamental insight that the degree of enforceability of prospective agreements is a key factor in the calculations actors make when deciding to commit to any agreement, we set out to investigate how the judicialisation of the WTO has affected the dynamics of cooperation in the international trade regime. However, we depart from standard analyses in cooperation theory in one important respect. We believe that an appreciation of these effects requires moving beyond a perspective that considers states as unitary actors. As Goldstein and Martin (2000: 603) rightly point out, 'domestic politics cannot be treated as an extraneous or as an irrational source of error that obstructs the purposes of legalization (*or judicialization*). Instead, politics operates in systematic ways and is the mechanism through which legalization (*or judicialization*) exerts its effects.' We therefore address whether, and if so how, judicial politics affect the prospects of lawmaking in the WTO by investigating their effects on the domestic politics of trade policymaking.

Our approach is in line with standard international political economy approaches. We conceive of governments' choices over trade policies as the result of the preferences and political pressures emanating from key economic interest groups within society, which are largely defined as a result of a rational calculation about the expected distributional consequences of cooperative agreements (De Bièvre and Dür 2005; Frieden 1991; Milner 1988; Rogowski 1989). On this basis, we address three broad questions and develop four sets of arguments.

The first question we address is how the greater enforcement of rules has affected the propensity of WTO members to commit to further reductions in tariff barriers to trade. Early accounts of the likely long-term effects of strengthened rule enforcement on processes of cooperation in the WTO argued that the prospects for further liberalisation in the WTO looked rather bleak. Judicialisation, it was argued, would lead to better information about the distributional consequences of trade agreements and, thus, empower protectionists relative to free traders. This would ultimately undermine the ability of the WTO to continue performing its legislative function, by reducing the incentives of domestic groups to support their governments in concluding new multilateral trade agreements for the further elimination and/or reduction of tariff barriers to trade (Goldstein and Martin 2000). At first glance, the failure of the Doha Round to produce a significant move forward in multilateral trade liberalisation, epitomised by the Bali 2013 mini-agreement on trade facilitation, would seem to provide straightforward evidence in favour of these claims. A closer look at the bargaining dynamics of the Doha Round, however, reveals that a systematic empowerment of protectionist forces across the board has not taken place. Some WTO members have actually pushed quite hard for a successful conclusion of negotiations, defending quite strongly the domestic constituencies who favour the opening up of foreign markets, even at the cost of making painful concessions that would entail significant losses for allegedly powerful domestic protectionist constituencies. These multifaceted dynamics of trade politics suggest that a more nuanced view is required about the effects of judicialisation on the preferences of domestic trade-related interests over agreements for the reduction and/or elimination of tariff barriers to trade.

The second question we address is whether, and if so how, the greater enforcement of rules has affected the propensity of WTO members to commit to a further broadening of the WTO's regulatory reach. The WTO is no longer exclusively a venue for the negotiation of commitments on the elimination of tariff barriers to trade. As tariff trade barriers have come down to low average levels for many sectors in the last half-century, the WTO has increasingly become a key global forum for the negotiation of new rules aimed at reducing barriers to international trade through regulatory cooperation over a wide array of issues. A crucial question is therefore also whether, and if so how, judicialisation has affected the capacity of the WTO to promote processes of international regulatory cooperation. At first glance, one might expect the issue to divide developed and developing countries, with the former group wishing to widen the WTO's regulatory scope because of the enhanced credibility of commitments brought about by judicialisation and the latter group fiercely resisting such a move for precisely the same reason. Yet, this is not in accordance with the preferences of members over regulatory harmonisation that have been observed before and during the Doha Round. Neither developed nor developing countries have had stable preferences over the inclusion of new regulatory issues in the WTO, at times resisting them and at other times welcoming them. Again, more systematic arguments are needed to grasp the causal links between judicial politics and the domestic politics underpinning WTO members' viewpoints over the expansion of the WTO's regulatory reach.

Both the first and second questions above can also not be fully answered without taking into account how the 'shadow of WTO law' has affected WTO members' preferences during negotiations on tariff and non-tariff barriers to trade. The interactions between the adjudicative and legislative functions of the WTO are perhaps more evident when one considers that, in current multilateral trade negotiations, WTO members often negotiate multilateral trade rules from a position of legal vulnerability; that is, they engage in multilateral negotiations while foreign partners can credibly threaten to resort and sometimes actually do resort to WTO litigation against them. Journalists' accounts, policy-oriented research, and even scholarly studies on the Doha Round of multilateral trade negotiations all stress the importance of the 'shadow of WTO law'. The threat and the actual use of litigation have been key determinants of the policy preferences, bargaining strategies, and tactics of members regarding a wide range of issues prior to and during the Doha Round. We therefore investigate in a systematic and theoretically informed way whether, and if so under what conditions and how, the decision by one WTO member to threaten to, or actually, initiate a legal dispute against another affects cooperative dynamics in the context of WTO negotiations on tariff and non-tariff trade barriers.

The third and final broad question that we address in this book is to what extent the creation of a stronger enforcement mechanism of agreed rules has affected lobbying patterns in trade policymaking. Judicialisation not only influences the balance between protectionists and free traders on tariff liberalisation and regulatory harmonisation. The institutional reform of the WTO dispute settlement system has also affected the way in which these interests are aggregated and represented. If it is true that policymakers largely represent the interests of key economic constituencies in societies, then the way in which interests are aggregated and represented crucially influences the ability of the WTO to perform its legislative functions.

Structure of the book

The book aims to answer the three broad questions discussed above with a view to developing a comprehensive analysis of the causal mechanisms linking judicial politics and lawmaking in the WTO. The book is organised as follows.

Chapter Two engages in a thorough discussion of the key concepts employed throughout the subsequent analyses and introduces the main arguments that will be developed throughout the book. In particular, the chapter describes the political system of the multilateral trade regime, takes stock of the literature on the politics of WTO settlement, and discusses the existing scholarly debate about the causal mechanisms acting between judicial politics and negotiated trade liberalisation in the WTO. In this broader context, the chapter sets out to distinguish between two concepts employed in the literature to describe the international processes of rule making and rule enforcement: legalisation and judicialisation. Both concepts denote an increased degree of enforceability of previously agreed rules. Yet, the two terms can be usefully employed to analyse two distinct properties of this evolution. The term legalisation is generally used to cover the broad social phenomenon of an increase in the use of formal–legal rules to regulate a particular domain, *in casu* trade. It suggests an increase in the degree of precision, obligation, and bindingness of the rules, as well as an increase in enforceability through adjudication by an independent third party. The term judicialisation refers more specifically to this latter aspect, namely the increase in enforceability through adjudication and the authorisation of sanctions by an independent third party. The terms legalisation and judicialisation are thus not entirely synonymous, but rather allow us to distinguish the broad process of increasingly subjecting trade matters to legally binding rules from the ways in which judicial institutions help enforce those rules. We explain that we work mostly with the concept of judicialisation because we are primarily interested in exploring the increasingly important phenomenon of strong enforceability of agreed rules in international trade relations.

Chapter Three discusses the question of how the judicialisation of the WTO has affected its members' propensity to commit to a further reduction of tariff barriers to trade. The discussion developed in this chapter takes issue with the argument that judicialisation reduces the incentives of domestic groups to conclude new multilateral trade agreements for the further elimination and/or reduction of tariff barriers to trade, as a result of the better information about the distributional consequences of trade agreements. More specifically, the chapter discusses cases in which these predictions have been shown to be inaccurate and advances the argument that the effects of judicialisation depend on the balance of interests in a given country in a given period of time. Greater enforcement of trade rules may well have the effect of empowering protectionists relative to free traders if the constellation of interests in that country is one in which exporters are already fully mobilised and import-competing firms are not. But it can also lead to the opposite outcome in cases in which protectionist interests dominate the domestic politics of trade. We support our argument with empirical evidence about patterns of political mobilisation in major trading countries concerning negotiations for the liberalisation of services and manufactured goods in the Doha Round.

Chapter Four investigates whether, and if so how, greater enforcement of rules has affected the propensity of WTO members to commit to a further broadening of the WTO's regulatory reach. This chapter offers an argument to systematically account for the variety of members' preferences that we observe regarding whether to pursue processes of regulatory cooperation in the WTO. More specifically, we argue that WTO members' preferences should be understood as a function of their level of domestic regulation and the type of regulatory harmonisation they wish to engage in. We show how these expectations hold by way of two in-depth case studies of WTO negotiations concerning regulatory harmonisation: on intellectual property rights and on environmental regulation.

Chapter Five addresses the question of how the legal vulnerability of members' domestic policies affects the prospects for cooperation in the trade regime. First, we show that, contrary to conventional wisdom, increased enforcement does not necessarily make actors shy away from further cooperation. Legal vulnerability can ignite a positive dynamic of cooperation because it can increase the set of feasible agreements for WTO members. Next, we set out how the nature of the issue at stake – that is, whether it can be easily disaggregated into negotiable units – crucially determines whether this positive dynamic of cooperation takes place. We illustrate the cogency of the argument by way of four in-depth case studies. The first two cases concern negotiations on the reduction of tariffs and on domestic support schemes regarding agricultural trade, typical cases of divisible issues. We show how the potential for, as well as the actual use of, legal disputes on agricultural policies between the US and the EU on the one hand and Brazil on the other has influenced their approach to agricultural trade negotiations in the Doha Round. In the two other cases, we consider indivisible issues, namely negotiations over the WTO-incompatible practice of zeroing in US antidumping policy, as challenged by Japan and the EU, as well as trade-and-environment negotiations between the EU and the US.

Finally, Chapter Six investigates how the creation of a stronger enforcement mechanism of agreed rules has affected patterns of lobbying in trade policymaking and how changes in these patterns have affected the ability of the WTO to perform its legislative function. In this chapter, we argue that the institutional structure of the WTO regime is key to understanding how interests get aggregated and represented. More specifically, we argue that the institutional setting of issue-linkage based trade negotiations creates incentives for firms to work through broad sector-wide lobbying organisations, while judicialised adjudication and enforcement in WTO dispute settlement stimulates the de-linkage of issues, and incentivises product-specific interest aggregation. We demonstrate how these two insights can explain the co-existence of both sector-wide and product-specific lobbying in the contemporary international trade regime. To corroborate our claims, the chapter provides evidence on interest aggregation for US- and EU-initiated WTO disputes, and on the EU and US domestic interest organisations that mobilise during multilateral trade rounds or are present at WTO ministerial conferences.

Chapter Two

Judicial Politics and the Litigation-Negotiation Nexus

Few would question that international institutions have become a central feature of contemporary international relations. To a greater or lesser extent, virtually all economic, political and social activities are now subject to rules decided upon, implemented, monitored and enforced by international institutions of various sorts. Domestic institutions have, of course, not gone out of business. The bulk of the regulatory process is still carried out by actors placed within the traditional boundaries of nation states. Yet, it is beyond doubt that elements of the regulatory process have increasingly migrated to the international level. Areas as diverse as trade, finance, the environment, human rights and even national security are more and more subjected to rules developed under the auspices of international institutions (Mattli and Woods 2009).

These international institutions vary a great deal. Some international institutions have a global reach and include virtually all existing states, while others have a membership that is explicitly restricted to particular subsets of states. International institutions also vary greatly in their scope, with some focusing on single issues while others regulate multiple issue areas (Hooghe and Marks 2014). Finally, some international institutions are designed to allow for a high degree of participation by non-state actors, while participation in others is strictly restricted to public officials (Tallberg *et al.* 2014).

In addition to these important dimensions, international institutions also vary hugely in the extent to which they impose constraints on the behaviour of governments. As widely acknowledged, international governance has witnessed a steady rise of legalisation in recent years (Goldstein *et al.* 2000). In a wide array of issues areas, states have increasingly subjected themselves to binding international legal constraints. In the most institutionalised forms of legalisation precise and obligatory legal commitments are backed up by effective and credible enforcement mechanisms. International governance has thus not only witnessed a move to governance by law, but also a flourishing of international tribunals and courts with powers largely independent of the states that established them (Alter 2012; Hooghe *et al.* 2013; Posner and Yoo 2005). While the world has not moved towards a single judicial system that resembles a domestic hierarchical judiciary, some international institutions are today characterised by a high degree of judicialisation; that is, they have established precise, obligatory and binding legal commitments in combination with credible enforcement mechanisms in the form of compulsory third party adjudication to resolve disputes and foster compliance.

Is this increasing judicialisation of international institutions good news for cooperation in international relations? There are two ways to address this question. The first, and more intuitive, is to assess whether these enforcement mechanisms make compliance with the rules by the states that have established them more likely. Logic and empirical evidence suggest that the answer to this question should be affirmative. In order to understand the probability of compliance with the rules embedded in international institutions one must consider the interaction of law with the probability of enforcement (Davis 2012). The stronger the enforcement mechanisms in place, the higher the probability of strict compliance. Moreover, a host of empirical studies has shown that institutions which possess stronger enforcement mechanisms indeed tend to induce greater compliance with agreed upon rules relative to those that rely on weak enforcement mechanisms (Tallberg and McCall Smith 2014; Zangl 2008; Zangl *et al.* 2012).

A second, and perhaps more fundamental, way to address this question is to assess whether the rise of judicial politics in international relations makes states more or less willing to further their cooperative arrangements. As regime theory has long taught us, international institutions can act as mechanisms to regularise interactions and play repeated games, which often leads to an amending or expansion of the initial cooperative arrangements. To put it simply, international institutions often also perform a legislative function. It gives the states that have created them a forum for bargaining which might lead to the adoption of new rules and to a deepening and an expansion of their mutual commitments. To paraphrase a seminal article of a couple of decades ago (Downs *et al.* 1996), the question is not only whether the rise of judicial politics in international politics is good news for compliance, but also whether the good news about compliance is good news for cooperation.

The WTO is an important case for assessing how judicial politics affects the prospects of cooperation in international relations. It is the most notable example of an international political system in which a quasi-judicial system for the enforcement of rules has been put in place to integrate and back up an already existing and highly successful institutional structure for deal-making, namely the multilateral trade rounds which had been the backbone of the trade regime since the creation of the GATT. As two decades have now passed since the DSM was put into place, it is time to take stock of whether, and if so how, the strengthening of enforcement mechanisms has exerted systematic effects on the international trade regime's ability to perform its legislative function.

The political system of the multilateral trade regime

Contemporary multilateral trade relations are governed by a stable and highly institutionalised international regime, the WTO. Created in 1995 as the successor to the GATT, which had been adopted in 1947 in the aftermath of World War II, the WTO governance system can be broken down into three components: a set of rules and commitments, a negotiating forum, and an institutional location for dispute settlement. The WTO embodies a set of principles and fundamental rules that provides the overarching legal framework under which trade relations should be carried out. While the principle of market liberalism, or the desirability of trade liberalisation, provides the underlying rationale for the entire system, the principle of non-discrimination gives market liberalism operational meaning. For an open international trading system to operate efficiently, members should not be allowed to provide special treatment to some trading partners at the expense of others. The Most Favoured Nation (MFN) and National Treatment clauses contained, respectively, in Articles 1 and 3 of the GATT translate the non-discrimination principle into binding legal commitments. The former article mandates that members of the regime automatically extend any privileges granted to individual members to all others, while the latter prohibits treating national producers more favourably than foreign ones.

Besides embodying these broad principles and rules that form the foundation of the multilateral trading system, the WTO performs two distinct functions. The institutional structure of the international trade regime has both a legislative function in the form of recurrent multilateral trade negotiations and an adjudicative function through the dispute settlement mechanism.

Since the inception of the GATT in 1947, the structure of reciprocal concessions in multilateral trade rounds has been the cornerstone of the regime. Trade rounds have for a long time essentially consisted of a series of deals aimed at lowering and eliminating tariffs to trade in industrial goods through reciprocal concessions. In the early phase of the GATT system, these reciprocal tariff reduction agreements consisted of deals struck bilaterally on a product-by-product basis (Jupille *et al.* 2013; Gowa and Kim 2005). This means that multilateral trade liberalisation in the trade regime was achieved thanks to bilateral agreements on market access that were extended to all members of the trade regime by virtue of the MFN. In the early phase of the GATT, the decision-making logic was therefore bilateral whereas the policy outcomes were multilateral (Martin 1992).

When members of the trade regime seek to coordinate their positions on general rules, particularly on matters of regulation, but also on questions of institutional design, the decision-making logic that applies is no longer bilateral but moves in the direction of multilateral consensus. As average tariff barriers to trade in manufactured goods were reduced to low levels, members of the trade regime started to realise that significant barriers to trade persisted in the form of distinct domestic regulatory practices. Hence, the international trade agenda has increasingly expanded into regulatory issues that have traditionally been within the scope of domestic institutions, and the need for multilateral consensus has, thus, become increasingly important over time. While the issue of non-tariff barriers first came onto the international trade agenda during the Tokyo Round (1973–9), it is the Uruguay Round (1986–94) that marked a real qualitative leap in the nature of cooperation in the trade regime. With the Uruguay Round and the creation of the WTO, cooperation in the trade regime forcefully moved beyond the traditional realm of negative integration by introducing positive obligations to adopt new measures in a host of different areas such as services, intellectual property rights, investments, technical standards and food safety and animal health issues (De Bièvre 2004). This form of market integration introduced regulation in areas of public policy that had traditionally been exclusively under the scope of sovereign nation-states, and often required the reform of domestic institutional arrangements. The expansion of the trade regime's scope of action has thus meant that consensus decision-making has gradually become more important within it.

So until the launch of the Uruguay Round in 1986, GATT rounds were characterised by the separation of issues into discrete negotiations, ranging from negotiations on a product-by-product basis, to negotiations on linear tariff cuts for all products within broad sectors, to negotiations on the adoption of regulatory standards. This means that members of the trade regime were allowed to choose whether they would sign up to the various codes negotiated (Daugbjerg and Swinbank 2008; Jackson 1998; Paemen and Bensch 1995). This logic of a 'GATT à la carte', however, dramatically changed with the launch of the Uruguay Round in 1986 when members of the trade regime decided that the launching, implementation and outcome of negotiations would be treated as a 'single undertaking' in which negotiations on the different issues would be bound into a single package via the 'nothing is agreed until everything is agreed' rule (Croome 1999).

With this move, the members of the trade regime systematically introduced linkages between negotiation issues. This move was forcefully pushed for by developed trading entities such as the US and the EU in order to ensure that concessions in areas such as agriculture and textiles could be offset by the gains that they could obtain as a result of new agreements on services and intellectual property rights. To ensure the success of this issue-linkage strategy, the EU and the US issued threats of exclusion towards recalcitrant members. They required that GATT membership be cancelled before accession to the WTO, so that non-discriminatory access to their lucrative markets would only be guaranteed to states subscribing to all agreements in the Single Undertaking (Steinberg 2002). All WTO commitments that members entered into from this point were to become characterised by a very high degree of stability, as any substantial change to them would have to be decided under the same multilateral consensus decision rule and would have to be part of a new overall package deal.

The third component of the WTO's governance system is the DSM. The DSM is the enforcement mechanism that the members of the trade regime devised to address two issues: first, when members of the trade regime conclude liberalisation agreements and subsequently disagree over whether a particular trade partner is complying with the terms of such agreements; second, and ultimately the main purpose of the DSM, to incentivise compliance with any agreed rules. Non-compliance with any rules may result from a failure to implement existing rules or from the imposition of new trade barriers that happen to be inconsistent with existing rules.

The existence of a mechanism for the enforcement of agreed rules is key to overcoming the problems of cooperation that are typical in international trade relations. Indeed, any cooperative equilibrium in the form of agreements on the liberalisation of trade is bound to remain unstable as long as robust and effective enforcement mechanisms are not put in place. States face ever-present and powerful incentives to renege on their trade liberalisation commitments, either by failing to implement the rules they have negotiated or by raising new trade barriers contravening the rules they have agreed. For instance, as long as a state has sufficient market power to affect the world prices of particular goods, it has an interest in using tariffs to improve its terms of trade while forcing the costs onto its trading partners. Also, states face powerful domestic pressures to cater to the preferences of import-competing producers that face intense competition as a result of trade liberalisation. Following on from the logic that trade represents a prisoner's dilemma, enforcement mechanisms are deemed necessary to avoid collectively sub-optimal outcomes. Indeed, cooperation on trade liberalisation is only possible as long as institutional mechanisms ensure that cheating in the form of trade protection generates greater costs than short-term benefits (Mayer 1981; Keohane 1984; Martin 1992; Staiger 1995; Bagwell and Staiger 2002). In trade agreements, the key enforcement tool is reciprocity: if you do not abide by your market opening commitments, I will respond in kind; if you do respect your commitments, so will I. It is, in other words, a simple tit-for-tat. This expectation structures bilateral interaction and actually makes trade agreements largely self-enforcing so that strictly speaking no international institution is necessary. Yet, the incentive to unilaterally misrepresent information or to abuse one's market power creates demand for the provision of reliable and more independent information about the nature of purported violations of previously agreed rules, a function that can only be reliably performed by the multilateral institution itself.

The dispute settlement mechanism of the multilateral trade regime thus helps states to commit to maintaining open markets (Davis 2012). In addition to the increased scope of trade rules, this enforcement mechanism of the multilateral trade regime has also changed significantly over time. With the creation of the WTO, members of the trade regime decided to strengthen the existing mechanism for rule enforcement by replacing the GATT's model of political–diplomatic dispute settlement with a quasi-judicial model. While the GATT did have a DSM, the ability of a defendant to block the establishment of a panel or the adoption of a ruling limited the enforcement capacity of states (Davis 2012). This does not mean that this institutional mechanism was ineffective. Dispute settlement procedures in the GATT period were activated in more than 200 cases and states generally complied with the rulings (Hudec 1993). The system was also quite effective in creating negotiated settlements during the consultation phase of the dispute settlement procedure (Busch and Reinhardt 2000, 2003). More generally, the largely bilateral commitments of the reciprocal tariff concessions of the GATT period were easily enforceable through the tit-for-tat withdrawal of concessions and thus to a large extent self-enforcing, especially between markets of approximately the same size (De Bièvre 2006a).

Yet, the largely political–diplomatic nature of this system was deemed insufficient for enforcing compliance with regulatory commitments that address barriers to trade located behind national borders. More specifically, when in 1988 the US Congress mandated that the US Trade Representative use Section 301 market access investigations more aggressively against 'unfair' regulatory trade barriers against American exporters, the Europeans proposed to reform the DSM in order to convince its US partners to commit to a new system of multilateral enforcement rather than to pursue the unilateral route (Hudec 2000; De Bièvre and Poletti 2014; Elsig and Eckhardt 2015). The result of these dynamics of institutional reform was a new DSM characterised by an automatic right to review, the formulation of legally binding obligations, a standing tribunal of justices, and the authority to authorise sanctions and even cross-retaliation against recalcitrant members (Goldstein *et al*. 2000; Stone Sweet 1997, 1999; Zangl 2008).

The process of reform that culminated in the founding of the WTO in 1995, however, unfolded through several steps. At the beginning of the 1980s, GATT contracting parties had already effectively abandoned the practice of vetoing GATT panel rulings (Hudec 1992). In 1989, GATT contracting parties also formally abolished the defendant's veto power against the establishment of a panel in a decision that took immediate effect, independently from any further progress in the Uruguay Round negotiations going on at the same time (GATT 1990). In 1994, all future members of the WTO approved the Dispute Settlement Understanding that incorporated these two crucial changes, while adding two further features: the possibility of appeal to an independent and permanent WTO Appellate Body, and the possibility of WTO panels authorising cross-retaliation by the complainant in cases of enduring non-compliance (WTO 1995).

By introducing the automatic right to review, the formulation of legally binding obligations, a standing tribunal of justices, and the authority to authorise sanctions and even cross-retaliation against recalcitrant members, GATT negotiators created one of the most effective global institutions in terms of constraining the behaviour of its constituent members towards respecting commonly agreed rules. This process of institutional transformation has commonly been captured by the terms 'legalisation' and 'judicialisation.'

The concepts of legalisation and judicialisation both denote an increased reliance on international law, yet they can be used to denote two distinct properties of this evolution. The term legalisation is generally used to cover the broad social phenomenon of an increase in the use of formal–legal rules to regulate a particular domain, *in casu* trade. It captures an increase in the degree of precision, obligation and bindingness of rules, as well as an increase in the enforceability of rules through adjudication by an independent third party (Abbott *et al*. 2000; Goldstein *et al*. 2000; Bernauer *et al*. 2014). The term judicialisation on the other hand refers more specifically to the increase in enforceability through adjudication and the possible authorisation of sanctions by an independent third party. The term judicialisation thus denotes a specific aspect of the broader concept of legalisation, drawing attention to the presence of judicial institutions that enhance the enforceability of previously agreed rules in international trade relations (Zangl, 2008; Stone Sweet, 1997, 1999; De Bièvre and Poletti 2015; De Bièvre 2006). The underlying assumption of our perspective is that precise, obligatory and binding rules need to be backed by credible enforcement mechanisms for such rules to significantly constrain the behaviour of trade actors.

The empirical record of WTO enforcement shows that transforming the WTO into an international institution with greater capacity for rule-enforcement has produced relevant and far-reaching consequences. Indeed, the DSM has been successful in fostering rule compliance. For one, the establishment of the DSM in the WTO has channelled more disputes into the rule-based system of the WTO. Unilateral retaliation has declined significantly and concomitantly formal complaints against violations of WTO law have increased (Davis 2012). Moreover, more than half of all WTO disputes are settled before the establishment of a panel and the issuing of a legal ruling (Busch and Reinhardt 2003), and the vast majority of those disputes that make it to the panel stage tend not to generate significant compliance problems (Wilson 2007), at least a greater majority than in the GATT era (Zangl 2008). Perhaps most importantly, the WTO's DSM has acted as a buffer against protectionist policies being put into place in the first place (Allee 2005). For instance, recent accounts stress the importance of the WTO's judicial arm in containing pressures for the large-scale imposition of protectionist politics in the aftermath of the 2007–08 financial crisis (Baccini and Kim 2012; Irwin and Mavroidis 2008). Of course, the DSM has not always been impermeable to problems. A few WTO disputes have proved particularly intractable, being highly politicised and the source of heated public debates at both the domestic level and the international, diplomatic level. Yet, despite notable exceptions, the WTO DSM has been remarkably successful as an enforcement mechanism of existing multilateral trade rules.

The politics of WTO dispute settlement

The WTO dispute settlement (DS) system is a legal system that unfolds in several discrete steps. The process begins when one or more members of the WTO file a formal complaint and request consultations on specific trade policy measures taken by another member. Consultations take place as confidential negotiations between the two parties, and, if they fail to solve the issue at this stage, the complainant can request the establishment of a panel of experts. The panel phase starts with the composition of the DS Panel as requested by the complainant, to which the parties present oral and written arguments. The panel members then proceed to prepare an interim report, about which the parties can negotiate during the process of writing. At this stage, the parties are encouraged to reach a mutually agreed solution, but, if they do not, the panel circulates its ruling in the form of its initial report (WTO 2004c). Both parties may accept the ruling and the dispute would end at that point. However, the respondent and the complainant also have the opportunity to appeal the ruling, and, if they do so, the dispute reaches the appeals phase where the standing Appellate Body (AB) reviews the dispute. The AB then issues a final ruling on the dispute, in which it may overturn or uphold the panel ruling in its entirety or in part. When the AB finds the defendant not to be in violation of its obligations, the dispute ends there. In disputes where the AB sides with some or all of the accusations of the complainant, the dispute moves to the implementation phase. At this stage, the respondent party is asked 'to bring the measures into conformity' with WTO law and it is asked to notify the Dispute Settlement Body of its implementation. In cases of enduring non-compliance, that body can authorise the complainant to put in place retaliatory measures against the defendant.

Two institutional features of the WTO enforcement mechanism are key to understanding the political–economic dynamics that underlie its functioning. First, member states are the enforcers of the WTO contract. Indeed, only government representatives can trigger review procedures, not the Secretariat of the WTO in the role of a supranational prosecutor, nor private actors. While the Trade Policy Review Mechanism of the WTO provides information on members' trade policies, it has not been used as a means to reveal non-compliance, and the WTO Secretariat remains explicitly neutral on member inquiries about compliance issues (Hoekman and Mavroidis 2000). In order to be able to file a complaint, governmental representatives crucially depend on information provided by private industry, in particular on lobbying by exporters who deem they are denied access to foreign markets as a result of WTO-incompatible trade policies in place in foreign countries. The literature has widely documented that the institutionalisation of informal public – private networks is key to determining the quantity of complaints and the effectiveness of members' litigation strategies in the WTO DSM (Shaffer 2003; Shaffer and Melendez-Ortiz 2010), and some members have undergone important formal institutional reforms to ease the flow of information between the two sides (Poletti *et al.* 2015). Although private actors play a key role in the process, state representatives alone remain the central actors of the enforcement process, as they are the only ones who possess the formal authority to initiate proceedings.

This institutional design has two important implications. On the one hand, members that do not have the necessary resources to hire the specialised legal staff to identify, analyse, pursue and litigate a dispute may be discriminated against in their ability to enforce their rights under WTO agreements (Horn *et al.* 1999; Bown 2005; Guzmann and Simmons 2005; Busch *et al.* 2009; Kim 2008; Davis and Blodgett Bermeo 2009). On the other hand, even when government representatives have such legal capacity at their disposal, enjoying the monopoly of the right to initiate a dispute provides them with a critical gatekeeping role in WTO litigation; they hold the power to select which issues should be litigated out of the much broader set of potentially targetable issues (Davis 2012).

Second, the ultimate remedy in enduring cases of non-compliance with a WTO ruling is retaliation by the complainant. The amount of retaliation has to be largely equivalent to the harm done by the violation in order to maintain the balance of concessions. Whenever a member is unwilling to implement a ruling or offer compensation in the form of better market access in other sectors, the WTO adjudicator can authorise the complainant to reciprocate with tit-for-tat retaliation, and suspend market access concessions previously made. Interestingly, non-compliance with the regulatory agreements adopted in the Uruguay Round – that is, its agreements on trade in services, intellectual property, health and consumer safety standards – may also be reciprocated with retaliatory tariffs. This right is known as the principle of cross-retaliation, meaning the applicability of retaliation across different WTO agreements. The implication of this institutional design is that the enforcement mechanism of the WTO remains, at least partly, skewed in favour of its powerful members. In the context of such a decentralised enforcement mechanism, where the responsibility of enforcement ultimately lies with the member states, it is clear that market size crucially affects enforcement capacity. Members with large markets can more credibly threaten to impose costly retaliation on defendants in the form of market closure in cases of enduring non-compliance than members with small markets (Guzmann and Simmons 2005; Poletti and De Bièvre 2014). Only when a member is valued by others as an attractive destination for exports, a probability that increases with the size of the domestic market, is it in a position to pursue or threaten to pursue policies that can generate concentrated losses for the other side's domestic producers in the form of retaliatory measures.

The enforcement mechanism of the WTO is thus largely bilateral and decentralised. If it were truly multilateral and WTO norms would apply *erga omnes*, retaliation would have to follow investigations by a supranational prosecutor and would be implemented collectively by all member states against the non-law-abiding member. These characteristics make the enforcement of WTO rules imperfect in important ways; most notably they make it skewed in favour of economically powerful members. Yet, the system is preferable to members than a completely decentralised purely unilateral system of enforcement for a number of key reasons. Most notably, two problems render unilateral strategies more costly than the WTO's DSM. First, it may be difficult to both detect misbehaviour and implement retaliatory measures. Regulatory issues are particularly problematic in both respects, as they tend to be more complex and difficult to ascertain and as a tit-for-tat strategy cannot be credibly threatened once domestic adjustment to existing regulations has already taken place among key producers (De Bièvre 2004). Second, and perhaps more importantly, diplomatic stakes represent a key reason for why a strategy of purely unilateral enforcement is more costly than the WTO system. Indeed, states may be deterred from enforcing rules unilaterally for fear of contributing to acrimonious rhetoric, harmful diplomatic relations and resentment from producers in the trade partner (Davis 2012). Compared to WTO adjudication, unilateral retaliation is more likely to be perceived as an arbitrary act of prevarication, which in turn is more likely to provoke a negative backlash in the form of popular opposition and to spiral into a trade war (Odell 1993). To put it in more general terms, the costs of sanctioning, and hence the probability of it taking place, tend to be lower when it takes place in the shadow of an institution such as the WTO's DSM because the political and reputational costs of sanctioning decrease dramatically when institutional devices can be activated to signal that a particular sanctioning strategy receives international support (Thompson 2009).

In light of the significance, visibility and far-reaching consequences of the reform of the mechanism of dispute settlement with the establishment of the WTO, it should come as no surprise that, since 1995, the so-called politics of WTO dispute settlement has become the subject of a rich and growing body of scholarly literature. These contributions have explored various aspects of the phenomenon, and have contributed significantly towards advancing our knowledge of the political–economic dynamics that underlie it. While it is difficult to do justice to the quantity and quality of this literature here, it is important to mention some of the most important lines of research to better situate the argument we develop in the following chapters.

To start with, a number of authors have shed light on the determinants of dispute initiation. They identify legal capacity, power configurations, the degree of economic interdependence, previous experiences with litigation and domestic lobbying as some of the most important factors that determine government representatives' choices over whether and against whom to initiate formal WTO complaints (Bernauer and Sattler 2011; Busch *et al.* 2009; Guzman and Simmons 2005; Kim 2008; Davis and Blodgett Bermeo 2009; Davis 2012). Others have analysed the political dynamics underlying the composition and behaviour of WTO dispute settlement panels and AB. In the former case, the literature highlights how WTO members seek to shape ex ante the endogenous preferences of judges (Elsig 2013; Elsig and Pollack 2014). In the latter case, the literature sheds light on how judges engage in strategic behaviour to enhance the probability of compliance by large and powerful members in order to maintain their own legitimacy, and to appease the wider WTO membership (Busch and Pelc 2010; Kelemen 2001). Other scholars have looked into the determinants of choice over multiple available institutional venues for resolving trade disputes, highlighting how political pressures from domestic interest groups and concerns about the impact of rulings on the wider WTO membership affect such venue choices (Davis and Shirato 2007; Busch 2007). The question of why disputes escalate from consultation to the panel stage has also been widely investigated and the political regime of the WTO members involved, the nature of the issue at stake, the involvement of third parties and, again, the intensity of lobbying have all been identified as important explanatory factors (Busch 2000, Busch and Reinhardt 2006; Davis 2012; Guzman and Simmons 2002; Johns and Pelc 2014; Poletti and De Bièvre 2014). An additional strand of literature has looked into the question of how WTO litigation affects trade flows among members of the trade regime (Kucik and Pelc forthcoming; Bechtel and Sattler 2015).

Finally, a large number of studies have looked into the conditions that foster compliance with WTO rulings and how WTO litigation affects the power balance between trade-related domestic interest groups. Besides acting as a conveyor of information and as a mechanism of commitment and socialisation, the reform of the WTO's DSM has also brought about greater compliance with WTO rules and constrained the emergence of protectionist policies in the aftermath of economic crises (Allee 2005; Irwin and Mavroidis 2008; Zangl 2008, Zangl *et al.* 2012; Baccini and Kim 2012; Davis and Pelc forthcoming). Some authors have sought to identify the conditions that determine the variation in the effectiveness of the WTO's enforcement mechanism to bring about compliance with WTO rules. The existing literature suggests that the complainant's retaliatory capacity and domestic decision-making procedures go a long way to explain different responses to WTO rulings both across and within WTO members (Bown 2004; Guzmann and Simmons 2005; Poletti and De Bièvre 2014; Young 2004). Other studies have sought to analyse the effects of WTO litigation. They show that the credible threat of retaliation by complainants generates the political mobilisation of exporters who are potentially hurt by such retaliatory measures and that this balances out the influence of import-competing producers, so that, ultimately, a constellation of domestic trade-related interests is created which is more prone to maintaining trade liberalisation (Goldstein and Martin 2000; Goldstein and Steinberg 2008, 2009).

This brief overview bears witness to the significant advances that scholarly research has made into understanding the political economy of WTO dispute settlement. And there is still ample room for this literature to advance even further, as important aspects of the politics of WTO dispute settlement certainly require further investigation. For instance, we still need to find appropriate ways of conducting large-N studies on compliance in WTO dispute settlement that overcome problems related to the measurement of compliance (Mavroidis 2012). More research would also be welcomed on the so-called non-cases, namely the cases which are not selected by litigants out of the total universe of potential cases (Bernauer et al. 2014).

However, we believe the almost exclusive focus of the existing literature on the politics of WTO dispute settlement has led scholars to overlook a number of issues that are key in order to acquire a comprehensive understanding of judicial politics in multilateral trade relations at large.

From disputes to deal-making

While understanding whether, and if so how, the reform of the DSM of the multilateral trade regime has fostered greater compliance with agreed rules is important, an exclusive focus on these questions risks leaving other key questions unanswered. Equipping international institutions with effective enforcement mechanisms does not only affect the likelihood of compliance with existing rules, but also the propensity of the members of these institutions to deepen and/or widen the scope of such rules in the future. That such a connection between enforcement and rule-making exists is quite intuitive: the calculations actors make whenever they have to decide on whether to commit to a common set of rules are likely to be affected by their expectations concerning the probability that such rules will be enforced.

The connection between enforceability and rule-making is a theoretically problematic one. To start with, the international cooperation literature highlights that some assurance regarding the credibility of enforcement of prospective rules is necessary for actors even to accept them in the first place. This is so because in prisoner's dilemma-like situations such as trade liberalisation any commitment gives rise to incentives for defection and thus cannot be credibly maintained without enforcement mechanisms that punish such defection. Standard cooperation theory thus suggests that whenever a credible enforcement mechanism exists – that is, one which casts a long shadow on the future with adequate monitoring capacities and appropriate technologies for responding to violations – actors should have little trouble arranging mutually beneficial agreements (Axelrod and Keohane 1986; Keohane 1984; Oye 1986; Snidal 1985). Following this line of reasoning, Downs *et al.* (1996) argue that the greater the depth of mutual cooperative arrangements, the greater the incentives to defect, and, consequently, the greater the magnitude of the punishment required to sustain a cooperative equilibrium. By extension, one should therefore expect stronger enforcement mechanisms to enable deeper cooperative arrangements.

In contrast, strong enforcement of prospective rules can also plausibly be argued to render cooperative arrangements more difficult to reach. Indeed, credible enforcement cuts two ways: though necessary to make cooperative deals sustainable, it nonetheless may ultimately impede cooperation. Fearon (1998) has shown how problems of international cooperation first involve a bargaining problem and then an enforcement problem, and that these two can interact in ways that cut across the received wisdom of cooperation theory. More specifically, his analysis highlights that actors' expectations about whether prospective agreements will be enforceable affect their bargaining strategies over the terms of such agreements; when they expect the terms of the agreement to be credibly enforced, it provides an incentive to bargain harder, possibly making cooperative agreements more difficult to reach. The argument does not suggest that cooperation under the shadow of credible enforcement is impossible. For instance, when the day-to-day opportunity costs of going without agreement are high relative to the size of the distributional shares at stake, the probability of a costly standoff in negotiations decreases. Yet, interestingly, when cooperation is modelled as a sequence of bargaining and enforcement problems in order to examine how they interact, the predictions regarding the probability of cooperation under the shadow of credible enforcement become exactly the opposite of those using standard cooperation theory: the probability of costly non-cooperative standoffs is expected to increase with stronger enforcement of prospective rules.

Other analyses have further elaborated on this central insight that stronger enforcement of prospective rules may make cooperative arrangements more difficult to reach, emphasising the role of political uncertainty (Downs and Rocke 1995; Goldstein and Martin 2000; Koremenos *et al.* 2001; Schwartz and Sykes 2002; Rosendorff 2005; Rosendorff and Milner 2001). More specifically, this strand of literature suggests that 'optimal imperfection' in the form of a certain degree of flexibility of agreements is required under conditions of political uncertainty in order to make sure that compliance with agreed rules remains politically feasible. In other words, this literature posits that strong and credible enforcement procedures that apply high deterministic penalties for noncompliance could backfire and lead to an unravelling of the process of liberalisation. If agreements are impossible to breach and elected officials operate in a condition of uncertainty about the political pressures for protection that may emanate from exogenous shocks – for example, in prices or supplies, in production technology, or in domestic political cleavages and/or institutions – they may find that the costs of signing such agreements outweigh the benefits. Flexibility measures in the form of 'legal' temporary deviations from agreed rules are therefore considered essential to maintaining political support for cooperative arrangements that would otherwise be perceived as too binding in the face of the inevitable uncertainties of the international market.

Given these sets of arguments, their subsequent applications, and the importance of both to the discussion we develop throughout the book, a brief discussion of how the key concepts of enforcement and flexibility relate to the political system of the WTO is in order. Indeed, the claim that the reform of the WTO's DSM has increased the credibility of rule enforcement in the multilateral trading system seems at odds with a number of analyses that view the WTO's dispute settlement system as a flexibility-enhancing device, which allows contracting partners to violate agreements, compensate the losers, and still retain immunity within the community of cooperating nations (Rosendorff 2005: 390; Rosendorff and Milner 2001). These latter contributions thus develop a line of argumentation that seems to contradict our view of the DSM reform as having *decreased* members' room for manoeuvre due to the increased enforceability of rules.

Shedding light on this apparent contradiction requires a short conceptual and empirical discussion. Conceptually, it is important to clarify that an agreement's flexibility should be conceived of as a function of two key elements: on the one hand what room for manoeuvre the rules of the agreement allow for (i.e. whether cooperation is deep or shallow), and on the other hand whether mechanisms exist to credibly enforce such rules. This means that effective constraints on actors' behaviour, or a lack of flexibility, arise when rules limit the range of acceptable conduct to a significant extent and when these rules can be enforced. So even when there are precise, binding and obligatory rules, these have little constraining power in the absence of a credible threat of sanctioning in cases of non-compliance, at least less power than when the threat of punishment is credible.

Hence, in order to ascertain whether flexibility has increased with the passage from the GATT to the WTO system, an empirical assessment of both the content of the rules and the nature of the enforcement of such rules is required. On the first topic, Pelc (2009, 2010) has convincingly argued that WTO rules have allowed members of the trade regime far less latitude than the GATT rules in escaping from trade liberalisation commitments, mainly through clarifying the criteria of escape and increasing the level of information required of potential escapees. Indeed, under the GATT members were able to suspend their obligations to prevent or remedy serious injuries caused by unforeseen developments (Art. XIX). First, a member contravening its liberalisation commitments could offer monetary compensation to the country suffering from its lost market access. Second, a country experiencing a sudden import surge could suspend its concessions by raising its tariffs, and the aggrieved country could respond in kind. Third, by threatening to suspend a wide range of concessions and thus to take away market access, a country could force a trading partner to impose so-called 'voluntary' export restraints on its exporters, in order to alleviate an import surge. The GATT criteria for escape were thus left under-defined and overly vague in order to allow members to retain a significant degree of flexibility.

As Pelc (2009) documents, the situation during the GATT period contrasts markedly with that observed in the WTO period. With the formation of the WTO, Article XIX was replaced by the Agreement on Safeguards. This completely banned voluntary export restraints, banned compensation or countermeasures for the first three years of the implemented safeguard measures, and also better defined criteria of escape, explicitly clarifying the meaning of 'serious injury' and 'threat of serious injury', providing clear criteria for identifying an increase in imports, and requiring a demonstration of the existence of a causal link between the increase of such imports and the suffered injury. In sum, the multilateral trade regime experienced a shift from a compensation-based system to an appeal to exceptions system that both heightened the requirements for escaping members to justify their escape and provided other members with greater legal means to challenge these attempts.

Perhaps more importantly, the introduction of these more stringent rules on deviations from trade liberalisation commitments only became effective and relevant since they were combined with a reform of the DSM that made punishment of non-compliance more probable. The problem with constraining escapees during the GATT period was not only that existing criteria for escape were too vague and difficult to challenge legally. The additional problem was that the weakness of the GATT dispute settlement system did not enable countries negatively affected by escape to effectively challenge it. Again, Pelc (2009) convincingly documents that after complainants found out in the early 1950s that they were unable to use the DSM of the GATT to meaningfully challenge measures taken by other members under Article XIX, not a single member ever activated the GATT dispute again to try to seek redress.

To conclude, relative to the GATT, actors operating within the WTO system can expect to be constrained more in their margin for manoeuvre. Having clarified, both conceptually and empirically, why it is more sound to see the WTO system as having decreased, rather than increased, flexibility, there remains the question of whether these greater constraints on members' behaviour have facilitated or obstructed cooperation.

The political economy of the litigation-negotiation nexus

The analyses we have reviewed so far have greatly enhanced our understanding of the causal connections between institutional design and cooperation. However, an important limitation of these analyses is that they miss detailed insight into how judicialisation has interacted with the politics of trade policymaking within WTO members. By treating WTO members as unitary actors that act one way or another in order to maximise aggregate welfare, these studies overlook the domestic politics that underlie trade policymaking. When considering the effects of design changes in international institutions, *in casu* the move towards a greater capacity to enforce rules, one needs to assess how such changes systematically influence the preferences, dynamics of political mobilisation and power of domestic organised groups.

The endogenous trade protection literature has long noted that the preferences, organisation and political action by domestic interests matter, showing how special interests can systematically bias trade policy towards protectionism, irrespective of whether trade liberalisation increases the aggregate welfare of societies (Schattsneider 1935; Magee *et al.* 1989; Grossman and Helpman 2001). This is so because trade policy is subject to systematic capture by politically influential groups who can, relative to diffuse interests such as consumers, more easily mobilise and lobby policymakers to attain their desired policies (Olson 1965). Ultimately, the ability of policymakers to commit to trade liberalisation depends on the relative balance of influence of those who favour and those who oppose a further opening of the economy to foreign products (Goldstein and Martin 2000).

Different theories have been developed to account for domestic preferences and patterns of political mobilisation over trade policy (Frieden and Rogowski 1996). For instance, the factor model suggests that the easing of trade restrictions increases returns to the factor a country has in abundance and conversely decreases the returns to the factor a country is poorly endowed with. Thus, that the political conflict underlying trade policy will pit factor-related interests against each other (Rogowski 1989). The sector model, setting out from the assumption that factors of production are specific to a sector, predicts that trade liberalisation imposes benefits and costs on different sectors, rather than on different factors of production (Alt and Gilligan 1994). The distinction between workers and capitalists thus loses its analytical usefulness, as both groups have similar interests within a particular sector. This model thus pits sectors benefiting from openness, or those which intensely employ an abundant specific factor, against those suffering from it, or those which employ intensely a scarce specific factor (Hiscox 2001). Finally, strategic trade theory assumes economies of scale and imperfect competition, and highlights how intra-industry trade – that is, trade of different varieties of the same product between countries with similar factor endowments (Krugman 1981) – may generate a political conflict between a small set of hyper-specialised producers, or even single firms, rather than between social classes or sectors of industry (Milner 1999; Verdier 1998; Gilligan 1997; Kono 2009). Irrespective of the content of these theoretical predictions, they all paint a picture in which trade policy is largely determined by the preferences and patterns of political mobilisation by trade-related domestic actors who either oppose or support trade liberalisation.

Of course, domestic organised groups do not act in an institutional vacuum. Domestic institutions are also key to understanding how such interests aggregate and weigh in the trade policymaking process (Rogowski 1987; Rickard 2010). Such attention to domestic institutions is necessary to explain why actors with similar underlying economic interests may end up adopting sharply different trade policies (Davis 2012). Similarly, we also cannot neglect the importance of the institutions of the international trade regime on the domestic politics of trade.

In order to develop our analysis of how judicial politics affects the likelihood of deal-making in the WTO, we thus believe it is more appropriate to conceive of trade policies as the result of a political process in which constituencies formulate demands to politicians, who then seek to satisfy these demands and convey these constituencies concentrated benefits because they depend on their resources for re-election or re-appointment (De Bièvre and Dür, 2005). Trade policies tend to confer concentrated costs and benefits on some organised groups, while conveying diffuse costs and benefits on all other sections of society. We expect policymakers to primarily seek to satisfy the demands of groups upon which trade policies bestow either concentrated benefits or costs, as these are more able to provide resources such as information, financial contributions or more general political support, essential to maintaining office. This means that diffuse interests can hardly be expected to critically influence trade policy decisions as they are less capable of organising effectively on trade issues and thus provide the resources that policymakers are in need of (Olson 1965). Following an established approach in the endogenous trade literature, we therefore conceive of policymakers as not having specific trade policy preferences but rather as political support-maximisers who seek to avoid the mobilisation of political enemies (Grossman and Helpman 1994). While many arguments have been developed to predict the conditions under which such domestic political conflict is more likely to lead to trade liberalisation or protectionism (Alt and Gilligan 1996), we simply want to underline here that we propose to look into the litigation-negotiation nexus by assessing how the stronger enforceability of rules in the trade regime has affected both the preferences and patterns of political mobilisation of groups favouring or opposing trade liberalisation and how these demands influence policymakers.

In the only study that has so far systematically looked into this question through these analytical lenses, Goldstein and Martin (2000) develop both the theoretical reasoning and the empirical support for a cautionary note on the domestic effects of strengthening enforcement mechanisms of rules in the trade regime. In fact, the authors portray quite a gloomy picture, suggesting that, while reducing incentives for cheating by individual nations, such an institutional reform could interfere with the pursuit of progressive liberalisation of international trade. In their cautionary note about the causal pathways linking judicialisation, domestic politics and liberalisation, the authors stress two elements that can be expected to decrease the domestic propensity to conclude new multilateral trade agreements. First, a more judicialised trade regime provides better information about the distributional consequences of trade agreements and thereby affects the incentives of groups to mobilise for and against trade agreements. More information, so the argument goes, empowers protectionists relative to free traders on issues relating to the conclusion of new agreements. The assumption this argument builds upon is that key economic interest groups are differentially mobilised prior to the process of judicialisation and, more specifically, that increased information will have a larger marginal effect on protectionist groups strengthening the incentives of antitrade forces to mobilise as compared to already well organised pro-trade groups. Second, judicialisation increases the predictability of trade agreements by reducing the ability of governments to opt out of commitments, making international trade rules more tightly binding. Increased bindingness, it is suggested, makes it difficult for leaders to gain support from free-trade majorities at home and, therefore, constrains their capacity to commit to new trade agreements. Since in a judicialised international trade regime it is more difficult for states to get around international trade obligations, governments may find that the costs of signing such agreements outweigh the benefits. As the authors point out, 'if enforcement is too harsh states will comply with trade rules even in the face of high economic and political costs, and general support for liberalisation is likely to decline' (Goldstein and Martin 2000: 620–1).

The evolution of multilateral trade negotiations since the creation of the WTO in 1995 clearly seems to corroborate these arguments. Precisely from the point the international trade regime equipped itself with stronger enforcement mechanisms, its capacity to deliver significant trade liberalisation through multilateral trade negotiations came to a halt. Has the creation of quasi-judicial mechanisms for the enforcement of rules been the cause behind the WTO's inability to deliver negotiated trade liberalisation? The next chapters of this book aim to address this fundamental question. While the cautionary note developed by Goldstein and Martin (2000) offers a provocative and important starting point to develop a systematic assessment of how judicial politics affect the dynamics of lawmaking in the WTO, we believe their work remains incomplete in many important respects. In particular, we develop four sets of arguments supported by original empirical evidence to offer a more comprehensive overview of the relevant causal mechanisms. While we very much agree with their statement that judicial politics affect deal-making in the WTO in systematic ways, we come to a much less pessimistic conclusion.

First, we explore the key argument that judicial politics affect the dynamics of political mobilisation by domestic pro and anti-trade liberalisation groups. In our view, the argument that an increased enforceability of rules empowers anti-trade groups relative to pro-trade groups across the board is overstated for two reasons. First, it is by no means clear that exporters would be more organised and mobilised than import-competitors prior to any such institutional reform. In fact, it is logical to expect the opposite to be true. Second, we believe that the traditional distinction between exporters and import-competing groups as the only two sets of concentrated interests with a stake in trade liberalisation no longer fully grasps the reality of trade policymaking in contemporary international trade relations. The conventional wisdom is that the only economic actors that stand to gain from trade liberalisation are export-oriented producers, as they gain from increased sales to foreign markets. However, in an international economy increasingly organised around global value chains (GVCs), import-dependent firms have also emerged as an additional set of actors, who sometimes have a clear stake in trade liberalisation. As we will illustrate in detail, for firms that operate within GVCs, trade liberalisation is highly beneficial because it leads to a reduction of the variable costs of their imports. Whether sourcing firms operate directly in a foreign country or simply import intermediate inputs from foreign suppliers is secondary, as in both cases import-dependent firms accrue benefits from cheaper imports (Manger 2012). Both arguments suggest that, under certain conditions, judicial politics incentivise the emergence of a strong coalition between exporters and importers in favour of multilateral trade liberalisation at the expense of anti-trade forces.

Second, we complement the cautionary note by adding regulatory cooperation to the picture. The bulk of trade liberalisation in contemporary international trade relations is not about lowering or eliminating tariff barriers to trade. Trade liberalisation today is largely about achieving greater compatibility between domestic laws across countries as they are directly related to the costs of doing business and, ultimately, affect the prices of the goods and services that are traded (Kim 2015). A central question is thus how, in addition to affecting patterns of political mobilisation concerning traditional tariff trade liberalisation, greater enforceability of rules affects the preferences of trade-related domestic actors over processes of regulatory deal-making. Regulatory trade liberalisation differs from traditional trade liberalisation in important ways (De Bièvre et al. 2014). The distributive effects of such agreements tend to be more diffuse and opaque. They are also more difficult to enforce through tit-for-tat strategies. In addition, regulatory agreements in the WTO are often nested within a wide array of international regimes across issue areas. Because of these fundamental differences between the two types of trade liberalisation, an investigation of the causal links between judicial politics and lawmaking in the WTO requires assessing in a systematic way the question of how the former affects the dynamics of regulatory cooperation.

Third, since the creation of a quasi-judicial mechanism of dispute settlement, WTO members have found themselves negotiating under the shadow of WTO law. Negotiations for the adoption of new trade liberalisation commitments in the Doha Round, regarding both tariffs and regulations, have taken place while WTO members have consistently threatened or resorted to WTO litigation procedures in order to pressure their trading partners into compliance with existing commitments. There is abundant empirical evidence about how WTO members use judicial mechanisms strategically to affect negotiations. The question of how the 'shadow of WTO law' affects the calculations trade-related domestic actors make in multilateral trade negotiations is thus clearly of central importance in acquiring a systematic understanding of whether, and if so how, judicial politics affect lawmaking in the WTO.

Finally, while judicial politics affect the relative balance of power of pro and anti-trade organised groups in the domestic politics of trade policymaking among WTO members, they also affect the very way in which these interests get aggregated and organised. It is not only a question of who mobilises to favour or oppose trade liberalisation. It is also a question of how they mobilise. The ability of lobby groups to represent a wide array of domestic interests has been deemed a crucial determinant of success in multilateral trade negotiations characterised by the linking of issues (Martin 1992). This is so because in such an institutional context lobbying success depends on the ability to provide the building blocks for the across-issue package deals that the negotiators seek to compose. Hence, the probability that a single firm's lobbying effort contributes to the outcome increases when mobilisation takes place in cross-sector business alliances and sector trade associations (Davis 2004). Yet, judicial politics have in practice actually called for more lobbying specialisation, and created disincentives for firms to join such cross-sector business alliances and trade associations (see Chapter Six). Assessing the way in which judicial politics affect how trade-related interests aggregate, both on the pro- and anti-trade side, is therefore crucial to understanding whether they undermine the conditions for effective deal-making in multilateral trade rounds.

Chapter Three

Judicial Politics and the Liberalisation of Tariff Barriers to Trade

While many commentators welcomed the replacement of the GATT's model of political–diplomatic dispute settlement with the WTO's quasi-judicial model of dispute settlement, some did raise concerns about the long-term effects of this institutional innovation. In an attempt to contribute to the understanding of how the increased capacity of the WTO to enforce rules would affect the likelihood of cooperation in the multilateral trade regime, Goldstein and Martin (2000) came to the rather gloomy conclusion that this institutional change could end up significantly interfering with the pursuit of the progressive liberalisation of international trade. The concerns of the authors were not so much about the effectiveness of the system in achieving its main objective, namely to foster compliance with existing rules. In this regard, the system could plausibly be expected to be successful. The more credible threat of retaliation in the case of non-compliance would lead to the mobilisation of potentially affected exporters and would thus create powerful political incentives for policymakers in non-compliant states to bring domestic rules in line with WTO law.

The analysis developed by these authors points instead to a more fundamental problem. While strengthening the enforcement mechanisms would lead to the desired goal of fostering greater compliance with existing multilateral trade rules, such an institutional innovation would also be likely to decrease the propensity of trade-related domestic interests to commit to new multilateral trade agreements. In particular, the authors suggested that two effects brought about by the strengthening of enforcement mechanisms of the trade regime, namely more transparency about the distributional consequences of trade agreements and an increased bindingness of trade rules, would be responsible for decreasing the propensity for cooperation among WTO members.

In this chapter, we elaborate on this argument in detail and seek to offer a more systematic account of the causal mechanisms linking the judicialisation of the trade regime and the domestic politics of negotiated traditional trade liberalisation, or the negotiation of new commitments on the reduction and/or elimination of tariff barriers to international trade. While the argument by Goldstein and Martin certainly provides a useful and provoking starting point for the debate on the processes through which domestic actors define their preferences over deepening and/or broadening their multilateral trade liberalisation commitments in a more judicialised international trade regime, we believe that it cannot account for how the domestic politics of negotiated traditional trade liberalisation has evolved in recent years. While it is true that the Doha Round has failed to deliver on its ambitious promises, it is by no means true that we have observed a decrease in the propensity of trade-related domestic interests to commit to new traditional trade liberalisation commitments across the board. There are important cases where the story is exactly the opposite and where judicialisation seems to have strongly incentivised the creation of pro-trade coalitions in the domestic politics of WTO members. In order to account for this mismatch between theory and empirical developments, we highlight problems with both the logical consistency and the completeness of the argument developed by Goldstein and Martin. We then proceed to present our own argument about the influence of judicialisation on multilateral trade negotiations and give some illustrative evidence to show its plausibility.

Judicialisation, traditional trade liberalisation and domestic politics: a pessimistic view

More than a decade ago, Goldstein and Martin (2000) engaged in the first attempt to systematically analyse how an increase in the judicialisation of the international trade regime interacts with the trade-related interests of domestic actors. Judicialisation, they argued, is likely to reduce the incentives of domestic groups to want cooperation with other members of the trade regime. In their cautionary note about the causal pathways linking judicialisation, domestic politics and liberalisation, the authors stressed two elements by which this reduction in incentives would occur.

First, a more judicialised trade regime provides better information about the distributional consequences of trade agreements, which affects the incentives of economic interest groups to mobilise for or against trade agreements. The ability of policymakers to commit to new trade liberalisation commitments largely depends on the relative balance of power between those who favour and those who oppose trade liberalisation. The mobilisation of these groups is a function of a number of factors, amongst which the most important are the costs of mobilising and the potential gains from collective action. These organised groups thus need to realise that they have an interest in seeking to influence governmental policy and that the prospective gains are larger than the costs of collective action. Judicialisation is important in this context as it increases the information available to actors about the distributional implications of trade agreements and thus affects the incentives these groups face when deciding whether to mobilise in favour or against trade liberalisation.

The central argument by Goldstein and Martin is that the better information under the WTO regime would have empowered protectionists relative to free traders on issues relating to the engagement in new agreements. While better information about the distributive effects of prospective trade agreements affects both import-competitors and exporters, the marginal effect of this better information is expected to be larger on those that are, on balance, less mobilised. And the authors presumed that exporters would have been more mobilised than import-competitors in the period prior to judicialisation, due to the reciprocity-based structure of the multilateral trade regime, the growing dependence on exports and the multinational character of the economic interests involved.

Second, judicialisation increases the predictability that trade agreements will be honoured by reducing the ability of governments to opt out of commitments. This increased bindingness, it is suggested, makes it difficult for political leaders to gain support from free-trade majorities at home and governments may conclude that the costs of signing any agreements outweigh the benefits they offer. As the authors point out, 'if enforcement is too harsh states will comply with trade rules even in the face of high economic and political costs, and general support for liberalisation is likely to decline' (Goldstein and Martin 2000: 620-1).

In sum, because WTO judicialisation has increased transparency about the effects of trade agreements and enhanced their bindingness, one should expect that economic interest groups have since then increasingly pressured policymakers to abstain from engaging in further multilateral trade cooperation.

A note of caution on the cautionary note

In our view, the argument developed by the authors of this important contribution leads to overly pessimistic predictions about the effects of the judicialisation of the WTO on the prospects for deal-making in the trade regime. We believe this is so because it is not entirely consistent with the standard logic of political-economy approaches to trade policymaking and because it is incomplete in its assessment of the organised actors that might have a stake in mobilising to affect government choices over trade policy. As we argue below, correcting for these two problems leads to a more nuanced view regarding how strengthening enforcement mechanisms in the trade regime might have affected the propensity of trade-related domestic actors to commit to new negotiated multilateral rules in the field of traditional trade liberalisation.

Empowering whom?

As already argued above, Goldstein and Martin (2000) believe that better information brought about by the judicialisation of the WTO has strengthened anti-trade forces relative to already well-organised pro-trade groups.[1] The key assumption for this argument is that, prior to the creation of the WTO, exporters were already fully or almost fully mobilised while import-competing groups were mobilised to a lesser extent. Following Gilligan (1997) and Milner (1988), the

---

1. Some authors have criticised the assumption that greater enforceability of rules should necessarily yield better information about the distributional consequences of prospective agreements (Finnemore and Toope 2001). While we agree with much of the substance of such critiques, we wish to show here some of the inconsistencies of the argument that Goldstein and Martin (2000) develop on the basis of this assumption, rather than problematise the choice of the assumption itself.

authors claim that this assumption is plausible given the principle of reciprocity upon which the multilateral trade regime has been based and the growing importance of multinational corporations in the contemporary international economy.

These studies have indeed convincingly shown that the principle of reciprocity and the increased internationalisation and multinationalisation of production processes have acted as important triggers for the emergence of powerful constituencies within developed countries with clear cut preferences for and an important political role in favour of international trade liberalisation. However, these studies do not provide a sufficient basis for assuming that exporters have been consistently more mobilised than import-competitors in the trade policymaking process. If anything, the opposite is more plausible. Standard political economy approaches concur in predicting that import-competing groups will dominate over export-oriented ones in the trade policymaking process.

The reasons for this expected structural imbalance in favour of protectionist interests have been widely documented in the literature and are actually acknowledged by Goldstein and Martin (2000) in various passages of their article. For one, exporters face more obstacles than import-competing interests when engaging in political action due to the costly activities of information gathering concerning market access opportunities, as well as the uncertainty about the amount and the distribution of the potential benefits that can be derived from lowering foreign trade barriers (Dür 2010). Also, because trade liberalisation requires changes to the status quo in the form of an affirmative action, namely the ratification of a treaty, incentives for political mobilisation are stronger for protectionist groups because there is a higher probability that their lobbying effort will lead to the desired outcome. More generally, experimental evidence has widely demonstrated that losses are more easily ascertained than gains and that actors tend to react more strongly to avoid prospective losses than to obtain prospective gains (Kahneman and Tversky 1986; Levy 1992, 1996).

If any generalisation were to be derived consistent with these observations, it would be more logical to expect that the balance of domestic forces between pro- and anti-trade groups prior to judicialisation has been tilted in favour of the latter group. It is therefore not surprising that most accounts of exporters 'winning' over protectionists are stories about why liberalisation occurs despite the expected bias in favour of import-competing groups in the domestic trade policymaking process. Indeed, studies that focus on how the institutionalisation of reciprocity has empowered exporters (Gilligan 1997; Goldstein 1993), on the growing multinational character of economic interests (Milner 1988), on changes in constituency interests and shifts in countries' comparative advantages (Hiscox 1999), and on the creation of preferential trade agreements and specific domestic institutional arrangements that insulate policymakers from societal pressures (Destler 1986; Meunier 2005; Rogowski 1987), all explicitly or implicitly start from the theoretical assumption that import-competing groups should be expected to dominate in the trade policymaking process, so that the choice for trade liberalisation is an exception in need for an explanation.

Neither prediction about which economic groups (import-competing or export-competing) dominates the policymaking process, however, is likely to reflect empirical reality. Different countries have different domestic power balances between interests and countries can experience changes in their domestic balances over time. A more logically consistent way to deal with the question of how judicialisation affects the domestic balance of economic interests is to argue that increased information has effects on both groups and that the overall effect of increased transparency resulting from judicialisation depends on the balance of interests in a given country. In fact, this is what Goldstein and Martin (2000) implicitly posit when they argue that increased information should lead to a relatively greater mobilisation of the less involved in the policy process. If this is true, WTO judicialisation would not have necessarily elicited greater opposition to multilateral trade liberalisation. Judicialisation may well have led to this outcome for a country in which the constellation of interests was one in which exporters were already fully mobilised and import-competing ones were not. But it could also have lead to the opposite outcome if the domestic politics of trade were dominated by protectionist interests.

What about importers?

In addition to the problems with its logical inconsistency noted above, we believe the argument developed by Goldstein and Martin (2000) is incomplete in that it overlooks the potential role played by an increasingly important group of economic actors within advanced and emerging economies: import-dependent firms. Since the turn of the century we have witnessed two important developments, namely a consolidation in the import and retail sectors and a transformation of a substantial number of producers into importers. Both processes are closely linked to the emergence and increasing importance of the internationalisation of the supply chain.

The internationalisation of the supply chain first began in the 1970s among developed nations (Baldwin 2011: 3; Milner 1988). However, the big transformation occurred when, supported by systematic advancements in international communications and technology and huge labour-cost differentials, the process of internationalisation also came to involve developing countries (Feenstra 1998; Ando and Kimura 2005). This 'new trade' that promoted the internationalisation of the supply chain involved production unbundling, known as outward-processing trade, or vertical-specialisation trade (Manger 2009; Hummels et al. 2001). While this vertical-specialisation trade was more important for Europe and North America until the 1980s, in the subsequent period North–South vertical-specialisation trade boomed, especially in Asia (Kim 2015).

So, while in the past retailers and producers in developed countries bought or produced the bulk of their products and inputs domestically, since the 1990s many retailers and producers have redefined their core competencies and turned their attention to 'innovation and product strategy, marketing, and the highest value-added segments of manufacturing and services' and outsourced labour-intensive, less value-added operations to lower income countries, mainly in Asia

(Gereffi *et al.* 2005: 79). This has been done through the creation of foreign subsidiaries – that is, by vertical foreign direct investment – or by relying on independent foreign suppliers (Lanz and Miroudot 2011). Hence, retailers have been increasingly buying their products from suppliers in Asia and elsewhere, while producers have been increasingly outsourcing and off-shoring a substantial part of their production overseas, again largely in Asian markets, which has turned many of these producers into importers in the European and American markets. These altered (production) structures, which have become particularly common in labour-intensive consumer goods industries (Gereffi 1999) and the food industry (Burch and Lawrence 2005), are usually referred to as GVCs.

In this context, the traditional distinction between import-competing groups and export-oriented producers makes it difficult to grasp the reality of contemporary trade politics both in advanced and in a number of emerging economies. As the retailers and the manufacturers that rely on imports have become an increasingly relevant set of economic actors, the preferences, patterns of political mobilisation and political influence of these firms also need to be assessed to acquire a comprehensive understanding of how judicialisation might affect the dynamics of lawmaking in the WTO.

In line with a number of different studies (Eckhardt 2011, 2013, 2015; De Bièvre and Eckhardt 2011; Eckhardt and Poletti 2015), we use the concept of import-dependent firms and define them as firms that rely on income generated by imported goods or on the import of intermediate products for their production process. Thus, two types of import-dependent firms can be identified: first, import-dependent retailers which are right at the end of the supply chain and carry out no production of their own, but purchase finished goods from foreign suppliers and resell those directly to end-users; second, import-dependent manufacturers, which are goods-producing firms for which imports play a pivotal role in the production process, either because they have outsourced production or because they use imported products as inputs.

While the conventional wisdom posits that the only economic actors that stand to gain from trade liberalisation are export-oriented producers, as they gain from increased sales to foreign markets, it is clear that import-dependent firms also stand to gain from trade liberalisation. For firms that operate within GVCs, trade liberalisation simply leads to a reduction in the variable costs of their imports. Whether sourcing firms operate directly in a foreign country or simply import intermediate inputs from foreign suppliers is secondary, as in both cases import-dependent firms accrue benefits from cheaper imports (Manger 2012).

Not only can these groups be expected to have clear-cut preferences for trade liberalisation, they can also be expected to be quite capable of mobilising politically. For instance, while exporters face collective action problems due to the relative uncertainty of the benefits they can accrue from trade liberalisation, import-dependent firms can anticipate with much greater precision the distributive effects of eliminating and/or lowering tariff barriers to trade with countries with which they are already in a trading relationship. So, import-dependent firms are more certain that they will stand to gain from reduced tariffs than exporters. What is more, as a result of mergers and acquisitions and vertical integration, many sectors dominated by import-dependent firms (e.g. textiles and clothing, footwear, consumer electronics) have undergone a dramatic move towards increased market concentration in the last decade and a half (Dunford 2004; Eckhardt 2015). Hence, in the contemporary international political economy, trade policymakers have an increasing incentive to take into account the benefits of trade liberalisation not only for potential exporters but also for domestic importers.

What does this mean for our reasoning about the effects of judicialisation on the preferences and influence of trade-related domestic interests over negotiated traditional trade liberalisation? In our view the implications are twofold. First, the traditional view according to which exporters and import-competing groups are the only relevant actors in trade policymaking no longer fully holds. As import-dependent firms such as in the EU have become better able to mobilise politically, they are just as capable of providing policymakers with crucial resources. Second, this third group of actors can be expected to be relatively less mobilised than the other two groups – exporters and import-competing groups – which have traditionally been active in the trade policymaking process. Accepting the assumption that increased information brought about by the institutional innovation of more judicialised enforcement in the WTO has empowered the relatively less mobilised among organised groups in the trade policymaking process, we should expect judicialisation to have acted as a trigger for a greater political role of import-dependent firms within it.

The reasoning we have developed so far offers quite a different picture of the causal mechanisms linking judicial politics and negotiated traditional trade liberalisation than the one painted by Goldstein and Martin (2000). For one, it is by no means clear that such an institutional innovation would have empowered protectionist groups across all WTO members. In fact, in some cases, namely when import-competitors are relatively more mobilised, the opposite outcome should be expected. In addition, in an international economy increasingly organised around GVCs, the preferences, patterns of political mobilisation, and influence of producers and retailers that stand to gain from cheaper access to imports from low-cost sources around the globe cannot be neglected. These actors can be expected to increase the political weight of the domestic coalition favouring trade liberalisation. The two arguments combined suggest that, while it may be true that in some cases judicial politics has created a domestic political environment more hostile towards new traditional trade liberalisation commitments, in other cases it may have acted in the opposite direction and fostered the political mobilisation of a coalition of exporters and importers actively pushing for comprehensive traditional trade liberalisation.

Evidence: patterns of political mobilisation before and during the Doha Round

In this section we offer some evidence to show the plausibility of the arguments developed so far. We do so in two ways. First we provide illustrative evidence of patterns of political mobilisation by organised groups in WTO Ministerial Conferences. While ideally we would compare patterns of political mobilisation before and after the strengthening of enforcement mechanisms in the WTO, data on the GATT period is unfortunately not available. However, data regarding the period after 1995 can also tell us something meaningful regarding the political dynamics that the judicialisation of the WTO may have engendered.

Second, we develop a case study of the EU domestic politics of trade prior to and throughout the Doha Round of multilateral trade negotiations. The rationale for the choice to look into the EU case is twofold. For one, given its pivotal role in international trade relations, the EU is an interesting case per se. Indeed, the EU has for decades been one of the world's two largest trading blocs and today accounts for roughly 20 per cent of global trade. With only 5 per cent of the world's population, it is the world's second largest importer and its largest exporter of goods and services. In addition to holding formidable power *in* trade, the EU has also exercised substantial power *through* trade, having been able to use a range of power tactics to generate support for cooperation in the trade regime (Meunier and Nicolaidis 2006; Steinberg 2002). The EU has thus consistently acted as a co-shaper of the multilateral trade regime together with the US (De Bièvre and Poletti 2014).

More importantly, the way in which the EU has approached the Doha Round and conducted itself during negotiations stands in stark contrast to the pessimistic view developed by Goldstein and Martin (2000). Despite the strength and traditional influence of key import-competing groups (i.e. farmers), the EU has fervently supported broad and comprehensive negotiations (Kerremans 2004; Van den Hoven 2004), an approach that is widely acknowledged as making it easier for negotiators to overcome societal pressures for protectionism (Davis 2004; Moravcsik 1994; Putnam 1988). Moreover, the EU has consistently taken a liberalising stance throughout negotiations on a wide array of issues. Finally, the EU has also undergone a transformation from being a reluctant leader during the Uruguay Round to a key sponsor of wide ranging liberalisation during the Doha Round. Indeed, after the adoption of the Uruguay Round commitments, Commissioner Lamy gave shape to the so-called 'multilateralism first' approach for EU trade policy and placed a moratorium on bilateral trade agreements (Elsig 2007). In sum, despite the expectation of increased obstacles on the path towards further multilateral trade cooperation, judicialisation has not deterred one of the most important trade actors from advocating for a new global round of comprehensive and liberalising trade commitments.

Hence, WTO judicialisation has not constrained the EU from supporting far-reaching multilateral trade cooperation and this case provides for sufficient room to question the validity of existing pessimistic claims about how WTO judicialisation has affected the prospects for further cooperation in the international trade regime. We therefore have used this case study as a plausibility probe, with the aim to demonstrate the empirical relevance of our argument by identifying one relevant case in which it can be concretely applied (Eckstein 1975). While plausibility probes fall short of systematically testing theoretical propositions, they are widely acknowledged to potentially play a crucial role in the process of theory development, particularly when used as preliminary studies on relatively untested theories and hypotheses such as the ones presented in this chapter, serving as an intermediary stage before moving from hypothesis construction to time-consuming empirical tests (Eckstein 1975: 108–13; George and Bennett 2005: 75; Levy 2008: 7).

Interest group attendance at WTO Ministerial Conferences

In order to subject the arguments reviewed and developed so far to empirical scrutiny, we first take into consideration existing evidence concerning interest group participation at WTO Ministerial Conferences. To do so, we rely on evidence that has appeared in various publications and comes from a large-scale project (see Hanegraaff 2014, Hanegraaff *et al.* 2011, Hanegraaff forthcoming, Hanegraaff *et al.* forthcoming; De Bièvre *et al.* 2016) which mapped all interest group participation at two international venues, namely at the World Trade Organisation's Ministerial Conferences (MCs) (between 1995 and 2012) and the United Nations Climate Summits (between 1997 and 2011). As far as the WTO is concerned, the project mapped and coded for each of the seven Ministerial Conferences between 1995 and 2012 all the organisations that were eligible to attend, not all of which actually attended. In total, the project identified 1962 different organisations, which were coded on the basis of a limited number of variables that were identified through organisational websites. This dataset with web-based information offers a comprehensive insight into the types of organisations interested in WTO policies, the regions and the countries where they come from, their respective areas of interest, how they are organised and so on. Most importantly for our purposes, because the dataset includes information on all Ministerial Conferences from 1995 (Singapore) to 2012 (Geneva), we are able to get an overview of how the characteristics of the interest groups population at WTO Ministerial Conferences has changed over time, which gives us a rough indication of the effects of the judicialisation of the WTO.

Two caveats on the nature of this illustrative quantitative evidence are in order. First, it does not give an overview of the evolution of the interest group population in the trade regime from the GATT to the WTO period. This is so because, during the GATT period, interest group presence during rounds was limited and not formalised, so that official and comprehensive sources on attendance are absent (Hanegraaff *et al.* 2011). Second, looking at the presence or absence of interest groups at WTO MCs leaves out of consideration the domestic lobbying that takes place in national capitals. While arguably this is where a substantial share of lobbying actually takes place, we believe evidence concerning interest group lobbying at MCs can nonetheless yield interesting insights, both because it is reasonable to expect that the distribution in the types of interest groups that lobby at the national capital should be fairly similar to what is seen at WTO MCs (De Bièvre *et al.* 2016), and furthermore because evidence on interest group presence at MCs allows for comparability and generalisability across different members of the world trading system.

Figure 3.1: Density of WTO population over time

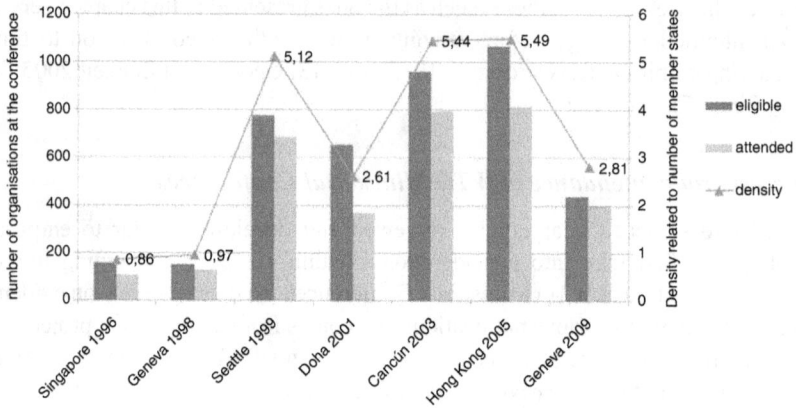

Source: (Hanegraaff *et al.* 2011)

The first question we address is whether there has been a rise in interest group activity in the context of multilateral trade negotiations since the creation of the WTO and the strengthening of the enforcement mechanisms it brought about. The expectation is that increased information about the distributive effects of prospective trade agreements should have fostered greater political mobilisation among interest groups. Figure 3.1 seems to corroborate these expectations.

Indeed, the figure shows that the density of the WTO population, operationalised as the number of organisations per member state that attended for a given MC, has increased over time. More specifically, the data indicates a process starting with slow growth, followed by a rapid growth that finally stabilises after a gradual decline. These ups and downs are neither particularly interesting nor surprising. Indeed, the observed evolution of the WTO interest group participation is quite in line with the expectation that, in an environment where a substantial number of organisations have mobilised, the increased constraints on realising political goals will lead to the exit of unsuccessful groups (Lowery and Gray 1995). What is interesting to note is that, when the WTO interest system reached a mature and stable composition, the density of interest groups was more than twice as large as in the early MCs. Thus, since the judicialisation of the WTO, the multilateral trade regime has clearly experienced a rise in the political mobilisation of interest groups. While a wide array of potential factors might have contributed to bringing about this evolution, it is just plausible to argue that the judicialisation of the WTO might be one of these important factors. And indeed, as we show in the next sections, many important interest groups were motivated to mobilise politically precisely to weigh in on the politics of the Doha Round in light of the predictability and transparency of prospective agreements ensured by the judicialisation of the WTO.

The next and more important question is whether such trends of political mobilisation have empowered pro or anti-trade liberalisation forces. Of course, answering this question is extremely different because one would need to dispose of specific data on the policy preferences of each interest group. Since such data is not available, we simply distinguish the population of organised groups attending WTO MCs on the basis of the types of economic sectors they represent. To do so, we consider four broad economic sectors: agriculture, manufacturing, services and wholesale and retail (which are grouped in the 'trade' category). We acknowledge that this type of evidence is limited in many important ways. Most importantly, the trade policy preferences of interest groups representing the same economic sector can change across WTO members, i.e. agricultural producers tend to have pro-trade preferences in countries like Brazil, while they tend to have protectionist preferences in the EU.

Table 3.1: Relative number of interest groups per economic sector per Ministerial Conference

	MC1	MC2	MC3	MC4	MC5	MC6	MC7	MC8
Agriculture	27%	40%	45%	40%	40%	43%	39%	40%
Manufacturing	35%	22%	29%	33%	31%	30%	28%	22%
Services	31%	32%	23%	21%	23%	20%	23%	27%
Trade	8%	6%	4%	6%	6%	7%	10%	11%

Source: (Hanegraaff 2014)

Figure 3.2: Relative number of interest groups per economic sector per Ministerial Conference

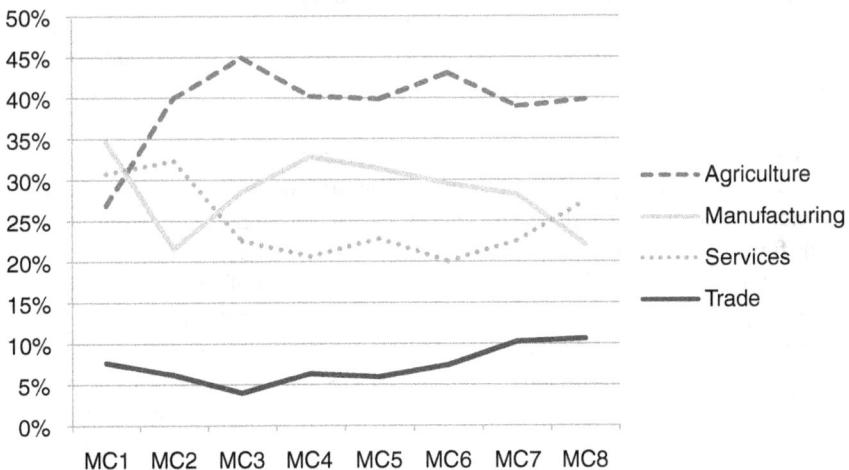

Source: (Hanegraaff 2014)

With these caveats in mind however, it is interesting to note how Table 3.1 and Figure 3.2 nicely show that the composition of the population of interest groups politically active at WTO MCs remains fairly stable over time. This is in line with our argument that judicialisation should not be expected to empower a particular type of interest but that its effects play out differently, depending on the existing relative patterns of political mobilisation in different countries. Perhaps, and in line again with our argument, the only economic sector that displays a consistent pattern of increase in political activity at WTO MCs is the 'trade' sector. This trend seems to corroborate our argument that judicialisation has acted as a trigger for the political mobilisation of importers in an international economy increasingly organised around GVCs.

The EU's domestic politics of trade policymaking in the Doha Round: The role of exporters and importers

In this section we briefly trace the policy preferences and patterns of political mobilisation of trade-related domestic interests in the EU to show the plausibility of the argument that judicialisation can empower a pro-trade coalition composed of export-oriented and import-dependent groups at the expense of import-competing groups when these latter groups are already well organised and traditionally influential in trade policymaking. We do so by concentrating on how judicialisation has affected the preferences and patterns of political mobilisation during the Doha Round of a key set of European exporters, namely service providers, and European import-dependent firms.

As far as European exporters are concerned, empirical evidence suggests that judicialisation has acted as a trigger for an increased political role by organisations representing these firms' interests. More specifically, the strengthening of the enforcement mechanism in the WTO seems to have strengthened the incentives of European services exporters to engage in costly collective action and push European policymakers to advance the liberalisation of the service trade in the Doha Round of negotiations. Indeed, while the European Commission's strategy for services liberalisation was met with indifference by services producers during the Uruguay Round, the capacity of the WTO to ensure transparency and predictability of commitments provided incentives for these groups to mobilise politically and strongly back the European Commission in the run up to the Doha Round. Comparing these dynamics with those of key import-competing groups, lends further support to the claim that judicialisation indeed has affected the power relations among principals, increasing the relative weight of actors with a stake in supporting agents' efforts to pursue multilateral trade cooperation

Services negotiations during the Doha Round have been intended to further the efforts towards the liberalisation of trade in services that took place in 1995 with the adoption of the General Agreement on Trade in Services (GATS). In accordance with the approach taken during the Uruguay Round, services were set as a priority of the EU's negotiating strategy in the run-up to the Doha Round (European Commission 1999). Negotiations on services have come up during the Doha Round, strongly paralleling the EU's requests, involving a mixture of concessions for reciprocal market access and rule-making (Woolcock 2005: 394). Although EU offers have varied greatly across modes of supply, it is fair to argue that the EU has taken a fairly liberalising stance throughout the negotiating process (Hoekman *et al.* 2007).

While the EU's negotiating stance on services has been fairly consistent across time, key economic groups have approached the Doha Round quite differently from the Uruguay Round. In contrast with the situation in the US, where negotiators were fully supported by corporate interests, the European services community was largely absent from negotiations during the Uruguay Round (Paemen and Bensch 1995; Van den Hoven 2002; Woll 2006). As has been noted, 'most business associations either showed no interest in the negotiations or were afraid to confront farmers' unions by supporting the Commission position' (Van den Hoven 2002: 15). After the signing of the Marrakech agreements and the creation of the WTO, however, things started to change.

During negotiations on financial services in the GATS (1995–7), for instance, there were major consultations with telecommunications providers and with the Financial Leaders Group, both of which had strongly lobbied the EU (Van den Hoven 2002). In the run-up to the new 'millennium round', service providers in several member states also strongly advocated further liberalisation of trade in services (Woolcock 2005). In 1999, for instance, the European Services Forum (ESF), a network of organisations representing the service industries across the EU, was established arguably with the primary aim of defending the sector's interests in the new WTO negotiations (Dür 2008). While the Commission itself had been unsuccessful in soliciting the creation of a coalition of service industries during the Uruguay Round (Paemen and Bensch 1995), this same attempt to build support for a new trade round was met with success in 1998 (Van den Hoven 2002). It is undisputed that these interests were keen to respond to these demands and since then the ESF has consistently lobbied for a strengthening of the GATS by monitoring and providing advice to the Commission and member states through detailed research and negotiation over proposals (ESF 1999, 2001, 2003, 2005). The Commission itself has acknowledged the key role the ESF has come to play during services negotiations in the Doha Round, both in terms of finding out where the problems lie and in advancing specific requests (Deere 2005). Interestingly, services negotiations in the new round have also been supported by industrial producers, which perceive them as essential to improving the competitiveness of European industry (UNICE 2000, 2001, 2003).

In sum, the patterns of business mobilisation with respect to negotiations on services have moved from relative indifference prior to judicialisation to active involvement in the subsequent phase. Of course, this is not to argue that judicialisation of the international trade regime has been the only cause of greater political mobilisation from these constituencies. Since the early 1990s, the services sector has also increasingly become an area of European comparative advantage with the greatest potential for growth in EU exports, and this has certainly influenced the readiness of businesses to mobilise politically. Nevertheless, the wording of various policy statements and policy positions brought forward by these organisations does seem to suggest that the increased transparency and enhanced credibility of commitments in the WTO have been key determinants of their policy preferences.

The ESF, for instance, justified its support for combining services and other trade-related issues in a new comprehensive trade round in a position paper in 1999 by stressing the precision, transparency and bindingness of WTO commitments (ESF 1999). This position was later further stressed by stating that 'services liberalisation with sufficient balances, certainties and transparency ... will only be achieved in the context of a wider and broad-based WTO round' (ESF 2001). The same line of reasoning can be seen in a number of position papers delivered by the organisation representing European industrial interests, the Union of Industrial and Employers' Confederation of Europe (UNICE). It has also pointed to the transparency and predictability of the WTO framework as a key reason to negotiate services liberalisation in the WTO rather than through bilateral or regional agreements (UNICE 2000, 2001).

Interestingly, these trends stand in stark contrast to patterns of political mobilisation in import-competing sectors. Farmers' groups, for example, are the interest groups with the longest and most successful record of political lobbying in Europe, and they lobbied EU policymakers as strongly during the Uruguay Round as they had before and during negotiations in the Doha Round (Daugberg and Swinbank 2009; Poletti 2012; Swinnen 2008). Thus, judicialisation seems to have had a larger marginal effect on the propensity of export-competing groups to mobilise politically, and thereby empowered them relative to import-competing ones.

We now turn to assessing whether import-dependent firms have played some role in the EU politics of trade policymaking during the Doha Round. There is ample evidence that associations representing the interests of European import-dependent firms, both retailers and manufacturers, have consistently supported multilateral trade negotiations, both before and throughout the Doha Round. As early as 1999, Eurocommerce and the Foreign Trade Association (FTA) delivered a joint statement to the WTO Secretariat expressing their support for the launch of a new and ambitious multilateral trade round to follow the Uruguay Round (Eurocommerce and FTA 1999). Since then, both associations have kept issuing a wide array of position papers and other documents expressing their support for deep and comprehensive multilateral trade liberalisation, particularly with a view to reducing the general level of protectionism to the benefit of retailers, manufacturers and consumers at large. For instance, in many different instances the FTA has expressed its broad support for a round that should address 'the range of issues that will have an immediate effect on the scope of action at home and abroad in the context of increasing internationalization' (FTA 2003), including the dismantling of customs and non-tariff barriers, the simplification of trade procedures, the further liberalisation of trade in services and the conclusion of a multilateral investment agreement (FTA 2002, 2003, 2004, 2006). When after the 2006 Geneva MC it became clear that an ambitious comprehensive trade deal was not in sight and that the ambitions of the negotiating parties would need to be significantly scaled down, the FTA continued to express support for a successful conclusion to the negotiations in order to overcome the protectionist tendencies following the global financial crisis and to reduce the impediments in global trade for the benefit of retailers and consumers (FTA 2011, 2011a, 2013, 2014). This support was justified by arguing that 'given the reality of international supply chains and production processes there is no going back to isolated domestic trade policy actions as today's market structures impose multilateral coordination and open borders' (FTA 2013: 1).

Similarly, Eurocommerce has continuously supported the conclusion of an ambitious multilateral trade deal to the benefit of retailers, wholesalers and importers (Eurocommerce 2003, 2005; 2009), in the conviction that 'import and export are two sides of the same coin. If Europe wants to stay competitive in the changing world market, it needs to import in order to be able to export to other parts of the world' (Eurocommerce 2013).

The positions of these organisations were echoed in the stance taken by another important organisation that represents the interests of European retailers and small and medium enterprises, the Association of European Chambers of Commerce and Industry (Eurochambres). It has on many occasions supported a successful outcome of the negotiations to provide a significant confidence boost to investors, importing companies and consumers (Eurochambres 2003, 2006, 2007, 2009).

Two issues are particularly interesting in the context of this analysis. First, it is clear that the institutional characteristics of the WTO, particularly the predictability and transparency of trade rules brought about by judicialisation, have been considered as key elements for these groups to engage in collective action in support of multilateral traditional trade liberalisation during the Doha Round. For instance, the FTA has forcefully called for the application of the DSM to all agreements that are eventually struck during the Doha negotiations (FTA 2003). In addition, it has explicitly stated that 'the WTO as the overarching global organisation for trade is best place to create simple and worldwide applicable rules … [M]ore multilateralism in trade and even more binding international rules are needed to protect economic policymakers themselves and the protectionist temptations' (FTA 2013: 2). Similarly, Eurocommerce has called for a successful conclusion of the Doha Round arguing that

> predictability and legal certainty are key prerequisites for economic operators to survive in the world market … [T]he WTO is the only multilateral organisation where the new world order has already started working, characterised by global governance, the respect for common rules and effective dispute settlement.
> (2009: 2)

In a similar vein, Eurochambres has called for success in negotiations in the light of the ability of the WTO's institutional framework to

> bring benefits in terms of stability and predictability … and to act as a shield for countries that have already started to impose any kind of barrier

and/or those who have started backtracking from their efforts to liberalize their economies.

(2009: 1–2)

In line with our expectations, the strengthening of enforcement mechanisms in the WTO has not been seen as an impediment for further commitments in WTO negotiations by European import-dependent firms, but rather as a key component of their consistent support for a successful conclusion of the Doha Round.

Second, and again in line with our argument, import-dependent firms and export-oriented producers have joined forces during negotiations in the Doha Round to push EU policymakers to create the conditions for success. For instance, a few days ahead of the WTO MC in Bali, the associations representing the interests of import-dependent firms – FTA, Eurocommerce and Eurochambres – issued a joint statement with the ESF calling for a finalisation of the deal on trade facilitation (Joint Statement Business Associations 2013). A year later, these three associations issued another joint statement with the Federation of European Exporting Goods Industry to urge the ratification of the agreement on trade facilitation, pointing out how

in a world of increasingly complex global value chains it is more important than ever that the international trade rule book keeps pace with a rapidly transforming business environment ... to reduce the cost and time of moving goods across national borders.

(Joint Statement by Business Associations Worldwide 2014)

Concluding remarks

In this chapter we have addressed the question of how the judicialisation of the international trade regime has affected the incentives and constraints domestic actors face when confronted with the choice of either supporting or opposing multilateral agreements on the elimination and/or reduction of traditional tariff barriers to trade. We have developed our reasoning starting from the argument that the institutional reforms which have strengthened the enforcement mechanisms of agreed rules in the trade regime could have acted as an impediment to the deepening of traditional trade liberalisation commitments in the WTO by having empowered import-competing groups relative to export-oriented ones in the trade policymaking process.

We have also offered a more nuanced view of the interactive dynamics linking judicialisation and the domestic politics of trade in WTO members' needs. Our argument ran along two lines. First, we showed that judicialisation need not tilt the balance of trade-related domestic groups in favour of anti-trade forces. In fact, we showed that under some circumstances the opposite outcome is equally plausible. Second, we contended that a proper understanding of the politics of trade policymaking in the contemporary international economy requires an appreciation of the role of import-dependent firms. In an international economy increasingly organised around GVCs, the politics of trade can no longer be usefully characterised as an exclusive conflict between exporters and import-competitors. In addition to these important economic actors, import-dependent firms also need to be taken into account as an important pro-trade liberalisation stakeholder in the trade policymaking process. Combining these two arguments suggests that, while in some cases judicialisation can indeed foster greater domestic opposition to traditional trade liberalisation, in other instances it may end up fostering the emergence of a pro-trade liberalisation coalition composed of exporters and importers more so than mobilising traditionally influential import-competing groups.

We have shown the plausibility of our argument by offering some illustrative evidence of interest group participation at WTO MCs and, most importantly, by tracing patterns of domestic political mobilisation before and during the Doha Round of multilateral trade negotiations in the EU. While our evidence was largely illustrative and only aimed to establish the plausibility of our argument, we believe our findings cast an important light on existing research on the link between judicialisation and cooperation in the WTO. The failure of the Doha Round to deliver significant trade liberalisation commitments would at first glance seem to corroborate the early pessimistic assessments about how the judicialisation of the WTO would affect the long-term stability of the trade regime by decreasing the propensity of WTO members to further commit to trade liberalisation within its framework. Showing that the outcome of negotiations has been consistent with such predictions, however, is not enough to corroborate them. The causal argument that underlies such a pessimistic view runs from the institutional reform of the WTO, to the domestic politics of its members, and only then to the outcomes of negotiations. Our argument and illustrative evidence have shown that the pessimistic view is not based on logically consistent reasoning and is incomplete in terms of the relevant economic interests it considers in the politics of trade policymaking. Instead, this chapter has suggested that an explanation of the inability of WTO members to reach an ambitious agreement for the liberalisation of traditional trade barriers to trade may be found in other factors and is not necessarily attributable to the constraints brought about by the judicialisation of the WTO.

Chapter Four

Judicial Politics and Regulatory Cooperation

The creation of the WTO in 1995 not only increased the bindingness and enforceability of international trade rules, but also their scope. Whereas before this time the trade agenda primarily concerned tariffs and quotas, or 'at the border issues', it was significantly expanded in 1995 to also include issues related to national laws and regulations, or 'behind the border issues'. This new coordination and cooperation in areas that had traditionally fallen within the universe of domestic economic regulation was triggered by the increasing economic integration between members of the international trading system (Young and Peterson 2006). The twin developments of a judicialisation of the enforcement of rules and the expansion of the regulatory scope of WTO agreements are intricately intertwined. It is certainly not a coincidence that members of the international trading system strengthened the WTO's rule enforcement mechanism at the same time as they enlarged the number of topics falling under its jurisdiction.

As expanded upon in Chapter Two, several key members of the GATT had become dissatisfied with the DSM's ability to tackle regulatory trade barriers in the late 1970s and early 1980s. At first sight, the GATT system would seem to have worked well at this time. Whenever disputing parties allowed the establishment of a panel, they were usually compliant with its ruling. Yet, many truly tricky disputes never made it to the panel stage at all. And when they did, they did not usually result in a ruling, as a defendant could veto the adoption of the panel report at the end of the dispute settlement process. As countries abandoned this veto practice at the beginning of the 1980s (Hudec 1992), attention turned all the more to the ability of members to veto the establishment of a panel at the very early stage of the procedure. As a consequence of this right, at the end of the 1980s and in parallel to the Uruguay Round negotiations, the United States especially began aggressively pushing a unilateral policy of deciding for itself whether regulatory, behind-the-border measures in intellectual property, health and safety rules, or services unduly hampered market access, and imposing retaliatory sanctions against trading partners when it deemed fit. The decision to abolish the defendant's right to veto the establishment of a panel when a complainant requested it in 1990 – expanded upon in Chapter Two (GATT 1990) – therefore established the automaticity of adjudication and the right to a panel, a decision that took immediate effect during a crucial phase of the Uruguay Round. Indeed, several regulatory chapters of the Uruguay Round negotiations received an enhanced impetus as a result, as negotiators now saw that regulatory agreements could be subjected to the strengthened dispute settlement system without the possibility of a veto, just like with traditional at-the-border barriers to trade.

In the previous chapter we analysed the relationship between judicial politics and the strategic calculus of domestic actors, key economic interest groups and policymakers on at-the-border issues. We now turn to the question of whether, and if so how, WTO judicialisation has influenced the preferences of domestic actors for WTO cooperation on domestic regulatory practices. Our main goal is to investigate how WTO judicialisation has affected the preferences of WTO members for international regulatory strategies. More specifically, we formulate hypotheses on the conditions under which WTO member states would choose a judicialised venue such as the WTO to pursue their regulatory strategies. Ultimately, we address the question of whether, and under what conditions, judicialisation would affect the propensity of WTO members to expand its regulatory reach.

Members of the international community of states have various courses of action at their disposal when deciding how to further their interests internationally on some particular issue through international institutions. They can use the existing focal institution that deals with such issues, if they deem it satisfactory, or, if they do not, they can select an alternative institution; they can thus engage in venue shopping as different institutional venues offer different incentive structures and actors tend to choose the venue in which they can achieve the greatest expected utility (Baumgartner and Jones 1993). They can also seek to create a new institution from scratch (Jupille *et al.* 2013). Although the empirical boundaries between these generic options are of course not always a priori clear, these categorisations help states navigate the universe of options they have at their disposal and choose among them. In this chapter, we are interested in the choice of 'selection' of international institution. More specifically, we want to gauge under which circumstances states tend to choose existing institutions with a high degree of judicialised enforcement for furthering their interests, and when they tend to choose those with a low degree of judicialisation. Doing so allows us to tackle the broader question of whether, and if so how, the judicialisation of the WTO has strengthened or decreased WTO members' incentives to commit to regulatory agreements within the WTO framework.

A key motive for venue shopping or institutional selection by the relevant actors – i.e. mainly states and interest groups on whose behalf they negotiate – is the enforceability of any rules agreed on during international negotiations. Rather than claim that the judicialisation of the world trade regime has hampered the propensity of all WTO members to commit to new regulatory agreements within it, we argue and illustrate that the key to understanding and accounting for states' venue choices for international regulatory harmonisation lies with the conceptual distinction between two different types of regulatory harmonisation: upward harmonisation and downward harmonisation.

Suppose a dyad of countries is considering whether to harmonise regulatory standards at a higher level, either by creating new rules or by upgrading existing rules. One country has domestic regulatory standards that are set at a high level, while the other country has a relatively low level of regulation. As the upward harmonisation of regulatory standards is advantageous to the country with high regulatory standards, we expect that it will prefer a venue with a high degree of judicialisation such as the WTO. In contrast, as upward regulatory harmonisation is disadvantageous to the country with a relatively low level of regulation, it will try to maintain the status quo. If upward harmonisation is unavoidable, however, it will rather prefer a venue with a low degree of judicialisation and thus resist the adoption of such regulatory agreements within the WTO framework.

This is not the end of the story, however. In a second scenario, the two states are considering downward harmonisation, or the question of whether to allow for exceptions and/or carve-outs to commitments that have been previously agreed upon. In this scenario, we argue that the constellation of preferences is reversed. As downward regulatory harmonisation is advantageous for countries with a low level of regulation, they will push for such measures in a judicialised setting such as the WTO. Highly regulated countries who naturally should oppose downward harmonisation, will either seek to preserve the status quo or prefer to locate such negotiations in a venue with a low degree of judicialisation.

The story we tell here is thus essentially about the WTO and the regimes within which it is nested. Since our discussion concerns preferences over global regulatory harmonisation and applies to situations in which there are at least two venues with an overlapping functional issue scope, one of which is highly judicialised and one (or more) of which is not, our empirical universe of cases boils down to situations in which states have to choose between the WTO and other international regulatory venues. Thus, our argument ultimately identifies systematic preferences over the choice of pursuing regulatory cooperation in the judicialised setting of the WTO.

Enforceability and regulatory cooperation

The literature on how WTO judicialisation has affected the regulatory strategies of states can be categorised in two groups. According to one view, judicialisation may have turned the WTO into an attractive institutional location for the governments of industrialised countries, as these are generally keen to negotiate regulatory issues due to the pressure of domestic constituencies (De Bièvre 2006). While regulatory agreements entail high implementation costs, especially with respect to enforcement, the WTO offers the possibility of retaliating against non-compliant countries, thereby giving more certainty, stability, and predictability to commitments and issue linkages. The industrialised countries that are keen to engage in international regulatory harmonisation are likely to value the increased credibility brought about by stronger enforcement of rules, and thus they will be prone to locate such rules in a highly judicialised venue.

However, drawing on the existing literature, one could also argue in the opposite direction, namely that strong enforcement might have reduced the propensity to commit to new agreements in the WTO. As discussed in Chapter Two, by increasing enforceability, judicialisation not only makes agreements more credible, it also makes them more tightly binding, decreasing flexibility and limiting the ability of governments to opt out of commitments. This in turn can lead governments to deem that the costs of signing such agreements outweigh the benefits. We might expect that stronger enforcement raises the stakes during negotiations, causing states to bargain harder and hold out in the hope of getting a better deal, or even to defect from cooperation entirely (Fearon 1998). Particularly when states face uncertainty about the distributional implications of a particular agreement, they are more likely to support negotiations in a setting with a high degree of flexibility. Because gains and losses of regulatory harmonisation tend to be difficult to ascertain (Wilson 1973), it is fair to expect actors to greatly value institutional flexibility.

It is important to note at this point that regulatory agreements possess an important property that sets them apart from simple at-the-border market access commitments: regulatory agreements are generally more difficult to enforce. Market access agreements on tariffs or quota can be implemented simultaneously, with countries enacting such agreements at an agreed date. They are enforceable through the bilateral, tit-for-tat withdrawal of market access or the threat thereof. If one country does not lower its tariffs, for example, the other country can revoke its own tariff reduction. Such an exchange of market access concessions can be conducted with specific products such as when all countries introduced zero tariffs for trade in pharmaceutical products. Alternatively, concessions can be exchanged across different types of products and sectors, such as the United States lowering its tariffs on manufactures in exchange for lower EU and Japanese agricultural barriers (Davis 2004).

Regulatory agreements by contrast display several characteristics that set them apart from classical trade treaties. First, the implementation of international regulatory agreements – on for instance intellectual property, health and safety rules, labour and environmental rules, procedural requirements, and the like – typically entails high transaction costs regarding policing, measurement, and especially enforcement (Majone 1996). Second, it is practically impossible to ensure simultaneous implementation. As countries implement their obligations at different points in time, reacting with the revocation of one's own implementation would be prohibitively costly in material and political terms. It would entail reversing changes to rules that affect domestic constituencies. Third, regulatory agreements typically cause asymmetrical implementation costs. Some states may have to drastically alter their existing regulatory regimes, while others may have to change very little or nothing at all.

For these reasons, regulatory agreements cannot be enforced easily in isolation. One way to make their enforcement more credible has been to link regulatory agreements to traditional trade liberalisation commitments in the WTO. In this way, market access commitments are exchanged for new international regulations. In the Uruguay Round, for instance, Western industrialised countries promised to lower barriers on textiles and agricultural products in exchange for the approval of agreements on trade in services and intellectual property.

Because of the greater difficulty of the enforceability of regulatory agreements, states are likely to pay even more attention to where to locate particular regulatory agreements than when they engage in the reciprocal exchange of traditional trade concessions. Where several institutions have the potential to deal with a given policy issue, negotiating over where to locate the negotiations in the first place becomes part and parcel of state interaction itself (Fearon 1998). This international regime complexity, namely the existence of multiple regimes with a similar issue scope, increasingly permits actors to apply venue shopping to achieve specific policy objectives (Alter and Meunier 2009). The existence of more and less judicialised institutions is thus a key factor in venue shopping for regulatory cooperation. Put differently, the judicialisation of the WTO political system has turned it into a more attractive institutional location for the conclusion of new regulatory agreements for some states, whereas for others it has become a much less attractive venue for concluding further agreements on behind-the-border issues.

The existing literature on regulatory cooperation still falls short of accounting for the empirically observable variation in state preferences for institutional venues for regulatory harmonisation. Developed countries with similar levels of domestic regulation do not have stable preferences for judicialised settings across the board. For instance, the preferences of the EU and the US over the inclusion of the so-called trade-and issues (i.e. trade-and-labour, trade-and-the-environment, the 'Singapore issues') in the Doha Round of multilateral trade negotiations greatly diverged. The former strongly supported the inclusion of these issues in the WTO framework, while the latter resisted such a move (Poletti 2012). Also, developing countries with a relatively low level of domestic regulation sometimes have a strong preference for international regulatory harmonisation in the WTO. For instance, developing countries have consistently sought to include new intellectual property rights rules concerning access to essential medicines within the WTO framework, whereas industrialised countries have opposed this strategy. How can this variation be accounted for? What are the underlying sets of incentives and constraints that determine this varying constellation of preferences both *within* and *across* countries? We contend that the key to understanding and accounting for states' venue choices over international regulatory harmonisation lies in the conceptual distinction between two different types of regulatory harmonisation.

Venue shopping and regulatory strategies: two scenarios

Actors engage in venue shopping or institutional selection when the possibility of moving around different access points exists (Baumgartner and Jones 1993; Jupille *et al*. 2013). Venue shopping can occur either between the same levels of government (horizontal venue shopping), across different levels of government (vertical venue shopping), or both (Princen and Kerremans 2008: 1137). Logically prior to any form of venue shopping is the existence of multiple institutions with a similar issue scope.

Diverging preferences between actors are linked to actual or perceived distributional costs or benefits of a particular regulatory initiative. Venue shopping takes place because actors hold diverging preferences over specific policies. Actors consequentially choose the venue where they expect to achieve their greatest expected utility. A particular venue will be preferred by those that support a given policy outcome if such a venue is expected to make that policy outcome more likely. Similarly, a venue that makes a certain policy outcome unlikely will be preferred by those that oppose such a policy outcome. In the next sections, we consider how the degree of judicialisation of a regime affects the venue shopping behaviour of states concerning international regulatory harmonisation. By developing systematic arguments on the conditions under which states are likely to be willing to pursue regulatory cooperation in judicialised international institutions, we aim to answer the question of how the judicialisation of the WTO can be expected to have affected the propensity of its members to expand the regulatory reach of the multilateral trade regime.

Upward regulatory harmonisation

States engage in upward regulatory harmonisation when they create new international rules to harmonise existing practices, or when they further tighten already existing international rules.

The literature dealing with the dynamics that underlies international regulatory competition offers useful insights about which actors will be likely to support upward regulatory harmonisation in judicialised regimes. This literature stresses the political economic dynamics that underlies governments' choices over international regulatory policies and argues that such choices are driven by a desire to satisfy the demands of organised societal groups. In essence, this view posits that states with stringent domestic regulatory standards have an incentive to export these costly regulations abroad: the more costly domestic regulatory standards are, the greater the incentives for both domestic producers and policymakers to support similar international standards to create a level playing field (Falkner 2007; Kelemen 2010; Kelemen and Vogel 2010). By exporting costly regulations abroad, domestic producers benefit because the competitive advantage of producers in countries with lower regulatory standards is reduced and because new market access opportunities are created in foreign markets. The incentives to spread domestic norms internationally are even stronger when producers and civic groups join forces in Baptist–bootlegger coalitions (DeSombre 2000; Vogel 1995).

While this perspective tells us why certain constituencies and the policymakers defending their interests may wish to have stringent domestic regulatory standards spread out to the international level, it leaves open the question of which institutional regime these states might prefer for coming to agreements. It seems plausible that their preferences for different institutional venues will depend on whether they expect their interests regarding regulatory export to remain stable over time. Such expectations may depend on a number of factors, such as the political salience of an issue, or the extent to which domestic institutional rules favour policy stability. For instance, when issues are highly politically salient and touch upon widely held and strongly rooted values and opinions within society, the preferences of different constituencies and policymakers over international upward regulatory harmonisation are not likely to fluctuate over time. Similarly, it seems fair to expect preferences for international upward regulatory harmonisation to be more stable in political systems where a high number institutional actors have a say in the decision-making process, so that the chances for movements away from the status quo are minimised (Scharpf 1988; Tsebelis 2002). Under these conditions, we can expect actors to value flexibility less, providing incentives for them to care more about the enforceability of commitments. Indeed, when actors anticipate that their preferences will not change in the future, they are likely to want to make sure opting out of agreed rules becomes more difficult.

In contrast, producers in countries with less extensive domestic regulatory standards have strong incentives to oppose the setting up of new international regulatory standards for exactly the same reasons. New rules for stricter domestic regulatory standards create adjustment costs for domestic producers and decrease their competitiveness in the international as well as the domestic market. It is true that, by a dynamic known as the 'California effect', countries with lower domestic regulatory standards may surrender competitive advantages voluntarily in order to follow states with higher regulatory standards that have large and attractive internal markets as well as high political influence (Vogel 1995; Young 2003). In normal circumstances, however, one should expect producers and policymakers in countries with relatively less stringent regulatory standards to oppose upward regulatory harmonisation because this would be likely to entail substantial adjustment costs and loss of competitiveness.

By extension, if the absence of any regulatory harmonisation is the preferred outcome for these actors, one should expect that, if there is to be upward harmonisation, they will prefer realising this in non-judicialised venues rather than in judicialised ones. If for some reason these countries are unable to veto these international regulatory initiatives, they should clearly prefer an institutional venue with weak enforcement, so as to allow for cost-free deviations from agreed rules. In other words, when actors cannot prevent regulatory action on a specific issue, they may grudgingly accept new substantive rules in a setting with a low degree of judicialisation in order to ensure that particular undesired policy outcomes never become binding standards.

Although the argument we develop in this chapter is primarily about the preferences of domestic actors for regulatory cooperation and how these might translate into regulatory strategies for states, we would like to highlight that, with regard to negotiation outcomes, bargaining power crucially depends on the costs of non-agreement (Moravcsik 1993). Whether developing countries with lower domestic regulatory standards give in to, or are able to resist, requests from developed countries to place new substantive rules in a judicialised venue is thus likely to depend on the outside options that are available for developing countries. If developing countries deem it more costly to resist the demands by developed countries than to accept the terms of the agreement, the agreement is likely to prevail. By contrast, if developing countries have a better alternative (i.e. if the costs of non-agreement for them are relatively low), they are likely to be able to resist and block initiatives from developed countries. In the range of cases we consider, the availability of outside options for developing countries mainly depends on whether advanced industrialised countries can make a deal attractive through issue linkage, or whether they can force reluctant developing countries to accept upward harmonisation through the threat of exclusion.

Downward regulatory harmonisation

Sometimes countries might wish to decrease, rather than increase, the level of international regulatory commitments they are bound to. This may be so for different reasons. States that had previously committed to regulatory agreements may find out that they are incapable of converging on stringent rules or perhaps changed economic circumstances may lead them to a change of preference. Whatever the reasons driving these preference changes, we empirically observe that many WTO member states are increasingly seeking to bring back some of the flexibility they gave up by committing to regulatory agreements in the WTO. Several initiatives have aimed at allowing for greater latitude and flexibility in the implementation of commitments.

Greater flexibility can be achieved in two ways. First, already agreed rules can be made more flexible by directly amending and/or replacing them. Second, flexibility can also be brought about indirectly by introducing new affirmative rights within the same judicialised venue that deviate from previously agreed rules, which has the concrete effect of amending such rules. We use the concept of downward harmonisation to describe both types of situation because, irrespective of whether the new rules take the form of limitations to existing rules or of new affirmative rights, the aim is to decrease the degree of stringency of the rules in place, thus enabling states to contravene such rules without suffering a cost.

In scenarios of downward harmonisation, the constellation of preferences has tipped over with respect to previous agreements. Countries with less stringent regulatory standards face compelling incentives to bring such negotiations to the most judicialised regime, whereas highly regulated countries are likely to strongly oppose negotiations in that venue. When states have already committed to binding agreements in the WTO or to commitments with long implementation periods, the state with the lower level of domestic regulation may have a stake in increasing the flexibility of such commitments to accommodate domestic rules that are likely to be found to be WTO incompatible and the change of which would entail high adjustment costs (Poletti and Sicurelli 2012, 2015). Domestic constituencies and policymakers are likely to anticipate that this can only be achieved by changing and/or replacing rules already agreed in the WTO.

In principle, downward regulatory harmonisation could also be pursued in other venues. Yet, the relationship between WTO rules and rules agreed in other non-judicialised regimes is inherently, although often implicitly, hierarchical. Indeed, when a clash between such rules emerges, WTO rules prevail because the WTO DSM can be invoked against non-compliant members and impose costs on them, whereas rules agreed in non-judicialised venues have no biting force (Eckersley 2004). In other words, countries with a low level of domestic regulation, usually developing countries, can only immunise themselves from already agreed binding rules in the WTO by changing and/or replacing rules in the WTO itself.

It is important to stress that this is so precisely because of judicialisation. In the absence of a venue with strong enforcement, countries preferring downward regulatory harmonisation have no particular preference for where to locate rules introducing flexibility. In the presence of a highly judicialised venue, however, it is simply not an option to shift to another venue or to create a new venue. When states have already committed to enforceable rules, they can only achieve downward harmonisation within the venue at which such rules were agreed. In sum, while in the absence of a judicialised venue actors could try to achieve downward harmonisation by addressing different venues, judicialisation restricts actors' room of manoeuvre, forcing them to pursue such strategy of downward harmonisation in the highly judicialised venue, because only then will the more flexible rule overrule the more stringent one.

Precisely for the opposite reasons, highly regulated developed countries are likely to prefer not having downward harmonisation at all and, in case they were unable to block such an initiative, are likely to acquiesce to the adoption of new rules only in a non-judicialised setting. The obvious reason for this is that they wish to retain the right to force their partners to comply with agreed rules. As they greatly value the enforceability of commitments, they are likely to oppose any attempt to bring flexibility in through the back door.

Again, whether developing countries with lower domestic regulatory standards manage to achieve their desired downward regulatory harmonisation through a negotiated outcome in the judicialised venue crucially depends on whether a better alternative to such an agreement is available to developed countries. If developed countries with higher domestic regulatory standards deem the costs of non-agreement to be higher than those resulting from the proposed agreement, they are likely to give in. The opposite holds when the costs of non-agreement for developed countries are low. In other words, whenever developing countries can link their approval of other issues to the introduction of flexibility for already existing stringent international regulation, they are likely to prevail.

Whether developed countries manage to keep the status quo or agree to the demands from developing countries to adopt new rules in a non-judicialised setting, is of secondary importance to them. Their primary concern is to avoid any change to the binding rules in the judicialised setting, and hence to keep their ability to enforce these rules.

Table 4.1: Regulatory cooperation and venue shopping behaviour of WTO members

	Upward harmonisation	*Downward harmonisation*
Highly regulated country	Judicialised setting	Status quo, or non-judicialised setting
Not highly regulated country	Status quo, or non-judicialised setting	Judicialised setting (WTO)

Venue shopping in the field of intellectual property rights protection

Having set out the strategic reasons for why states may engage in venue shopping in a systematic way, we now turn to the empirical testing of our argument. We illustrate the explanatory force of the argument by way of in-depth case studies of two instances of global intellectual property rights regulation, one in the area of genetic resources and one in the area of public health and access to medicines. We look into the politics of regulatory cooperation in the field of intellectual property rights protection for two important reasons. First, intellectual property rights protection has become an important component of contemporary international political economy. Whereas formerly nation states were the relevant loci of regulation that steered the allocation of intellectual property rights and obligations and thereby affected the socio-economic conditions of many, nowadays these matters are largely decided upon at the international level. Second, the regulatory framework governing the global intellectual property rights regime is spread across a host of international venues. The World Intellectual Property Organization (WIPO) holds sway over this area of global regulation, as does the WTO, the United Nations Food and Agricultural Organization (FAO), the World Health Organization (WHO), the United Nations educational, scientific and cultural organization, the Convention on Biological Diversity (CBD), and the International Union for the Protection of New Varieties of Plants (UPOV). While the WIPO and the UN special committees and agencies are characterised by a low degree of judicialisation, the WTO has judicialised dispute resolution, which makes its rules binding and enforceable. The wide array of institutional venues dealing with global intellectual property rights regulation and their different degrees of judicialisation thus make this field particularly fit to test the explanatory force of an argument about how different institutional features of regulatory regimes affect the venue shopping behaviour of states.

Since we conduct an analysis with a factor-centric research design, we picked case studies so as to provide for the needed variance on the side of the explanatory conditions (Gschwend and Schimmelfennig 2007).[2] In both case studies, we consider situations in which states could choose among different institutional venues and draw on process-related evidence to show the plausibility of the contention that the venue preferences of states are affected by both the level of domestic regulation and the type of regulatory harmonisation. In addition, we adopt an inter-temporal approach that allows us to multiply the observation points of the empirical analysis and hence strengthen the internal validity of the case studies. Indeed, in both instances of global intellectual property rights regulation we are able to trace how the preferences of states have evolved over time in response to changes in the value of one of the key explanatory conditions, namely the type of regulatory harmonisation.

---

2.   A factor-centric research design is primarily interested in the explanatory power of causal factors, whereas an outcome-centric research design is primarily interested in explaining policy outcomes.

Genetic resources and biological diversity

The Agreement on trade-related aspects of intellectual property rights (TRIPS) considerably expanded the range of economic sectors and technologies subject to intellectual property rights protection. This expansion of property rights has shifted the boundary between 'the public domain and the realm of property' (Boyle 2004). However, one regulatory area where safeguard devices such as patents have not been fully adopted at the international level is the field of biotechnology. Advancements in biotechnology have given rise to the question of whether living organisms and their genetic resources, which include genetic codes, seed varieties or plant extracts, can be subjected to intellectual property rights protection.[3]

For most of the twentieth century, the view was that private ownership over plants and animals and their genetic resources per se should not exist and that they should belong to the common heritage of mankind, meaning that open access to these resources should be guaranteed (Raustiala and Victor 2004: 281). Advocates of patentability, in contrast, argue that biotechnology is a means to secure the sustainable development of agriculture, to yield higher results with less use of pesticides and other environmentally harmful products, and to meet the challenge of soaring international commodity and food prices. In order to achieve this, investments in technologies that make use of genetic resources and other biological material have to be protected and secured through the allocation of private property rights.

The evolution of states' preferences for venue choice in the field of the intellectual property rights protection of plant genetic resources is consistent with our theoretical expectations. In the first phase, it was a typical case of upward harmonisation. Developed countries with a high level of intellectual property rights protection initially sought to secure the interests of commercial plant breeders through the adoption of international rules, which could then be placed under the framework of the WTO with its strong enforcement mechanism. Instead, biodiversity-rich developing countries with low levels of intellectual property rights protection first sought to oppose the adoption of strongly enforceable rules that would harm their interests. Once these rules were agreed, however, this turned into a case of downward harmonisation with a new constellation of preferences. As expected, developing countries began seeking to incorporate new rules in the WTO to increase flexibility in the rules and to allow for the greater public availability of plant genetic resources, while industrialised countries resisted this move and tried to locate this agenda in other non-judicialised venues.

The preferences of industrialised countries for upgrading global intellectual property regulation on plant genetic resources have developed gradually throughout the last half century. In the 1970s, many of the agricultural innovations had been brought about through improvements in wild plant genetic resources

---

3.   According to the CBD, biotechnology is 'any technological application that uses biological systems, living organisms or derivates thereof, to make or modify products or processes for specific uses.'

or those stored in seed banks (Raustiala and Victor 2004: 281). Industrialised countries regulated plant genetic resources at this time through so-called plant breeders' rights, meaning that it was not allowed to simply copy innovations in plant varieties, but that breeders did have the right to use another breeder's innovations for their own new variety.

Industrialised countries had first brought their concept of plant breeders' rights with limited intellectual property protection onto the international stage in 1961 through the UPOV Convention.[4] Since plant breeders were almost exclusively located in industrialised countries, this so-called *sui generis* system of intellectual property protection set up within the venue of UPOV mainly mirrored the interests of commercial plant breeders in the developed world (Helfer 2004). Indeed, the UPOV Convention of 1961, as well as its 1978 amendment, only conferred property rights over modified plant genetic resources and left the natural and unmodified ones in the domain of the common heritage system. Basically, this implied that commercial and non-commercial plant breeders had access to this resource. While biodiversity-rich developing countries mostly provided raw plant genetic resources, plant breeders in industrialised countries commercialised them. In the 1991 revised version of the UPOV convention, plant breeders' rights were strengthened, whereas the so-called farmers' privileges – the saving of seeds for re-use – were restricted (UNCTAD-ICTSD 2005), which further strengthened the intellectual property rights of agro-technical industries in industrialised countries.

Meanwhile, a group of developing countries raised the topic in the FAO in 1983, which lead to the adoption of the non-legally binding FAO International Undertaking on Plant Genetic Resources (Raustiala and Victor, 2004: 286). This agreement stated that all plant genetic resources – whether modified, found in nature, or stored in seed banks – belong to the common heritage of mankind (Correa 2001). This is clearly a case of downward regulatory harmonisation which stood in clear contradiction with the UPOV conventions.

In addition, state representatives within the UN Environmental Program also developed a redistributive system of benefit sharing for commercial research and development on plant genetic resources within the framework of the Convention on Biological Diversity (CBD) which entered into force in 1993. The CBD upheld the principle of national sovereignty over genetic resources, and developing countries set up the benefit sharing principle with the objective to offset the effects of increased intellectual property protection.

Thus, over the years two competing international sets of rules were juxtaposed next to one another without any hierarchy when it came to their degree of enforceability. This all changed, however, when representatives of industrialised countries introduced intellectual property rules on genetic resources during the Uruguay Round negotiations. While the GATT contracting parties already had a relatively effective dispute settlement mechanism by 1989, they had decisively

---

4.   UPOV is the French abbreviation for Union for the Protection of New Varieties of Plants. Even though formally independent, the UPOV is closely associated with the WIPO.

increased the degree of judicialisation of that venue in the early 1990s by introducing compulsory jurisdiction and by increasing the independence of its so-called panels (GATT 1990, Hudec 2000). By the end of the round in 1994, they also added the multilateral authorisation of sanctions in order to pressure non-compliant states into implementation, and created the WTO Appellate Body. These moves had, thus, turned the WTO into the most highly judicialised international venue when the issue of intellectual property rules on genetic resources were introduced.

With the explicit motivation of bringing more stringent intellectual property rights under the WTO's dispute settlement jurisdiction, industrialised countries drafted the TRIPS agreement (Sell 2003). More specifically, they wanted to insert Article 27.3(b) into this particular WTO treaty, which would require members to grant patents for microorganisms and would establish a *sui generis* system for genetically modified plant-based micro organisms. This meant that all microorganisms, and non-biological and microbiological processes could be patented, even though the treaty did not provide a clear definition of these terms (Wissen 2003: 5). Industrialised countries with high levels of intellectual property rights protection considered the UPOV Conventions as an adequate *sui generis* system for worked plant genetic resources. Most developing countries, in contrast, were opposed to this attempt to locate such stringent intellectual property rules in the highly judicialised venue of the WTO. Yet, in the end, they had to grudgingly accept its adoption, as it constituted one of the building blocks of the single undertaking of the Uruguay Round (Steinberg 2002). In other words, the cost of non-agreement was too high for them, as developed countries with higher domestic regulatory standards could resort to the threat of exclusion from the pre-existing market access commitments that were embodied within the GATT.

At the same time, this was not a complete victory for industrialised countries. The TRIPS section on the patentability of animals and plants was left vague. It did not explicitly incorporate any preexisting intellectual property agreements such as the UPOV, and because not all countries had signed up to the UPOV Convention, this particular section was made subject to a later review process (Raustiala and Victor 2004).

When the contentious Article 27.3(b) was later reviewed during the Doha Round, the industrialised countries initially sought to get agreement on the interpretation that the UPOV should be considered as the only *sui generis* system. Soon after, however, preferences for venues switched. Developing countries no longer only pursued their policy objectives in the FAO and the CBD, but also tried to pursue these objectives in the WTO, as their efforts in the other venues would remain without tangible effects. Industrialised countries, instead, began arguing strategically that the complexity of the matter demanded discussions to take place, not within the framework of the WTO, but in more specialised and, more importantly, less judicialised venues.

The strategy by developing countries to bring flexibility back into the TRIPS agreement consisted of developing new rules in the FAO, the CBD, and the WIPO with a view to establishing a definition of what qualifies as a *sui generis* system of patentability in line with their preferences, and then to have such a definition incorporated into the TRIPS agreement during its review process. In 2000, developing countries concluded the Cartagena Protocol on the possible dangers that might arise out of the use of biotechnology and genetically modified organisms (Raustiala 1997). In November 2010 in Nagoya, the CBD parties also agreed on a protocol for access and benefit sharing regarding genetic resources used in inventions, but postponed negotiations on enforcement to a later stage – perpetuating the low degree of judicialisation of this international venue. Developing countries with a preference for a relatively low level of regulatory harmonisation on the topic also engaged in negotiations about the specification of the CBD provisions on plant genetic resources in the FAO Commission on Plant Genetic Resources for Food and Agriculture. This led to the International Treaty on Plant Genetic Resources for Food and Agriculture (IT/PGRFA) in 2001, which revised the earlier FAO undertaking. This treaty outlined farmers' rights and established a fund to which private parties needed to contribute a part of their profits realised through the commercial products made from a communal seed treasury (Helfer 2004a: 39). Yet, the treaty also left implementation and enforcement to the discretion of member states (Zerbe 2007: 104). Finally, the regulation of genetic resources was also dealt with in the WIPO Intergovernmental committee on intellectual property and genetic resources, traditional knowledge and folklore.

Having developed rules in these non-judicialised regulatory venues, developing countries then sought to put a number of them on the negotiation table of the WTO review process, knowing that the desired flexibility with respect to TRIPS could only be achieved if these CBD and FAO rules could be made part and parcel of WTO law. They asked for a clarification of the term microorganism, a determination of what should be considered an effective *sui generis* system of plant variety protection, an incorporation of the CBD into WTO law, especially with regard to benefit-sharing, potential disclosure requirements for the use of genetic resources in order to prevent what they called bio-piracy, and the protection of traditional knowledge (Wissen 2003).

In the face of this attempt to bring flexibility back into the TRIPS rules, industrialised countries argued strategically that the complexity of the matter demanded that discussions on the new legal concepts – such as benefit sharing, traditional knowledge, farmers' rights, or prior informed consent – should be conducted in a venue with more specialised expertise on the subject, while knowing perfectly well that the WIPO had already abandoned any attempt to introduce judicialised enforcement in 1997 (Gurry 1999). While developing countries preferred the maintenance and extension of the public availability of plant genetic resources to be discussed during the TRIPS review process, industrialised countries – most notably the US and Japan – wanted to keep these issues within the WIPO – a venue where any decision would not become subject to a highly judicialised form of enforcement. In other words, as the costs of non-agreement were low for developed countries, they could resist the other side's demands.

Public health

The debate concerning how to allow deviations from WTO TRIPS rules to protect the public health in poor countries also well illustrates our theoretical reasoning. In the first phase, advanced industrialised countries introduced and defended the high level of intellectual property rights protection for their patent-based pharmaceutical companies under the TRIPS Treaty in the highly judicialised venue of the WTO. Developing countries had to grudgingly accept this discussion of intellectual property rights rules within the WTO instead of at the less judicialised WIPO or the WHO. Yet, in a second phase, developing countries with public health crises began seeking exceptions to existing rules *within* the WTO TRIPS Council, and later demanding these exceptions as a precondition for the start of the Doha Development Agenda negotiations. Simultaneously, industrialised countries began to try to shift the topic to non-judicialised international venues such as the World Bank, the UNAIDS (Joint UN programme on HIV/AIDS) and the Global fund to fight Aids, tuberculosis and malaria.

In the 1970s and 1980s, patent-based manufacturers of medicines and their allies within the national public administrations of industrialised countries pushed their governments to engage in venue shopping in international intellectual property protection. Companies with bases in the US, the EU, and Japan were among the most active in the international coalition that advocated a shift from the granting of national *privileges* to the provision of global property *rights*, and sought institutional change to achieve this substantive shift in international regulation (Correa 2000; Maskus 2002; Sell 2003). These actors had been especially disappointed with the lack of substantive and obligatory intellectual property rules under the WIPO, whose rules more resembled guiding standards with implementation left to the discretion of signatory states. And even if an upgrading of substantive intellectual property rules could be achieved within that organisation, the WIPO did not (and still does not) possess the high degree of judicialisation that would enable the enforcement of those rules. The WIPO negotiations on a draft substantive patent law treaty failed in 1992, and those on DS in intellectual property failed in 1997. For developing countries, the cost of non-agreement in these venues was nil, as industrialised countries could not offer issue linkages, or credibly threaten exclusion from any benefits in the WIPO. Instead, industrialised countries began advocating a shift to a venue with a greater promise of judicial enforcement, the GATT/WTO, where the threat of trade sanctions would allow states to link the issue of market access to the implementation of stricter intellectual property legislation (Sell 2003). Intellectual property became part of an overall package deal in which intellectual property protection worldwide was linked to enhanced market access in goods and services for developing countries.

The TRIPS agreement effectively introduced the positive obligation to adopt national patent legislation and grant 20 years of exclusive rights [to what?], and it empowered domestic courts to enforce those rights. Moreover, the establishment of the WTO dispute settlement system established compulsory jurisdiction whenever a member state filed a dispute regarding non-compliance with these rules, created the WTO Appellate Body, and provided for the (threat of) the imposition of trade sanctions in cases of continuing non-compliance after a WTO ruling. Although developing countries expressed concerns about the creation of an institutional setting that developed countries could use in order to impose costs on them, they were forced to accept the terms of the agreement, because developed countries could resort to the threat of exclusion from the WTO (Steinberg 2002).

Soon after the adoption of the TRIPS agreement, non-governmental public health organisations and developing countries raised objections to the high degree of intellectual property protection and the shadow of hard enforcement. Developing countries raised the topic in the WTO TRIPS Council as well as in the WHO (Helfer 2004a), expressing concern that the TRIPS agreement did not provide for the sufficient degree of flexibility necessary to ensure easy and affordable access to medicines in countries with public health problems.

The TRIPS agreement already included provisions that allowed states to partially overrule the payment of patent royalties through the granting of so-called compulsory licenses.[5] The agreement also stated, however, that production under compulsory licensing was predominantly intended for the domestic market, which hampered the ability of countries that were unable to produce pharmaceutical products from importing cheaper generics from other countries. Developing countries with insufficient or no manufacturing capacities in the pharmaceutical sector thus protested that the flexibility offered by the TRIPS agreement was of no use to them. As the TRIPS implementation period of ten years for developing countries and fifteen years for the least developed countries was fast approaching, they argued that they would not be able to deal with health emergencies, such as outbreaks of diseases like HIV/AIDS, malaria, and tuberculosis. India and Brazil, countries with manufacturers of drugs without patent protection, so-called generic pharmaceuticals, joined the ranks of least developed countries and started to advocate that the exportation of their products to countries with a health emergency should be explicitly allowed.

Thus, those actors who had a stake in increasing the flexibility of already agreed rules sought to modify those rules in the highly judicialised venue of the WTO, rather than in other non-judicialised venues more specialised in the issue areas of intellectual property and health. In contrast, those who opposed increased flexibility tried to shift negotiations to international venues outside the WTO, which lack judicialised enforcement.

Developing countries thus raised the issue of compulsory licensing in the WTO TRIPS Council and in the negotiations leading to the launch of the Doha Round. In 2001, the Doha Declaration on the TRIPS Agreement and Public Health mandated WTO members to find an 'expeditious solution' to the problem. In 2003, WTO members agreed to a waiver from TRIPS obligations making sure that production under compulsory licensing would not only be allowed for the domestic market, but

---

5.   States must still compensate owners at a lower fixed percentage.

also for foreign markets. In 2005, this decision was made permanent in the form of an amendment of the TRIPS agreement, which two-thirds of the membership ratified. Developing countries thus achieved their preference for negotiating rules relaxing the strictness of the TRIPS agreement within the judicialised WTO. Developed countries attached a high value to a successful launch of the Doha Round, making them prepared to concede much in order to ensure that the developing countries would be on board. The 9/11 attacks made the US particularly keen on reiterating their commitment to multilateral cooperation (Blustein 2009), while the pending expiration of the peace clause on agricultural subsidies created incentives for the EU to broaden the scope of negotiations in the Doha Round as much as possible (Poletti 2010). Since the costs of non-agreement were high for developed countries, they were willing to concede to developing countries on a prima facie relaxation of TRIPS provisions concerning access to medicines.

In the course of these negotiations, the US, the EU and other industrialised states tried, yet failed, to include an exhaustive and hence limiting list of diseases for which developing countries could declare a health emergency. The agreement reached thus specified the general conditions under which compulsory licenses would be possible and the procedure to be followed.[6]

In the following phase, countries that had wanted to maintain the status quo, such as the US and the EU, tried to shift the issue of access to medicines to international venues without judicialised enforcement, foremost the WHO, the World Bank and the UNAIDS. They strategically argued that the main problem of access to medicines was a question of public infrastructure and resources, rather than of intellectual property. WHO documents started to adopt a compromising tone with regard to public health and intellectual property, while cooperation between government agencies, pharmaceutical companies and public health NGOs was formalised in the Global Fund – first established under an administrative services agreement with the WHO, but since 2009 an autonomous international financing institution.

In sum, countries that sought to bring flexibility to rules agreed in judicialised settings anticipated that their goals could only be achieved by changing and/or replacing those very same rules. On the contrary, those who wished to maintain the status quo tried to resist this move and, when this turned out to be impossible, preferred to shift the issue onto a non-judicialised venue in order to retain as much as possible their right to exert pressure on their partners to comply with their obligations.

Concluding remarks

In this chapter we have sought to answer the question of whether the judicialisation of the WTO has made regulatory cooperation more or less likely within its

---

6. In fact, the tricky detail of its implementation revealed that this 2005 amendment of the TRIPS treaty was a Pyrrhic victory for developing countries, as the procedure for compulsory licensing turned out to be so excruciatingly difficult as to de facto severely limit its feasibility (Third World Network 2010).

framework. We first developed an explanation for how an institutional characteristic of different international venues, namely their degree of judicialisation, affects the venue shopping behaviour of states interested in international regulatory cooperation. While our argument that states anticipate whether the prospective agreement will be highly enforceable is a key factor in their propensity to commit to such agreements is not new, we sought to better specify how and under what conditions the enforceability of prospective rules influences the attractiveness of specific venues. We have argued that distinguishing between different types of regulatory harmonisation is key to making sense of the empirically observable variation in the venue shopping behaviour of states.

The first situation we took into consideration was one in which states consider either establishing new rules or tightening already existing rules in the WTO. We argued that, in such cases of upward harmonisation, highly regulated states stand to benefit from spreading domestic norms onto the international level and will value the enforceability of commitments, while countries with a relatively low level of domestic regulation stand to lose from the prospective agreement and will prefer to cooperate outside the WTO in a non-judicialised venue if the status quo cannot be maintained. The second situation we considered was one in which states confront the question of whether to allow for a loosening of already agreed WTO rules. We contended that, for such cases of downward harmonisation, state preferences will reverse: highly regulated states will prefer cooperation outside the WTO in venues with low degrees of rule enforceability if the status quo cannot be maintained, while countries with a relatively low level of domestic regulation will seek to replace and/or change existing WTO rules from within. The in-depth case studies of two instances of global intellectual property rights regulation lend support to our argument, showing that negotiating actors clearly took into account the degree to which a prospective agreement would subsequently be enforceable.

While we have illustrated the cogency of our argument by relying on empirical evidence concerning different instances of global intellectual property rights regulation, there is no reason to limit the applicability of our hypotheses to the analysis of this particular field of international regulation. In the mid-1990s, the WTO became a key venue in international regulatory governance, and an attractive institutional location for states striving to locate new rules. Since then, debates on global regulatory harmonisation in a number of different issue areas have often confronted state actors with the choice of whether to locate these rules within the WTO or in other more specialised and non-judicialised venues. Because our argument reveals that there will be systematic preferences in cases where actors face a choice between a judicialised and a non-judicialised institutional venue for global regulatory harmonisation, we suggest that our line of reasoning could shed light on such choices in other issue areas.

For instance, some industrialised countries with a preference for an upward regulatory harmonisation of labour standards have attempted to make the core labour standards codified within the International Labor Organization enforceable by bringing them under WTO jurisdiction. This move has been fiercely and successfully resisted by the developing countries that have subscribed to these International Labor Organization conventions, as these value their flexibility and their low degree of enforceability. Similarly, efforts by advanced industrialised countries towards the idea of a multilateral treaty on investment have been hampered in part because they cannot offer an attractive issue linkage package to developing countries (Walter 2001). The question of whether or not to introduce environmental standards into the WTO negotiations has followed a similar logic. As we will explain in detail in Chapter Five, to preserve its ban on imports of hormone-treated beef and genetically modified crops, the EU has long sought to increase the scope of legitimate exceptions to WTO rules.

As it turns out, the pessimistic prediction that the 'legalisation' or judicialisation of the WTO has led to a generalised reticence of member states to cooperate on new regulatory commitments is not borne out by the evidence. Instead, reality seems more complicated. We have stipulated that under some conditions judicialisation indeed has this interactive effect with cooperation. We have also identified conditions, however, under which this interactive effect is not seen, but where there are incentives for actors to pursue further cooperation within the institutional framework of the WTO.

The arguments we have developed in this chapter also shed light on additional important aspects of the international political economy of international regulatory cooperation. It is fairly well established that the expansion of the international trade regime's regulatory reach with the conclusion of the Uruguay Round was possible because the developing countries which reasonably stood to lose from this move were confronted with the threat of exclusion from previously agreed traditional market access commitments (Steinberg 2002). Our argument, however, suggests that, in the absence of this threat of exclusion, the prospects for further regulatory cooperation in a highly judicialised setting such as the WTO are bleak, as states with relatively low regulatory standards are likely to oppose it. The inability of key developed countries to bring developing countries to agree to negotiate on the Singapore issues or on trade-and-labour, as well as the lack of significant advancements in negotiations concerning international property rights or trade-and-environment in the current Doha Round bear witness to the obstacles that stand in the path towards upward regulatory harmonisation in the WTO. The breakdown of the comprehensive Doha package into a small set of separately treated negotiation items has merely led to a minor agreement on trade facilitation at great difficulty and cost.

What is more, our analysis suggests that these same states are likely to exert pressure on the WTO to bring flexibility in through the back door to avoid the adjustment costs that regulatory harmonisation would bring about. This has important policy implications. Increasing flexibility may be an attractive way to deal with the increased diversity of preferences that the ever-larger membership of the WTO has brought about – witness, for example, the failed attempt by a limited set of WTO member states for an anti-counterfeiting trade agreement, or the demand by developing countries to extend the TRIPS implementation deadline yet another time. A high degree of judicialisation and strong enforcement of rules may well be feasible and stable over time only in small clubs composed of countries with similar levels of domestic economic regulation. It should come as no surprise, therefore, that states increasingly prefer making preferential trade agreements, bilateral and regional, on regulatory harmonisation. Indeed, analysts have rightly observed that, within preferential trade agreements, negotiations on the institutional design of dispute settlement systems and the enforceability of regulatory harmonisation commitments have also moved centre stage (Allee and Elsig 2015).

Chapter Five

Legal Vulnerability and Cooperation

When members of the WTO negotiate, they often do so under the shadow of WTO law. Multilateral negotiations in the WTO may concern new rules on entirely new areas, yet very often concern the further specification or change of existing rules and commitments. As widely discussed in the previous chapters, the subject of these negotiations can be the reduction and/or elimination of tariffs and quantitative restrictions on trade in goods, as well as the harmonisation of existing domestic regulatory practices. One of the implications of the judicialisation of the trade regime is that WTO members increasingly negotiate multilateral trade rules from a position of legal vulnerability; that is, they engage in multilateral negotiations while foreign partners can credibly threaten to resort, and sometimes actually do resort, to WTO litigation against them on the basis of already existing legal commitments.

The fact that WTO members can resort to litigation while multilateral negotiations are ongoing has important implications for how they define their positions and policy preferences in such negotiations. Indeed, when they negotiate under the shadow of WTO law, the issues on the table are not always just confined to the acceptance of new agreements on tariff reductions or regulatory practices. Instead, these negotiations often also spill over, sometimes more tacitly than explicitly, into discussions about non-compliance on existing commitments. Member states often face stark choices in such cases. A legally vulnerable actor might, for instance, have to choose between getting sucked into litigation by foreign partners, and (re)negotiating the potentially targetable policies. Journalists' accounts, policy-oriented research, and scholarly studies have often hinted that the 'shadow of WTO law' has been a key determinant of policy preferences, bargaining strategies, and tactics prior to and during the Doha Round (Blustein 2009). Several studies concur, for instance, that the expiration of the 'peace clause' of the Uruguay Round Agreement on Agriculture (URAA) and the subsequent disputes about EU and US agricultural subsidies strongly influenced the Doha Round negotiations concerning agriculture (Porterfield 2006; Sumner 2005). The peace clause stipulated that, between 1995 and 2002, WTO members would not activate the WTO DSM to challenge policy measures in the area of agriculture. Once this moratorium expired, strategic considerations changed, just as they had changed from 1995 onwards in all other policy areas in which the possibility of dispute settlement for measures that did not conform to WTO agreements was present. Similarly, many have observed how the WTO disputes against EU regulations based on the precautionary principle have exerted a decisive influence on negotiations on so-called trade-and-environment issues (Kelemen 2010; Skogstad 2003).

In this chapter, we draw inspiration from these empirical observations and seek to systematically investigate whether, and if so under what conditions and how, the potential for legal dispute affects cooperative dynamics in ongoing WTO negotiations. We develop our argument in two steps. First, we show that, contrary to conventional wisdom, increased enforcement does not necessarily make actors shy away from further cooperation, as it can increase the set of feasible agreements for WTO members. More specifically, we contend that legal vulnerability can increase the set of feasible agreements for both sides, thus potentially increasing the likelihood of cooperation in multilateral negotiations.

Next, we explain that the nature of the issue at stake crucially determines whether legal vulnerability can trigger this positive dynamics of cooperation. When the issue at stake is divisible – that is, when it can be easily disaggregated into negotiable units – potential disputants will tend to prefer negotiation to litigation. However, when the issue is indivisible – that is, when it is very difficult or impossible to disaggregate the issue into separate negotiable units – legal vulnerability does not increase the set of negotiated agreements that the two sides are ready to accept.

The chapter proceeds as follows. Having defined a number of key concepts, we develop a game-theoretical argument about the effects of legal vulnerability on the choice of negotiation or litigation within the WTO. We then illustrate the explanatory potential of the argument with an in-depth qualitative analysis of how parties to actual WTO disputes in the Doha Round responded to the incentives brought about by legal vulnerability. We look into four specific cases in total.

Legal vulnerability, issue divisibility and multilateral trade negotiations

As widely discussed in the previous chapters, the prospective enforceability of any future WTO agreements affects the propensity of trade-related domestic actors to commit to such agreements. In Chapter Three we looked into how judicialisation has affected the preferences and patterns of political mobilisation of trade-related domestic actors on issues concerning traditional trade liberalisation. In Chapter Four we looked into how judicialisation has affected the propensity of WTO members to widen organisational jurisdiction to new regulatory issue areas. The discussion in these chapters has, however, neglected an important characteristic of the interplay between judicial politics and negotiations in the contemporary multilateral trade regime, namely that the presence of legal vulnerability with regard to already existing commitments also affects current negotiations. WTO member states thus not only face a choice of whether to commit to new binding agreements, in the way in which we have framed the discussion so far, but are also already bound by a wide array of agreements. This means that member states sometimes negotiate under the shadow of WTO law: they may, in other words, engage in multilateral negotiations over issues already governed by WTO law that are either in the process of being litigated or at least at risk of being litigated. A central question in the study of how judicialisation affects the dynamics of negotiated liberalisation in the WTO is thus how exactly the shadow of WTO law affects multilateral trade negotiations. Does it increase the bargaining space in negotiations, or does it create new obstacles on the path towards agreement? And when does it empower a complainant?

A few studies have delved into this important question, yet they remain incomplete in important ways. For instance, while Poletti (2010) highlighted that potential defendants may have an interest in drowning potential disputes in broad-based multilateral negotiations, the exclusive focus on one side of the dyadic relationship leaves open the question of why the (potential or actual) complainant in a WTO dispute would acquiesce in letting a judicial case rest that it can reasonably expect to win, and opt for negotiations with a more uncertain outcome. In addition, while Busch and Reinhardt (2000) show how uncertainty about each side's preference in a WTO dispute might encourage settlement before the dispute escalates, the question of how the threat or use of litigation affects bargaining dynamics in multilateral trade negotiations remains unaddressed.

The argument we develop in this chapter offers a systematic assessment of the dynamics of cooperation under the shadow of WTO law. The key concepts we use for our analysis are legal vulnerability and the degree of issue divisibility. First, a WTO member is in a position of legal vulnerability when one or more WTO members can credibly threaten to resort to and/or actually make use of WTO litigation against them while multilateral trade negotiations are ongoing.

Next, issue divisibility denotes how easily the issue at stake can be disaggregated into tradable units to enable transfers between the two parties. Many issues that are discussed during WTO negotiations and challenged in WTO litigation are highly divisible; that is, they have a relatively continuous character such as tariffs, quotas and subsidies. However, not all issues can be easily disaggregated into tradable units and some tend to have an 'all or nothing' character (Guzmann and Simmons 2002). Other important issues that are discussed during WTO negotiations and challenged in WTO litigation are thus characterised by a relatively low level of divisibility, in that they feature discontinuous properties, such as product and process regulations. Broadly speaking, the distinction between divisible and indivisible issues mirrors the distinction between traditional and regulatory barriers to trade. In general, traditional barriers to trade tend to be characterised by a high degree of divisibility, while regulatory barriers to trade tend be characterised by a low degree of divisibility.

In the next sections, we make two arguments. First, we are argue that, when a member state has the option to challenge another member (successfully) through WTO DSMs during multilateral trade negotiations, the set of feasible agreements for both sides may increase and overlap, which strengthens the chance of agreement.

This argument is presented in a simple game below in which two states bargain over the reduction of a trade distorting measure characterised by a high degree of issue divisibility under the shadow of judicialisation. Within the multilateral trade regime, negotiations on the liberalisation of international trade have traditionally taken the form of exchanges of reciprocal concessions between trading partners. Exporters in one WTO member state would mobilise and demand that their government seek the removal of trade-distorting measures, which were providing import-competing producers in the other state with protection from foreign competition. Whether an agreement was struck would depend on whether the sets of feasible agreements for the parties involved in the negotiations overlapped at a particular point in time.

WTO negotiations still retain these features to a certain degree, but the introduction of a quasi-judicial mechanism of dispute resolution in the trade regime has also given governments an important additional tool to target trade-distorting measures that are incompatible with WTO rules. Indeed, member states that enjoy the benefits of protectionism through legally vulnerable policy tools can no longer consider the status quo as a cost-free strategy, as those seeking the removal of WTO-incompatible policies can impose adjustment costs on them through the imposition of retaliatory measures by a WTO panel or the Appellate Body. Defendants thus not only run the risk of a condemnation by the WTO Dispute Settlement Body, but also of having to withstand the adverse consequences of foreign trade barriers imposed by the complainant in retaliation against enduring non-compliance.

As the analysis of our game-theoretical model shows, when a WTO member successfully takes legal action (or can credibly threaten to take legal action) against another member state, it can significantly affect negotiations by increasing the set of feasible agreements both sides are ready to accept. We show that while the ability to impose costs on a defendant by way of litigation can increase the complainant's bargaining power, the complainant's preference for loss-mitigation over gains from retaliation also augments the defendant's leverage. The balance between these two forces opens a bargaining window, and ultimately increases the chances for cooperation in multilateral trade negotiations. However, it is important to note that the complainant's increased bargaining power is conditional, to some extent, upon the belief that litigation will produce a compliant response on the part of the defendant. If the defendant is not expected to comply with an adverse ruling, then, although a bargaining window will still exist, the complainant will be able to extract fewer concessions from the defendant. The degree to which the complainant expects the defendant to comply helps to explain where in the feasible range of agreements the parties are likely to settle. This last condition influences the choice between litigation and negotiation, and is in turn largely dependent on the potential of domestic interest groups in the defendant member state to mobilise and oppose compliance.

In our second argument, we show that legal vulnerability generally can only ignite a positive dynamic of cooperation between two potential and actual disputants when the issue is characterised by a high degree of divisibility. In the second simple game we present, two states bargain over the reduction of a trade distorting measure characterised by a low degree of issue divisibility. When it is impossible to reach a middle ground compromise that falls between the preferred outcome of a potential or actual defendant (i.e. the status quo) and the preferred outcome of a potential or actual complainant (i.e. the full removal of WTO-incompatible trade barriers), the potential for negotiation disappears and the issue at stake leads to protracted WTO litigation. Thus, the simple game shows that the indivisibility of a litigated issue tends to forestall cooperation on it.

It is important to note that these arguments about the effects of legal vulnerability hold only when two scoping conditions are met. First, we need to assume that the two sides involved in a (potential) dispute value the other's market as a destination for their exports, and are in a position to pursue or to threaten to pursue policies that can generate losses for the other side. We call this an interdependent trading relationship. Second, we need to assume that the potential complainant has legal capacity, defined as 'resources available to identify, analyze, pursue, and litigate a dispute' (Guzman and Simmons 2005, 559). If it is lacking the capability to use the DSM, then judicialised enforcement should be regarded as non-existent.

Model setup: divisible issues

Suppose that, during multilateral trade negotiations, a WTO member state A demands concessions from a trading partner B who has implemented some trade-distorting measure. Let the present size of the trade-distorting measure be normalised to 1 and let 0 represent full compliance with A's demands, so that any position on the open interval between 0 and 1 represents a corresponding percentage reduction in the barrier size. Assume that A and B have linear, monotonic, and competing preferences over the trade barrier, so that B's utility is strictly increasing with barrier size, while A's is strictly decreasing. Suppose further that B can be of two types: the non-compliant type (B_{NC}), for whom there is some additional penalty to be paid for full compliance, and the compliant type (B_C), for whom there is no additional cost. Let this additional cost for the non-compliant type be represented by ϵ (where $\epsilon > 0$). State B's type is the result of an initial draw by nature, such that B is compliant with probability p and non-compliant with a complementary probability $p-1$ (where $0 < p < 1$). This type is private information for B, but the distribution of types is common knowledge.

State A's beliefs about state B's type are potentially based on two factors. First, they are affected by the prior probability that state B is of the compliant type. Empirically, this probability is a function of the state's ties to import-competing industries that will attempt to punish governments that concede too much. A government that is able to preserve some or all of its trade violation will not face any punishment from import-competitors, while one that completely concedes to the opponent's demands, without getting anything in return, is seen as selling out the domestic industry and pays a cost premium. Second, state A will take into account any previous observations of state B's behaviour. In cases in which A has previously observed B complying or not complying with judicial rulings, it will incorporate this information according to Bayesian principles.

The game is depicted in Figure 5.1 below. It begins with Nature drawing B's type, following a demand by A that B remove its trade-distorting policy. State B can then either concede to the demand or refuse to concede. If it concedes, then the game ends and both states receive payoffs according to their valuation of the full concessions outcome. If B does not concede, A can either accept this decision or threaten to litigate. We assume here that the complainant, state A, wins any litigation process with certainty and that this outcome is common knowledge. As discussed later, relaxing this assumption does not meaningfully change the substantive results. If A accepts, then the game ends, and both states receive the status quo payoff.

If A threatens to litigate, then B can choose to refuse to comply completely or it can offer a negotiated settlement. If B complies then both states receive the full compliance pay-off. If B completely refuses to comply, then litigation occurs and A acquires the ability to impose retaliatory measures against B. These measures will be equal in magnitude to the initial trade-distorting measure imposed by B, and will thus harm state B's exporters to the same degree that the initial measure benefits B's import-competing industries. Therefore, it will cancel out any gains from the initial measure. Retaliation may also provide a similar benefit to A's domestic industries. However, because A's import-competing industries did not mobilise for the benefit, the ultimate value of retaliation for the state is reduced by some factor α between 0 and 1.

If B chooses to negotiate, then it makes a proposal to A of $N \in [0,1]$, where N represents the percentage size reduction of the distorting measure. State A can choose to accept or reject this offer. If it accepts, then the two states agree to reduce the trade-distorting measure to N. We assume that the round ends successfully, that the settlement is implemented, and that both states receive their respective payoffs from negotiation. If A rejects the offer, then A proceeds with litigation. Again, we

Figure 5.1: Bargaining in the shadow of WTO law over divisible issues

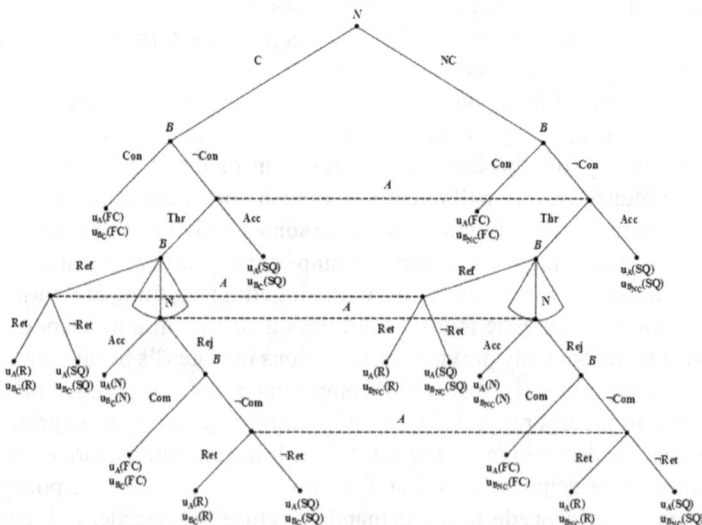

assume that, if litigation occurs, the complainant A wins with certainty.[1] Given this outcome, B can comply with the judgment or it can opt not to comply. If it complies, then the two states receive the full compliance payoff. If it refuses to comply, then A is authorised to retaliate and can choose whether or not to do so. If it does, then the states receive the retaliation payoff; otherwise, they receive the status quo payoff.

Each player's preferences over outcomes are as follows. For A, the ideal outcome is full compliance by B, which it prefers to retaliation, wherein it will recover only a proportion α of the cost. Retaliation is in turn preferred to the status quo. Formally, $u_A(FC) > u_A(R) > u_A(SQ)$. A's preference with respect to a negotiated settlement depends on where the settlement falls. It prefers offers in which N is low to those for which it is high. B, by contrast, most prefers the status quo, as it continues to enjoy the benefits of its trade-distorting measure. It prefers this to retaliation by A, which will eliminate any such benefits. The compliant type, B_C, is indifferent between retaliation and full compliance; the non-compliant type, B_{NC}, strictly prefers retaliation to compliance. Formally, $u_{B_C}(SQ) > u_{B_C}(R) = u_{B_C}(FC)$ and $u_{B_{NC}}(SQ) > u_{B_{NC}}(R) > u_{B_{NC}}(FC)$. Like A, B's preference with respect to N depends on its value. It prefers larger values of N to smaller ones.

This is a game of incomplete information, which requires a Perfect Bayesian Equilibrium. It can be solved using backward induction. We make the assumption that, when indifferent, a state has a preference for the more peaceful choice (i.e. concession, negotiation, compliance, or non-retaliation), and that in the case of play that is off the equilibrium path (OTEP), A believes B to be of the compliant type. We discuss the latter assumption below.

Analysis: divisible issues

Given our assumptions, the players have dominant strategies at each node, so that there is a unique pure strategy equilibrium. Moreover, there are no non-degenerate mixed strategy equilibria. Beginning from the final node, the equilibrium strategies of the players follow. If litigation has proceeded and B refuses to comply, A strictly prefers retaliation to non-retaliation, so that it can recoup some of the costs of the barriers. Given this strategy, when faced with an adverse judgment, B_C will prefer to comply, while B_{NC} will refuse, strictly preferring retaliation to compliance. Because A is unaware of what type of B it is facing, its decision following a negotiated offer by B will be a function of the probability that B is compliant (p). In particular, it will accept any proposed barrier level, $N \leq p(0) + (1 - \alpha)(1 - p)$, and reject any larger

---

1.   Both assumptions above can easily be relaxed by assigning some exogenous probability to the outcomes. Doing so will not affect the substantive results of the model, but rather will alter B's optimal negotiated offer N^*. Uncertainty about the outcome of litigation increases the bargaining power of state B and reduces the value of N^*. Uncertainty about the end of the negotiating round makes litigation more attractive, which increases the bargaining power of A and the optimal N^*. Indeed, as the probability that the round ends successfully approaches 1, the incentive to negotiate disappears. In such a case, state A would always prefer to litigate, as even a successful negotiation, if not implementable, would result in a status quo outcome.

proposal. Given these preferences and A's beliefs, the optimal offer for both types of B will be at A's reservation value, $N^* = (1 - \alpha)(1 - p)$.[2] Because this value must be strictly positive, both types will prefer to offer N^* rather than to negotiate. The feasible equilibrium values of N^* span the open unit interval. Because $N^* < 1$ in equilibrium, A will prefer (the threat of) litigation to acceptance of the status quo. Finally, given the initial choice between concession and refusal to concede, the fact that $N^* > 0$ will lead both types of B to refuse concessions initially. The equilibrium beliefs for A are simply that B is of type B_C with probability p, and of type B_{NC} with probability $1 - p$. Because both types behave similarly on the equilibrium path, state A's prior and posterior beliefs are equivalent in equilibrium. Given any play off the equilibrium path by B, A believes B to be of type B_C with probability 1.

The equilibrium outcome in this game is a negotiated proposal by B, $N^* = (1 - \alpha)(1 - p)$, which is accepted by A. The equilibrium offer depends on the distribution of types of B and on the benefit to A of retaliatory barriers. As the likelihood that B is of the non-compliant type increases, the equilibrium value of N^* also increases, leading to a larger portion of the trade-distorting measure remaining in effect. On the other hand, as the benefit from retaliation grows, the equilibrium value of N^* decreases, leading to a reduction in the agreed trade distortion level. In all cases, however, negotiation is expected to occur, with each state's beliefs about the outcome of litigation influencing the agreed settlement.

The driving force in the model above is the authorisation to retaliate, which A receives from successful litigation. This authorisation is issued by the multilateral authority invested in the WTO Dispute Settlement Body. We can contrast this to the situation depicted in Figure 5.2, in which trade negotiations do not occur under the shadow of litigation. In such a scenario, A lacks any sort of stick with which to coerce B into reducing its trade distortion. Its only option is simply to demand that B complies with WTO rules. If state B agrees, then it receives the concession outcome, and if it does not, the status quo remains in place. Faced with the simple choice between reducing and maintaining its level of protection, with no other consequences, both types of B would prefer to keep the measure intact. Judicialised enforcement, backed with multilaterally authorised retaliation, therefore provides A with an important weapon in multilateral negotiations that can induce cooperation (if not full compliance) without actually ever being used.

Model: indivisible issues

The game unfolds in a different manner when the two parties are confronted with indivisible issues, that is, issues that are very difficult to disaggregate into

---

2.   This is the only point at which A's beliefs about OTEP behaviour are payoff relevant. Because A's decision to accept or reject B's offer is a function of A's posterior belief about B's type ($\hat{p}$), an OTEP proposal that leads A to believe that $\hat{p} < p$ will mean that both types of B will have an incentive to deviate towards $N = (1 - \alpha)(1 - \hat{p})$, and no equilibrium can be sustained. Thus, an equilibrium only exists if A's posterior belief about the probability that B is compliant is at least p. We choose $\hat{p} = 1$ for simplicity.

Figure 5.2: Bargaining in the absence of legal vulnerability

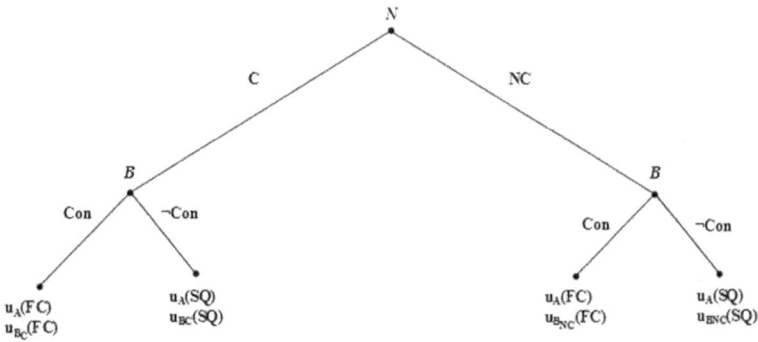

negotiable units. Many steps in the game are of course identical, yet the game differs in crucial respects.

Suppose that, during multilateral trade negotiations, a WTO member state A demands concessions from a trading partner B, who has implemented some trade-distorting measure. Let the present size of the measure again be normalised to 1 and let 0 represent full compliance with A's demand. Assume again that A and B have linear, monotonic, and competing preferences over the trade barrier, such that B's utility is strictly increasing with the barrier size, while A's is strictly decreasing. Suppose further again that B can be of two types: the non-compliant type B_{NC}, for whom there is some additional penalty to be paid for full compliance, and the compliant type B_C, for whom there is no additional cost with full compliance. Let this additional cost for the non-compliant type be represented by $\epsilon > 0$. As in the game with divisible issues, state B's type is the result of an initial draw by nature, such that B is compliant with probability $0 < p < 1$ and non-compliant with the complementary probability. This type is private information for B, but the distribution of types is common knowledge.

State A's beliefs about state B's type are again potentially based on two factors. First, they are affected by the prior probability that state B is the compliant type. Empirically, this probability is a function of the state's ties to import-competing industries that will attempt to punish governments that concede too much. A government that is able to preserve some or all of its trade violation will not face any punishment from import-competitors, while one that completely concedes to the opponent's demands, without getting anything in return, is seen as selling out the domestic industry and pays a cost premium. Second, state A will take into account any previous observations of state B's behaviour. In cases in which A has previously observed B complying or not complying with judicial rulings, it will incorporate this information into its beliefs about B's type according to Bayesian principles.

The game is depicted in Figure 5.3 below. It again begins with Nature drawing B's type, following a demand by A that B remove its trade-distorting policy. State

Figure 5.3: Bargaining in the shadow of WTO litigation over indivisible issues

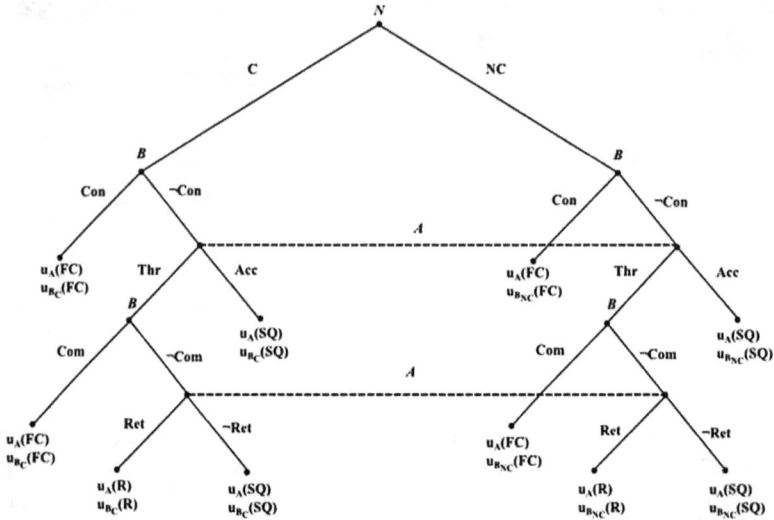

B can then either concede to the demand or refuse to concede. If it concedes, then the game ends and both states receive payoffs according to their valuation of the full concessions outcome. If B does not concede, A can either accept this decision or threaten to litigate. We assume here, just as before, that the complainant wins the litigation process with certainty, and that this outcome is common knowledge. As discussed later, relaxing this assumption does not meaningfully change our substantive results. If A accepts, then the game ends, and both states receive the status quo payoff.

If A threatens to litigate, then B can choose to refuse to comply completely, or simply to comply. This is so because B is unable to offer a negotiated settlement N, which represents some reduction of the measure, as the issue under litigation is indivisible. If B complies then both states receive the full compliance payoff. If B refuses to comply, then litigation occurs and A acquires the ability to impose retaliatory measures against B. As in the game with divisible issues, these measures will be equal in magnitude to the initial trade-distorting measure imposed by B, and will thus harm state B's exporters to the same degree that the initial measure benefits B's import-competing industries. These retaliatory measures will thus cancel out any of B's gains from the initial measure. Retaliation may also provide a benefit to A's domestic industries. However, as explained above, because A's import-competing industries did not mobilise for the benefit, the ultimate value of retaliation for the state is reduced by some factor $\alpha \in (0,1)$.

Analysis: indivisible issues

In the case of the game depicted in Figure 5.3, the demand to remove the trade-distorting measure is effectively a non-negotiable ultimatum. Although this is a game of incomplete information (state A is unaware of state B's type), the lack of an issue over which to bargain means that state A has a strictly dominant strategy, and that the game can easily be solved by backward induction. Assume that the preference ordering is the same as before: $u_A(FC) > u_A(R) > u_A(SQ)$, $u_{B_C}(SQ) > u_{B_C}(R) = u_{B_C}(FC)$, and $u_{B_{NC}}(SQ) > u_{B_{NC}}(R) > u_{B_{NC}}(FC)$.

To solve the game, we begin by considering the final stage. Because $u_A(FC) > u_A(R) > u_A(SQ)$, A will strictly prefer retaliation to maintaining the status quo, regardless of state B's type. State B's choice at the preceding node depends on its type. First, suppose B is of the non-compliant type. Then $u_{B_{NC}}(SQ) > u_{B_{NC}}(R) > u_{B_{NC}}(FC)$, which implies that B strictly prefers not to comply with the panel's ruling. Now suppose that B is of the compliant type. Then, because $u_{B_C}(SQ) > u_{B_C}(R) = u_{B_C}(FC)$, state B will be indifferent between its two options at the penultimate node. Thus, it is free to mix over the two options, compliance and non-compliance, with any set of complementary probabilities q and $1 - q$.[3] Given this set of preferences, state A's choice at the previous node is between accepting non-concession, which will maintain the status quo, and threatening B, which will lead to a retaliation outcome with probability $p + (1 - p)(1 - q)$, and a compliance outcome with a probability $q(1 - p)$. Because A prefers both possible outcomes of this expected utility calculation (retaliation and compliance) to the status quo, the expected utility from any convex combination of the two possible outcomes will be strictly greater than the utility from the status quo. Thus, A will always prefer to threaten. Given this strategy, state B's initial choice will be between conceding and taking the full concession outcome or not conceding and dealing with the retaliation outcome. Again, the non-compliant type of B has a strict preference for retaliation, and so it will opt not to concede, while the compliant type is free to mix with any set of complementary probabilities, $\{r, 1-r\}$.

When an issue is indivisible, we are left with an infinite number of equilibria. However, these equilibria can be characterised easily. State A's equilibrium strategy will always consist of *{Threaten, Retaliate}*. A non-compliant type of B will always play the strategy *{Not Concede, Not Comply}*. A compliant type of B will play one of the mixed strategies possible over the alternatives at both choice nodes in equilibrium. Thus, we have two possible equilibrium outcomes: retaliation, which can always occur, and full compliance, which can only occur if state B is a compliant type.

Empirically observable implications

In the previous sections, we explored how litigation in the WTO affects ongoing multilateral trade negotiations using game-theoretical modelling. From our discussion, we now derive a series of empirically observable implications, which will guide the empirical analysis of the controlled comparative case studies below. Note that one of the key premises of our game-theoretical discussion was that a WTO member or group of members is in a position to credibly threaten the

---

3. We assume here that B chooses to comply with probability q. We could also simply assume that indifferent types always (or never) comply.

imposition of concentrated costs on another WTO member in the case of non-compliance. The empirical implications of our discussion are thus conditioned on this assumption.

First, we expect to observe that legal recourse is a key factor that influences the strategic calculus of any WTO member state involved in negotiations. This means that we should be able to trace the presence of legal recourse through to an increase in the set of feasible agreements between the two disputants in the context of multilateral trade negotiations.

Second, when issues can be easily divided into separately negotiable units, the complainant(s) and the defendant(s) should be able to identify a bargaining space for a negotiated settlement; on the other hand, when the issue under litigation is indivisible, they should not be able to do so, and end up continuing on the path of (further) litigation.

Third, the location of a negotiated agreement on divisible issues should be a function of the credibility of the first state's threat to litigate and the probability that the second state is of the compliant type. A state should be able to extract greater concessions through negotiations when its threats are believed and when its opponent is likely to comply with an adverse ruling. Factors such as the level of organisation of various domestic groups will cause the likelihood that a given state is compliant to vary across issue areas. Additionally, an opponent could be able to infer something about a state's likelihood of compliance on a given issue given its compliance behaviour in previous cases.

Fourth, our argument does not suggest that the existence of legal recourse affects the likelihood of success for multilateral trade negotiations. Our analysis is limited to an examination of how the presence of legal recourse affects the likelihood of agreement between the two sides involved in a dispute. For this agreement to be implemented, the dyad's overlapping set of feasible agreements would have to intersect with the win-set of *all* other participants – a negotiation outcome analysis that is beyond the scope of this analysis. Thus, we are more interested in the nature of dyadic interactions than in negotiation outcomes per se.

Doha negotiations under the shadow of WTO law

We demonstrate the empirical plausibility of our theoretical arguments by analysing the interactions between the complainants and defendants in four WTO disputes. We examine how these interactions have affected bargaining dynamics in the Doha Round. All four cases meet the scope conditions of our argument. They first concern pairs of WTO members with large and attractive markets in a position of trade interdependence, a necessary condition for a potential defendant to worry about the threat of retaliation by a potential complainant. Additionally, all the complainants possess sufficient legal capacity to bring disputes against the defendants.

One attractive feature of these four cases is temporal in nature. All the cases occurred around the time that litigation became an option for WTO disputants, providing us with important variation between cases. They all thus display similar values on one of the key independent variables we look into, namely the presence of legal vulnerability. At the same time, these cases vary on the key independent variable of the nature of the issue at stake. Two cases deal with relatively divisible issues – agricultural export subsidies and domestic support schemes – while the other two deal with relatively indivisible issues – consumer and health safety regulations, and rules concerning anti dumping. With regard to the two divisible issue cases, we show how two defendants in WTO disputes, the EU and the US, and a challenger of their WTO-incompatible policies, Brazil, did indeed identify areas of common agreement in the Doha Round negotiations. With regard to the two indivisible issue cases, we trace the trade-and-environment negotiations between the EU and the US, where the EU's health and safety regulations were legally challenged by the US negotiators, and the US negotiations with Japan and the EU over the WTO-incompatible practice of zeroing in US antidumping policy. We show how legal vulnerability generated a positive dynamic of cooperation in the cases with relatively easily divisible issues, while this was not so with the cases concerning issues that were very difficult to divide, a fact which forestalled negotiators in finding an area of common agreement and left them little choice but to resort to further litigation.

Cooperation and the expiration of the peace clause: the EU and Brazil

The URAA was concluded in 1994, and bound WTO members to a set of clear commitments regarding the agricultural sector. It limited the use of export subsidies, domestic support schemes, and import tariffs, and addressed formal barriers to market access. The direct impact of the agreement was rather marginal. The quantitative impact of the tariff reductions enhancing market access was limited because the cuts in import tariffs took place from a base value that was frequently inflated – a practice known as 'dirty tariffication' (Tangermann 1999). In addition, the major developed countries were only required to make minor changes to their domestic support policies to bring them into conformity with the rules of the agreement (Josling 1998).

Yet, the agreement contained the seeds for the deeper trade liberalisation that was to be obtained in the long run. First, in order to meet the concerns of those WTO members that were aware of the rather limited direct effect the URAA would have on agricultural trade liberalisation, the text also included a so-called 'built-in agenda' (Article 20). This agenda mandated WTO members to start a new round of negotiations on agriculture by the end of 1999. Second, the agreement contained an important provision, the so-called 'peace clause' (Article 13), which granted immunity to countries from legal actions on the basis of the provisions of the agreement on subsidies and countervailing measures (SCM) until 2003. This particular agreement penalised the use of subsidies and regulated the actions countries could take to counter their effects. In essence, the peace clause protected domestic and export subsidy programmes that were actionable on the basis of the SCM agreement until the end of 2003, provided that states at least complied with the reduction commitments contained in the URAA.[4] The expiration of the peace clause at the end of 2003 would then open up the possibility of WTO members challenging the agricultural domestic and export subsidies of other member states through the DSM (Steinberg and Josling 2003; Swinbank 1999).

Middle-income agricultural exporting countries such as Brazil were expected to reap the largest share of the benefits from further agricultural trade liberalisation (OECD 2005). It is, therefore, unsurprising that, by the late 1990s, numerous agricultural interest groups in these countries began organising intense lobbying efforts to push for further agricultural trade liberalisation, particularly with an eye to increasing market access opportunities to the highly protected markets of developed high-income countries, such as those of the EU, and the US (Cairns Group Farm Leaders 1998, 1999, 1999a, 2000; OECD 2005).

Credible threats of litigation and retaliation

The prospect of the peace clause expiration was deemed by both interest groups and policymakers to provide Brazil with an effective tool to extract concessions in the negotiating game, as our model would suggest. But, although the threat to resort to the DSM after 2003 certainly seemed a powerful tool in the hands of Brazilian policymakers, it was not certain that Brazilian agricultural exporters would actually be better off because of it. As agricultural policy reform was known to be particularly difficult to achieve within the EU (Swinnen 2008), the possibility that non-compliance would follow an adverse WTO ruling was a scenario that needed to be contemplated by Brazilian policymakers. Hence, they opted for a constructive engagement in negotiations, maintaining a credible threat to resort to litigation, instead of resorting to immediate litigation. In the period preceding the launch of the Doha Round, private sector representatives and policymakers in Brazil combined calls for an ambitious agenda aimed at the elimination of all trade-distorting subsidies and a substantial improvement in market access with an explicit reference to the prospect that the expiration of the peace clause would eliminate all constraints against the use of the DSM to challenge developed countries (Cairns Group 2000a, 2000b; Cairns Group Farm Leaders 2001; Cotta 2001; Raghavan 2001).

As the largest provider of trade-distorting agricultural subsidies, the EU was one of the main potential targets of Brazil and other middle-income agricultural countries. Organisations representing the interests of European farmers, as well as public decision makers from the EU's Directorate General (DG) for Agriculture and Rural Development, knew that these domestic policies were likely to be deemed WTO incompatible by any ruling from the DSM.[5] It is estimated that in

---

4.   The peace clause (Article 13 of the URAA) relates only to the domestic subsidy provisions listed in Annex 2 (the Green Box) and Article 6 (covering, *inter alia*, Blue and Amber Box payments), and to the export subsidy payments detailed in Part V of the Agreement.

5.   Interview by the authors at COPA-COGECA, Brussels, 16 June 2010, and with the DG Trade Official at the European Commission, Brussels, 22 February 2009.

the late 1990s roughly 45 per cent of the EU's producer support estimate[6] was vulnerable to legal challenges (Poletti 2010). As was noted at the time, compliance with a succession of hostile panel reports following the expiration of the peace clause might lead to the death of the European Common Agricultural Policy (CAP) by a thousand cuts (Swinbank 1999: 45).

Their position of legal vulnerability was among the reasons why European farmers and EU policymakers aligned in their support for the strategy of comprehensive negotiations in the Doha Round. This type of negotiation appealed to these actors, as trade-off deals increased the likelihood of a compromise entailing fewer agricultural concessions (*Agra Europe*, 2 November 2001, All to play for on agriculture as Doha WTO meeting beckons; Brittan 1999; COPA-COGECA 1999a, 1999b[7]).

A deal on the agenda of the new round of trade negotiations was reached at the Doha WTO Ministerial meeting in November 2001, and agricultural negotiations had been agreed to be part of a single undertaking, scheduled to end by January 2005. Although the text was understandably vague and ambiguous, it identified the parameters within which a future agreement would have to be based: improvements in market access, reductions of (with plans to phase out) all forms of export subsidies, and substantial reductions in trade-distorting domestic subsidies (WTO 2001).

A bargaining window opens

In the first phase of negotiations, the two sides took very different positions. The first proposal tabled by the EU in February 2003 was defensive and sought to keep the structure of the URAA intact (WTO 2003). The position adopted by Brazil and other members of the Cairns Group was, instead, much more aggressive, and included requests for a complete phasing out of export subsidies over a three-year implementation period, the elimination of blue and amber box direct payments over a five-year implementation period, a tighter definition of green-box payments, significant tariff cuts, and opposition to any extension of the peace clause (Cairns Group 2000, 2000a, 2000b). Yet, two developments connected to the EU's legal vulnerability contributed to a softening of its bargaining position, and led to a partial convergence towards the positions of countries such as Brazil.

First, in late 2002, Brazil (together with Australia and later Thailand) initiated a WTO dispute against the EC sugar regime, arguing that the EU was subsidising exports in excess of the volume and expenditure limits set down in the Uruguay Round (WTO 2002). The explicit aim of the dispute was not simply to seek a

---

6.   An indicator created to provide a summary measure of the producer subsidy that would be equivalent to all the forms of support provided to farmers, including direct farm subsidies that may or may not encourage production domestically, as well as market price support provided by import tariffs and export subsidies.

7.   Interview by the authors at COPA-COGECA, Brussels, 16 June 2010.

favourable WTO ruling, but rather to communicate to the EU the unfairness of its agricultural policies and Brazil's readiness to use all instruments at its disposal to extract concessions in the Doha Round (Camargo 2008). By the summer of 2003, the EU realised it would lose the case (Ackrill and Kay 2009), and would be forced to comply with WTO rules or face retaliation; and indeed, both in 2004 and in 2005, the WTO AB ruled in favour of Brazil (WTO 2004, 2005). As Anania and Bureau (2005: 548) note, the dispute had two main consequences for negotiations: it enhanced the bargaining power of developing countries such as Brazil who now realised they could obtain significant benefits by resorting to the WTO DSM, and it weakened the position of countries that were legally vulnerable to such disputes, such as those in the EU.

Second, in parallel to and in connection with these developments, the EU began implementing further significant reforms of the CAP in June 2003 with the so-called Fischler reforms. The most direct aid was decoupled from production requirements, which turned the largest share of potentially actionable policy instruments into WTO compatible ones, while reducing the support provided to European farmers only marginally (Swinnen 2008). Overcoming the likely effects of the expiration of the peace clause was clearly a key factor behind this reform. First, the reform was adopted only a few months before the expiration of the peace clause. Second, it had the most pronounced impact on the likely targets of legal challenges in the WTO, and was explicitly aimed at enabling the EU to allocate the new direct payments into the WTO-compatible green box (European Commission 2002).[8] It should come as no surprise that, after the adoption of the reform, EU negotiators stressed that the agreement represented a 'significant decision for WTO talks' (*Agra Europe*, 18 July 2003, EU prepares WTO offensive as Cancun talks draw nearer). Indeed, Commissioner Fischler declared that 'today we have largely said goodbye to an old system of support which distorted trade. The new agricultural policy is trade friendly... [T]his will put us on the offensive at the WTO negotiations' (Fischler 2003).

These developments paved the way for a gradual convergence between the EU and Brazilian positions. Having realised that Brazil was both willing and able to use litigation to its advantage, and using domestic reform to increase its room to manoeuvre, the EU began to soften its position in August 2003 and joined the US in launching a proposal to eliminate export subsidies on products that were of particular interest to developing countries.

The proposal prompted an immediate response from what has since become known as the G20 group of developing countries.[9] The G20 presented a framework proposal for directing agricultural negotiations, proposing a number of drastic

---

8. An interview by the authors with the DG Trade Official at the European Commission, Brussels, 23 February 2009 confirms this point.

9. In the months preceding the WTO Ministerial Conference in Cancun in September 2003, Brazil had undertaken a shift in strategy to increase pressure for agriculture liberalisation. While remaining a member of the Group, Brazil led the G20, an issue-based coalition of developing countries that aimed to bargain jointly during the MC and beyond.

measures such as the abolishment of the blue box, a tighter discipline on the green box and the elimination of export subsidies for all products.[10]

As the September 2003 MC in Cancun ended in failure, the G20 made clear that it was in a position to extract substantial concessions from the EU and did not want to approve an extension of the peace clause (*Agra Europe*, 8 August 2003). As a result, the EU took a further step in the negotiations by putting export subsidies on the table.

Sets of acceptable agreements start to overlap

In May 2004, in an attempt to re-launch negotiations, the EU made itself available to discuss a complete phasing out of export subsidies (European Commission 2004; WTO 2004a). This decision was largely motivated by a desire to forestall being forced to dismantle these instruments as a result of legal rulings, which the EU feared in the wake of the sugar case.[11] The willingness to discuss export subsidies was greeted by the Brazilian government as a victory that would entail significant cost reductions for the domestic agricultural industry, while serving as the beginning of the end of agricultural subsidies (*Agra Europe*, 6 August 2004, EU satisfied with WTO farm deal).

Meanwhile, the EU had started an internal discussion about how to change its sugar regime to implement the WTO ruling. This culminated in a reform, adopted by the Council of Agricultural Ministers in November 2005, which ensured that the EU largely complied with the far-reaching requirements of the WTO ruling (Daugbjerg and Swinbank 2008). The EU's willingness to comply with the WTO ruling against it on sugar subsidies allowed Brazil to update its beliefs about the EU's type: its compliance on one issue suggested that it would be likely to comply on related issues. In terms of the model, following EU compliance with WTO rules on sugar subsidies, Brazil expected p to be higher, and thus believed that it could demand more.[12]

Indeed, in 2005, Brazil sought to extract significant concessions on market access and domestic support (G20 2005). The Fischler reforms had, of course, reduced the scope of issues on which the EU remained legally vulnerable: Brazil

---

10. The URAA codified different types of subsidy to farmers according to their impact on production. Subsidies with minimal links to the quantities produced, the inputs used, or the prices paid were classified as belonging to the 'Green Box', and not subject to reduction commitments. Specific payments that were linked to quantities produced but subject to output controls were classified as belonging to the 'blue box' and were also not subject to production controls. Other types of subsidy, including market price support subsidies, were classified as belonging to the 'amber box'. Amber box subsidies are subject to an overall limit called the Aggregate Measure of Support (AMS).

11. Interview by the authors with former DG Agriculture Official at the European Commission, Brussels, 25 June 2010.

12. The EU's compliance with the sugar ruling affected Brazil's posterior belief about its likelihood of compliance in subsequent disputes. However, this outcome did not lead Brazil to believe that the EU would comply with certainty. Thus, a litigation strategy still would have entailed a risk of non-compliance, and negotiation remained optimal for Brazil.

would be able to extract additional concessions from the EU, but only within the parameters set by the Fischler reforms. But among those issues that remained legally vulnerable, Brazil and the G20 were able to gain significant concessions. In Hong Kong, with regard to domestic support schemes, the G20 asked for a reduction of both the total Aggregate Measurement of Support (AMS) and overall trade distorting support by 80 per cent, while the EU offered to cut both by 70 per cent. On market access, the G20 asked for a 75 per cent reduction in the highest tariffs, while the EU offered a maximum cut of 60 per cent, an average cut of 46 per cent coupled with a request to be able to designate 8 per cent of tariff lines as sensitive. Further convergence would be achieved at the subsequent July 2006 MC in Geneva, when the EU improved its offer on market access, getting close to the tariff reductions demanded by the G20 group (an average tariff cut of 54 per cent) and lowered its demands on sensitive products to 5 per cent of total agricultural tariff lines (Blustein 2009). While in Hong Kong, the two sides were still somewhat remote from each other, by the July 2006 MC in Geneva, the EU Trade Commissioner Mandelson positioned himself as an ally of the G20, and Brazil de facto accepted the reality that the concessions it had extracted on issues on which the EU was legally vulnerable – namely, export subsidies and domestic support schemes – were a sufficient basis for a deal (*Agra Europe*, 28 July 2006, EU offered WTO farm tariff cut of 48%; Blustein 2009).

A negotiated deal within reach

Although a deal could not be struck in Geneva – mostly as a result of the US inflexibility in both asking for greater market access concessions from the EU and refusing to meet EU demands for greater domestic support scheme reductions – Brazil continued to strive for a negotiated compromise with the EU in the Doha Round, rather than shift to litigation. Although its updated beliefs about the EU suggested an increased likelihood of compliance, some fears remained that powerful farm lobbies in the EU might encourage a less compliant attitude were Brazil to litigate on these agricultural matters (Camargo 2008).

Further developments in the negotiations corroborate the claim that the parameters of an eventual compromise had already been identified. Indeed, in the last document that sets the limits of a potential compromise in the agricultural negotiations, the Revised Draft Modalities for Agriculture of December 2008, the figures were roughly similar to those identified in the July 2006 Ministerial Conference, namely an average tariff cut of 54 per cent with the possibility of designating 4 per cent of tariff lines as sensitive products, a 70 per cent reduction of the AMS and an 80 per cent reduction of overall trade distorting support (WTO 2008).

The prospects for a successful conclusion of the Doha Round have been bleak, if not non-existent, since 2008. The narrative developed so far, however, shows that the two sides have been able to move closer to each other throughout the negotiations, and that, both in terms of content and timing, such convergence was largely due to the legal vulnerability of the EU. While an agreement on the further liberalisation of agricultural trade may not be reached due to the difficulty of finding common ground among the positions of all negotiating partners, it is clear that legal vulnerability acted as a trigger to increase the set of agreements on agriculture acceptable to both the EU and Brazil. Had Brazil been unable to litigate, it is unlikely that any mutually acceptable agreements would have existed.

Cooperation and the expiration of the peace clause: the US and Brazil

Much like the EU position on agriculture, the US position in the Doha Round's agricultural negotiations was an attempt to strike a delicate balance between significant pressure from Congress to protect farm subsidies and the constraints of a judicialised WTO. And, as in the EU case, a variety of analyses before the expiration of the peace clause demonstrated that a wide array of domestic support schemes for farmers in the US would likely become challengeable by third parties in the WTO once it expired (Josling *et al.* 2006; Kennedy 2008; Porterfield 2006; Steinberg and Josling 2003; Sumner 2005). Consistent with our expectations, the US negotiating strategy was largely affected by legal vulnerability.

With the approval of the 1996 Farm Bill, agricultural domestic support schemes were substantially transformed. Deficiency payments were eliminated and replaced with production flexibility contract payments, fixed payments that would gradually decrease over a period of seven years. While the US Department of Agriculture projected that this new approach to farm subsidies would keep the US far below the $19.1 billion URAA limit, these estimates proved inaccurate. When commodity prices collapsed in the late 1990s, Congress responded with a series of supplemental bills that provided market loss assistance payments to producers of the same commodities that were eligible for production flexibility contract payments (Porterfield 2006).

Agricultural domestic support schemes were further boosted by the 2002 Farm Bill. It permitted spending to increase by about $8 billion per year above the levels projected by the 1996 Farm Bill and institutionalised additional payments that were tied to commodity prices, thus creating larger production incentives (Sumner 2005). The 2002 Farm Bill established that the bulk of US subsidies would be provided through market loan programme payments, direct payments, and countercyclical payments.

Credible (threats of) litigation and retaliation

Both bills made US domestic farm subsidies vulnerable to WTO legal challenges, but this was particularly so with the 1996 Farm Bill. The famous WTO ruling on US cotton subsidies clearly showed that, with the 1996 Farm Bill, the US was contravening WTO rules. In 2002, Brazil initiated a WTO dispute against the US over various cotton support programmes enacted between 1999 and 2002 (WTO 2002a). After two years of consultations, filings and panel meetings with the parties, a WTO panel decision released in September 2004 and an AB ruling in 2005 upheld Brazil's claims (WTO 2004b, 2005a). The dispute settlement panel and the AB found that certain programmes that the US claimed were WTO compatible green-box subsidies (production flexibility contract payments and direct payments) were, in fact, more than minimally trade distorting, and that the US was also exceeding the $19.1 billion cap on permissible amber-box support. For these reasons, US policies were ruled to have caused harm to Brazil's interests, as they would have suppressed prices in the world market for cotton (Sumner 2005). Notably, the US declined to comply with the WTO ruling, so that Brazil was eventually allowed to impose sanctions. Ultimately, the dispute was not resolved until 2010 when, following a number of compliance complaints by Brazil, the two parties agreed on a negotiated settlement to settle the controversy (USTR 2010).

Interestingly for our analysis, this case can be considered as the first post-peace clause challenge to farm subsidies (Josling *et al.* 2006). It had significant implications for the US. With the 2004 and 2005 rulings in the cotton case, it became clear that a wide array of farm subsidies provided under the 2002 Farm Bill would also be vulnerable to legal challenges. Marketing loan programme payments, counter-cyclical payments, and, to a lesser extent, direct payments, for instance, all seemed challengeable under the SCM Agreement on the grounds that they cause serious prejudice to foreign competitors in the US domestic market and in international markets (Schnepf and Womach 2007; Steinberg and Josling 2003).[13]

That the cotton ruling would open up the possibility of challenging a wide array of US domestic farm subsidies was clear to the relevant actors in both the US and Brazil. In 2003, the President of the American Farm Bureau Federation Bob Stallman expressed concern that the US could face further challenges, leading him to support an extension of the peace clause (Inside US Trade, 15 August 2003). After the issuing of the AB ruling in 2005, the US Secretary of Agriculture Mike Johanns noted that 'the US has two choices: it can sit back and watch as our farm policy is disassembled piece by piece, or begin WTO talks on a new policy that would provide a safety net for US producers' (Inside US Trade, 7 October 2005). After the failed meeting of the MC in Geneva in 2006, both the US Trade Representative Susan Schwab and Secretary of Agriculture Johanns again expressed their concerns, claiming to expect an upsurge in legal challenges against US farm programmes (Inside US Trade, 24 July 2006).

Brazil's government was obviously also aware of this situation and, as a result, was keen on conveying the message that it considered WTO litigation to be a powerful weapon at its disposal. After the adoption of the 2005 AB ruling, Pedro Camargo, the former Brazilian Secretary of Production and Trade in the Ministry of Agriculture, forcefully stressed the link between the cotton case and other potential cases against US farm subsidies when, in the face of the US refusal to implement the WTO ruling, he argued that 'the dispute settlement system will again have to produce essential jurisprudence on levels of trade-distorting support acceptable in international competition. Potential cases on rice, wheat or dairy would also have to go this route' (Camargo 2005: 4).

---

13. It is estimated that the most vulnerable programmes were those for the following commodities: corn, wheat, rice, feed grains, corn, and oilseeds.

A bargaining window emerges

In this context, and consistent with our model's predictions, the US considered multilateral trade negotiations as the best venue to deal with its legally vulnerable trade-distorting policies in agriculture. The most visible effect of the cotton dispute on the Doha talks was the US agreement in August 2004 to begin negotiations on the so-called 'Cotton Initiative', a proposal by a group of least-developed cotton exporting countries (Benin, Burkina Faso, Chad and Mali) to deal with questions such as cutting cotton subsidies and tariffs to support farm productivity growth in Africa. The initiative led to two significant commitments by developed countries in the Hong Kong WTO MC in 2005, namely to eliminate all forms of export subsidies for cotton in 2006, and to provide duty-free and quota-free access for cotton exports from least-developed countries (WTO 2005b). These concessions were, of course, conditional on the successful conclusion of the Doha Round.

Furthermore, and more generally, the US conceived of multilateral negotiations as an opportunity to engage in trade-off deals that would allow it to minimise concessions on legally vulnerable policies and, at the same time, push its offensive interests. More specifically, after the initiation of the so-called 'upland cotton dispute' by Brazil, the United States attempted to protect farm subsidy programmes by linking limited concessions on permissible levels and classifications of subsidies under the Agreement on Agriculture to counter-concessions on market access, while also attempting to secure a new peace clause that would limit challenges to farm subsidies under the SCM Agreement (Porterfield 2006). For instance, the July 2003 joint EU–US proposal preceding the Cancun MC called for an expansion of the scope of the blue box so as to enable the US to shift some of its previously labelled amber box spending into the blue box (Kerremans 2004). Moreover, in successive proposals the US took a strong position on market access while it sought to minimise concessions on domestic support schemes. The proposal presented by the US in October 2005 in the run-up to the December Hong Kong WTO MC included bold requests on market access, such as a cut of 90 per cent on the highest agricultural tariffs and to limit the number of 'sensitive products' to 1 per cent of tariff lines. Yet, the proposal was very timid regarding the domestic support pillar, where it offered to cut its AMS spending by only 60 per cent and its *de minimis* spending by only 50 per cent. These concessions in the US plans could be met by shifting most of the previously labelled amber-box support into the WTO compatible blue box (USTR 2005).

Brazil did not passively accept these proposals offered by the US. Indeed, Brazil fought hard to resist the US strategy of shifting trade-distorting and legally vulnerable domestic farm subsidies into WTO-compatible spending categories. Moreover, while siding with the US in its requests for large cuts in agricultural tariffs, Brazil sought to push the US towards greater concessions with respect to the actual percentage reductions in domestic support (G20 2005).

Unwillingness to comply due to strong domestic lobby

Despite the limited concessions it was able to extract on domestic support from the US, Brazil continued to deem WTO multilateral negotiations the best venue for dealing with US domestic farm subsidies, and chose not to pursue litigation. The reason for this was likely to be in part due to the aforementioned noncompliance of the US on the cotton issue. Observing the unwillingness of the Americans to comply with previous WTO rulings, Brazil updated its beliefs about the US type, and attributed a smaller value of p in terms of the model. Thus, Brazil was ready to accept a smaller negotiated settlement to avoid the risks of litigating against a non-compliant trading partner. Indeed, in 2002, immediately after filing the complaint on US cotton subsidies, Brazil's government explicated that

> [t]he threat of new subsidies cases after the expiration of the peace clause would eventually serve as an incentive for members to agree to new reductions in domestic subsidies and agricultural tariffs. Even a deal that is not exactly what Brazil wants would ward off subsidies cases since such a deal would be preferable to a series of disputes.

> (*Inside US Trade*, 1 November 2002)

Even in the aftermath of the 2005 AB ruling against the US, when it was clear that the concessions that could be extracted from the US were limited, the Brazilian government reiterated on different occasions that it preferred seeking convergence on domestic farm support rules during the Doha Round negotiations over resorting to WTO litigation (Cairns Group 2005, 2006, 2007). For Brazil, negotiations in the present were clearly also preferable to litigation in the future (Camargo 2005), especially if the ultimate outcome of the strategy – even if Brazil would be victorious in litigation – was unclear.

These reactions are very much in line with what our model suggests. As it had done in the case of the challenge against EU sugar export subsidies, Brazil used the cotton dispute to get a better deal in the Geneva negotiations. Brazilian officials, however, knew that the road towards the implementation of the WTO ruling was loaded with political landmines because of the tremendous political influence of farmers in the US system and the visibility that the cotton issue had acquired in the US (Goldberg *et al.* 2004). The political resistance to the implementation of WTO rulings in the US proved that these expectations were justified (*see* Schnepf 2011 for a timeline) and that the US was relatively unlikely to comply with adverse WTO rulings. In other words, the US was perceived to be (and acted as) a non-compliant type of disputant. In this context, it is not surprising that, although Brazil could revert to a credible strategy of litigation against the US, it preferred to continue engaging in negotiations that would be likely to lead to some small concessions over a strategy which risked US non-compliance with WTO rulings.

Preferring negotiations rather than litigation

As noted above, the Geneva 2006 WTO MC failed to identify common ground for compromise. Among the many contentious issues that remained unresolved, the US insistence on greater market-access concessions by the EU and its refusal to improve its offers on domestic support stand out as major bones of contention. The positions of the key players had not changed substantially by December 2008. The lack of any actual agreement in agricultural negotiations, however, does not run directly counter to our argument. Reaching an agreement would require a compromise between all the major stakeholders involved in the negotiations process. As for the dyadic relationship between the US and Brazil considered here, it seems likely that the chance of any overlap in the negotiating positions of the two parties would have been even less likely in the absence of legal vulnerability. Consistent with our expectations, both parties preferred to tackle existing barriers to trade through negotiation rather than litigation and gradually moved towards a compromise (though one that entailed relatively few concessions). Eventually this allowed them to minimise the costs for the US and to reduce at least some of the costs incurred by exporters in Brazil.

Negotiations on food and consumer safety: the EU and the US

As the EU had become a global precautionary superpower in the course of the 1980s and 1990s, it was subject to serious legal vulnerability under the WTO rules from 1995 onwards. The evolution of European food safety regulations and their troubled relation with the WTO rules bear witness to this fact.

In the 1980s, economic and political pressures arose for the EC to adopt common rules on the use of hormones in raising beef that effectively resulted in a ban of all hormones (Princen 2002). Similarly, throughout the 1990s, the EU approved a series of regulations that culminated in the adoption of a tight regulatory structure, which ultimately imposed a moratorium on the production and import of genetically modified (GM) food products (Skogstad 2003). Whereas these rules and regulations could generally be employed without much consequence during the GATT regime, they made the EU legally vulnerable under the new WTO regime.

Litigation and retaliation

As expected, the EU food safety regulations became subject to external challenges soon after the formation of the WTO. In 1996, the US requested a dispute settlement panel case against the EU, claiming that its ban on hormone-treated beef was inconsistent with the Sanitary and Phytosanitary Standards agreement. Both the WTO dispute settlement panel and the AB supported these US claims, in April 1997 and February 1998 respectively. The European moratorium on GM crops that was put in place in 1997–8 also raised concerns in the US, home to major producers and exporters of genetically modified organisms (GMOs).

The US eventually threatened to take legal action in the WTO against the EU's regulatory regime for GMOs on the grounds that it provided for unjustified trade restrictions (Kelemen 2010).

After the US threatened to initiate a WTO case against the European GMO regulation, farmer associations in the EU started expressing their concerns and asked for new WTO rules. Indeed, expecting the US to take legal action, both small farmer associations and the COPA-COGECA took a stance in favour of WTO rules that would immunise the EU from legal challenges and provide guarantees to European consumers (COPA-COGECA 1998, 2000). These requests from producers added up to the pressures already coming from environmental NGOs (Friends of the Earth 1999; WWF 1999, 2001).

In 1999, concomitantly with the US threat to initiate legal proceedings in the WTO against European GMO regulations, trade and environment became a priority for the EU in the new round of trade negotiations (Poletti and Sicurelli 2012). In line with the requests of both farmers and environmental NGOs, the European Commission started to strongly advocate the integration of environmental principles within WTO rules. This would grant de facto immunity from legal challenges against its food and consumer safety regulations (European Commission 1999; WTO 2000).

While in previous sections we have shown that complainants were willing to consider negotiation as an alternative to litigation, in line with our theoretical expectations, the US did not accept starting negotiations on the terms proposed by the EU. The issue at stake was indivisible in nature; that is, the choice was either to allow US exports to enter the EU market or not. Consequently, the US could not gain anything by entering into negotiations and relied on WTO litigation instead. The European attempt to lend legal cover to its domestic rules was clear to US negotiators, as they explicitly expressed their 'concern that Europe might use the negotiations in Doha to justify illegitimate barriers to trade, particularly trade in biotechnological products and application of the commercial clauses of present or future multilateral agreements on bio-security'.[14]

While it agreed to include a trade-and-environment chapter in the Doha Declaration, the US narrowed the scope of any future negotiations concerning the relationship between WTO rules and Multilateral Environmental Agreements by attaching the provision that they would only affect the parties to such agreements and by refusing to discuss the incorporation of the precautionary principle into WTO law (Eckersley 2004). In this way, the US made sure that any future agreement on trade and environment would not prejudice its right to challenge the rules of WTO members that were not compatible with the Sanitary and Phytosanitary Standards agreement, which it deemed to be illegal non-tariff barriers.

Meanwhile, given the strong popular support for existing food and consumer safety regulations and consensual decision-making rules, EU policymakers could not proceed with bringing domestic legislation in compliance with WTO rules. The WTO ruling on the EU's ban on hormone-treated beef and the subsequent

---

14. Inside US Trade, 23 November 2001

imposition of retaliatory measures by the US did not lead to a substantial policy change within the EU. Indeed, when policy change did take place in 2003, the EU simply introduced comprehensive risk assessment procedures and did not actually lift the ban (Daugbjerg and Swinbank 2008). Similarly, the reform of its regulatory framework for GMO approvals that the EU started in 2000 culminated in the adoption of Directive 2001/18 and Regulation 1829/203, which further tightened existing GMO regulations. Thus, these directives actually made things worse for US growers (Pollack and Shaffer 2009).

Although these political developments had made it crystal clear that compliance by the EU was not to be expected, the US insisted on relying on WTO litigation rather than seeking a compromise in negotiations. In 2003, the US finally initiated a formal WTO complaint to challenge the EU's de facto moratorium, due to the increased frustration of US producers over lost sales to the EU and concerns over the impact of EU regulatory restrictions on regulatory developments in other countries. It is important to stress that, unlike Brazil's strategy with the sugar and cotton disputes, the US did not conceive of WTO litigation as a tool to maximising leverage during negotiations.

The complainant refuses to negotiate on an indivisible issue

In September 2004, in response to the US move, Pascal Lamy tried again to argue in favour of negotiating new WTO rules that would allow members to deviate from WTO obligations when they clash with domestic policies that reflect values which are strongly rooted in a given community. He listed environmental protection, food safety and precautions in the field of biotechnology among Europe's collective preferences (Lamy 2004). Once again the EU was trying to change international trade rules to lend legal cover to its own domestic regulatory framework. Because of the indivisible nature of the issue, however, no middle ground compromise was possible between the two sides. So the US refused to engage in these negotiations and deemed WTO litigation as the best tool to achieve its aims. To put it simply, WTO litigation did not trigger a convergence of negotiating positions between the EU and the US because there was no space for a middle-ground compromise due to the character of the issue at stake.

Rules negotiations and the zeroing practice in antidumping: the US and Japan

In our fourth and final case study, we show how the indivisibility of the issue was at the root of the failure to find a compromise over the US zeroing practice in antidumping. For years, US antidumping authorities have used a particular method for calculating antidumping margins, known as zeroing, a legally vulnerable practice under extant WTO law. Indeed, the WTO Antidumping Agreement sets limits on the leeway domestic authorities have to label a practice dumping and to the antidumping duties they can impose whenever a foreign exporter has engaged in dumping. When domestic antidumping authorities investigate whether dumping has taken place, they typically assess the difference between the average price in the home market (the normal price) and the average price asked by the foreign exporter (the export price). For each transaction, if the export price is lower than the normal price, then the dumping margin is positive; if the export price is higher than the normal price, then the dumping margin is negative. The export and normal price levels are then compared using the average dumping margin from all transactions. With zeroing, however, a margin of 'zero' is counted for those transactions where margins were actually negative, which, of course, substantially influences the outcome when averaging all transactions to arrive at the average dumping margin.

This method clearly leads to higher dumping margins and thus to higher antidumping tariffs. Understandably, exporters to countries that apply this zeroing method disapprove of it, as they suffer concentrated losses from it. For years now, WTO members with many such exporters have challenged this practice. They have already caused the EU to stop its use of the simple zeroing method, and have been pressuring the US to move along the same path.

The defendant seeks negotiations

Seeing how its zeroing policy was subject to legal challenge by the EU, Japan, Korea and other WTO members, the US assertively put its position on the table during the Doha multilateral trade negotiations, namely that zeroing should be turned into a WTO-compatible policy.[15] Since the 2001 Doha MC had decided to clarify and improve disciplines in the WTO Antidumping Agreement,[16] the US actively engaged in getting the so-called rules committee to put a 'legalisation' of zeroing methodology on the negotiating agenda, in order to undermine pending WTO cases challenging its policy, to forestall future ones, and to cater to the vocal domestic lobby of import-competing industries benefiting from the inflated average dumping margins that the zeroing methodology provides.

A group of 12 WTO members led by Japan, however, vehemently opposed any such move, filing briefs to the chair of the rules committee on behalf of the Friends of Antidumping group while the EU, not a member of that group, also voiced concern. It was eminently clear to the US as well as to many targets of US antidumping duties, that zeroing was legally vulnerable. Panels and the AB had ruled several times against the use of zeroing in US antidumping investigations, especially in so-called administrative reviews and sunset reviews (Vermulst and Ikenson 2007). In 2006, the AB ruled against sixteen such US administrative reviews on EU products and deemed them in violation of the Antidumping Agreement. In reaction to these WTO rulings, the US consistently argued that it would be better to negotiate rather than litigate about this legally vulnerable part of its antidumping policy. The other side, the Friends of Antidumping group

---

15. *Inside US Trade*, 3 August 2007.
16. *Inside US Trade*, 5 October 2002.

led by Japan, remained diametrically opposed to any loosening of WTO rules on zeroing, and by mid-2007 no agreement between them and US negotiators could be found.

The complainants refuse to negotiate on an indivisible issue

At the end of 2007, Guillermo Valles, the chair of the rules committee, tried to move his part of the Doha negotiations forward by putting forward a proposal to rule out zeroing methodology in initial antidumping investigations. Flatly rejected by Japan, the negotiations stalled, especially since American Congressmen had come under ever more pressure from import-competing industries, such as the steel industry, to instruct the US Trade Representative not to cave in to demands for the abandonment of zeroing.[17]

As by now litigation had run its complete course (Prusa and Vermulst 2011), the EU and Japan were entitled to respond to US non-compliance with the imposition of retaliatory tariffs against US exports. The US side now invested its time and energy in trying to convince the EU and Japan not to proceed with retaliation. It proposed not to use zeroing in future reviews, but to leave the existing antidumping tariffs based on zeroing in place and leave it open as to whether they would use zeroing in future initial antidumping investigations. At the same time, the US was as unwavering as the other side of the negotiating table, and reiterated its conviction that all forms of zeroing should be made WTO-compatible through a revision of the antidumping agreement in the ongoing, but by then very moribund, Doha negotiations.

Concluding remarks

In this chapter, we have investigated how legal vulnerability to WTO rules affects multilateral trade negotiations. We have demonstrated formally that the availability of legal recourse provides countries with a weapon that they can use during negotiations against trading partners who are engaging in unfair practices. The credible threat to use this weapon can encourage concessions from otherwise obstinate trade distorters. Negotiated agreements can be beneficial to both parties, as the defendant can bargain for a smaller reduction than would be required under an adverse judgment, while the complainant can still attain relief for its exporters. This logic, however, only holds when the issue at stake is divisible. When the issue at stake is indivisible, then the possibility of coming to overlapping sets of agreements lapses. Issues of domestic regulation in particular display this indivisibility characteristic. Furthermore, the complainant's beliefs about the defendant's willingness to comply with a judgment against it matter a great deal. Complainants are willing to accept fewer concessions from trading partners who are likely to be non-compliant. The complainant's assessment of whether the defendant is of the compliant or of the non-compliant type is heavily conditioned

---

17. *Inside US Trade*, 5 October 2007.

by the mobilisation potential of the domestic groups within the defending state who are opposed to the removal of the disputed trade barrier.

Empirically, we have illustrated how the possibility of legal challenges has affected the negotiations on trade-distorting agricultural subsidies between Brazil on one side and the EU and the US on the other side. In line with our model, the empirical analysis shows that Brazil's ability to challenge the trade-distorting policies of its trading partners and to impose costs on them significantly affected the behaviour of the US and the EU. When Brazil could not yet credibly threaten to litigate on these issues because of the peace clause, neither the EU nor the US was willing to bend in negotiations; Brazil's litigation threat became credible, however, as soon as this peace clause lapsed, and both were then willing to offer concessions that would not otherwise have been on the negotiating table. In line with our model's predictions, the US was able to concede less than the EU, due to Brazil's beliefs about the lack of willingness to comply among the Americans, constrained as they were by a strongly mobilised farm lobby. The bargaining space for a negotiated settlement arose, however, because the issues at stake were divisible.

In cases when WTO members are in dispute over indivisible issues, however, the possibility of negotiated settlements should turn out to be elusive. In such cases, the judicialisation of the WTO actually does not enhance incentives for cooperation in the negotiating branch of the organisation. Indeed, in the disputes in which the US complained about EU food and consumer safety measures, and where Japan and other WTO members complained about the US practice of zeroing in antidumping investigations, no bargaining window opened up, as issue indivisibility foreclosed any such possibility.

The mechanism we have highlighted in this chapter assumes that the issue under dispute is sufficiently important to the defendant to induce some non-zero probability of non-compliance. In those cases in which the costs of compliance are sufficiently low or broadly distributed, compliance may be a foregone conclusion, and a complainant can simply opt for litigation with the assurance that it will receive everything it desires. While this limits the cases for which we can expect legal vulnerability to increase the chances of cooperation, those that remain can reasonably be assumed to be among the most relevant and important.

The discussion we have presented has important implications for the study of the effects of international trade institutions on preference formation and state behaviour. First, our analysis raises the question of why prominent GATT members cooperated on the judicialisation of the world trade regime in the first place. If they could have anticipated the potential loss in relative bargaining power, why then would the US and the EU have agreed to strengthen the WTO enforcement mechanisms? As we focus primarily on the ways in which changes in structure can affect the optimal strategies for WTO members in negotiations, this question falls beyond the scope of the present chapter. Suffice it to remark that the US, which supported the judicialisation of the GATT dispute settlement system from the beginning, initially expected to be a beneficiary of the new system, while the EU went through a process of experiential learning that ultimately led it to support institutional reform, despite its initial reluctance (Eckhardt and Elsig 2015).

Second, our analysis advances the debate on the conditions for international cooperation. The conventional wisdom posits that the odds of defection from cooperation are greater when actors engage in negotiations concerning prospective agreements that they expect to be highly enforceable (Fearon 1998; Koremenos *et al.* 2001). In line with this argument, some have suggested that increased enforceability of rules may have ended up endangering the stability of the world trading system by decreasing the propensity of WTO members to further commit to trade liberalisation (Goldstein and Martin 2000). This analysis may well be correct. The opposition of key players to the expansion of the WTO's regulatory reach to a host of areas such as labour standards and the so-called Singapore issues, as well as the reluctance of other members to deepen existing trade liberalisation commitments indeed seem to support the view that stronger enforcement of rules may be impeding cooperation in the trade regime. Our analysis, however, has complemented this argument in an important way. While judicialisation may well have increased reluctance to commit to binding agreements in new areas, it may also have increased the willingness to deepen *already existing* commitments, given the shadow of WTO law. So far, observers and analysts have generally concurred that the DSM is efficient because more trade disputes get resolved and compliance with WTO rules has been strengthened (Zangl 2008). Our analysis shows that the DSM may be efficient in an even more fundamental way. Not only can more disputes be resolved, but the opportunity for legal recourse may actually ignite a dynamic of cooperation on issues in which certain members are legally vulnerable, at least when these issues are easily divisible. While the prospects for a negotiated agreement in the Doha negotiations are very slim because of a number of factors such as the rise of Brazil, the outright resistance from India, the deteriorating trade positions of the US and the EU, and the complex nature of negotiations on regulatory issues, our argument implies that, in the absence of the shadow of WTO law, the chances of success would be even smaller.

Third, in addition to showing that bargaining under the shadow of WTO law may enhance the prospects for a negotiated agreement, our argument reveals interesting aspects about bargaining power in the WTO. We show that a defendant enhances the credibility of its non-compliance threats by disregarding WTO rulings, which can ultimately improve its bargaining position in future negotiations.

Finally, our analysis casts doubt on whether the expansion of the WTO's regulatory reach is sustainable and desirable. Since the positive effect of legal vulnerability on cooperation in the WTO disappears when it comes to regulatory commitments concerning indivisible issues, one should expect little cooperation in this area. In fact, the legal vulnerability of domestic regulatory arrangements is even likely to stall, rather than foster, the future prospects for further cooperation in the multilateral trade regime.

Chapter Six

WTO Judicialisation and the Specialisation of Interest Mobilisation

In the final chapter of this book, we explore how the institutional structure of the WTO has affected the character of interest mobilisation in the domestic politics of the members of that multilateral trade regime. As we have shown in Chapters Three and Four, the judicialisation of the world trade regime has significantly affected the incentives of trade-related economic interests to advocate further liberalisation and/or regulatory harmonisation within the WTO framework. Yet, the judicialisation of the WTO may also have affected the incentives of those trade-related economic interests with regards to how they mobilise. In this chapter, we develop a set of arguments on how the judicialisation of the WTO has furthered trade lobbying specialisation at the expense of broad sector-wide lobbying.

The level at which economic interests are aggregated within policymaking institutions affects the degree to which they are likely to produce public policies beneficial to a larger group or even society at large, rather than policies tailored to the special interests of small groups. The question of why some interests are more easily mobilised than others has received a great deal of attention within the political science literature (Olson 1965, 1982; Lowery and Gray 1995; Grossman and Helpman 1996, 2001; Baumgartner and Leech 2001; Coen 1998). This substantial attention to the politics of collective action is not surprising because the consequences of these processes often directly affect policy outcomes and have important consequences for the democratic legitimacy of political systems (see Baumgartner and Leech 1998; Dür 2008; Hojnacki *et al.* 2012).

Within this literature, one recurrent finding is that specialised, or specific, interests mobilise more easily than more encompassing interests. As already argued by Mancur Olson in the 1960s, the incentive to free ride is so powerful among the latter groups that mobilisation often does not materialise (Olson 1965). By contrast, organisations that represent small and specialised segments of the economy, such as firms in a specialised sector, face considerably fewer obstacles to getting their act together and to effectively mobilise over a more sustained period of time (Olson 1965; Grossman and Helpman 2001; Coen 1998; Dür and De Bièvre 2007). Interest group systems may thus run the risk of falling prey to an over-specialised, narrowly focused interest representation system, and consequently of becoming captured by specific interests (Olson 1982; Lowery and Gray 1995).

For this reason, many political systems, although to a varying degree, have built in certain safeguards to make sure a broader set of interests will be politically organised (Lowery and Gray 1997; Greenwood and Dreger 2013). Given the varying success of these safeguards around the world, interest group systems vary widely in terms of the nature of interest mediation. A well-known distinction is the one between corporatist systems, in which the representation of encompassing interests is highly institutionalised, and pluralist systems, in which interest representation is less centrally organised and in which interest groups are more competitive in their search for influence (Mahoney 2008; Woll 2012). As a result, corporatist systems are often perceived as being more receptive to broad interest representation, while pluralist systems are usually seen as more open to specialised kinds of interest mediation.

As we will argue later, the judicialisation of the WTO may eventually erode the capacity of trade-related economic interests to mobilise on a broad-based sector-wide level within the negotiation venue of the organisation. Hence, analysing the causes for specialised rather than broad-based collective action in trade policy acquires particular relevance, as it may inform us about the extent to which the WTO can produce goods of a public rather than a private nature, as well as the prospects for successful future cooperation within the WTO. In fact, if our analysis is not entirely mistaken, and viewed from the perspective on incentives for interest mobilisation, the prospects for the attainment of public goods such as further multilateral trade liberalisation or multilateral regulatory agreements look rather bleak.

In essence, our argument is that the judicialisation of the world trade regime has given additional impetus to the specialisation of trade policy lobbying. While the negotiation venue of the World Trade Organisation has continued to be mainly characterised by broad sector-wide lobbying, the judicial arm of the organisation has attracted more specialised collective action. We argue that this so because *judicial* enforcement through WTO dispute settlement litigation de-links issues and stimulates product-specific lobbying. Since exporters know that WTO Dispute Settlement Body rulings, and the possibility of trade sanctions, increases the likelihood that a foreign government will remove trade barriers that do not conform to the WTO rules, they have an incentive to mobilise. Yet, the case-by-case logic of judicial proceedings triggers product-specific interests to lobby their government, and makes them less eager to pay the high coordination costs of sector-wide collective action. The judicial venue within the WTO thus sets incentives different from those set by issue-linkage based multilateral trade *negotiations*, which create incentives for firms to lobby through organisations that represent and aggregate the interests of entire industrial sectors, or even across multiple sectors. In such a context, fruitful lobbying depends on the ability to supply the building blocks for the across-issue package deals that the negotiators will generally seek to attain. Since the probability that a single firm's lobbying effort affects outcomes is likely to increase when mobilisation takes place in cross-sector business alliances and/ or sector trade associations, individual firms will seek to represent their interests through organisations representing such encompassing interests.

Our analysis has several implications for the literatures on the political economy of trade policy, interest group mobilisation, and global governance.

First, we complement existing accounts on trade policy lobbying, which suggest that an important driver of lobbying specialisation in trade policy has been the decades-long increase in intra-industry trade at the expense of inter-industry trade. We complement this existing explanation by specifying how international trade institutions have influenced firm incentives for political mobilisation.

Second, we add to the literature on patterns of interest group mobilisation on domestic governance issues in advanced liberal democracies. In the domestic realm, rule generation and law making – or, the legislative function of states – calls for political organisations that are able to aggregate interests at a broad level, whereas rule application and enforcement – or, the adjudicative function of states – calls for case-by-case treatment and the mobilisation of specialist expertise (Shapiro and Stone Sweet 2002; Bouwen and McCown 2007). Our analysis shows that the institutional structure of international trade governance, constituted as it is by a highly judicialised form of adjudication and recurrent multilateral trade negotiations, has systematic consequences for patterns of political mobilisation, and, in fact, leads to patterns that resemble those found in domestic governance systems.

Third, we complement the interest group politics literature by showing that business associations often act as defenders of special interests. This has important consequences for how we value interest mediation systems that favour these types of interest (Olson 1982; Grossman and Helpman 1996 and 2001; Baumgartner and Leech 2001). Additionally, we add to the literature on interest representation in EU trade policymaking. Lobbying concerning EU trade policy has traditionally been carried out by European-wide associations representing the interests of entire sectors of industry or of several sectors simultaneously (Dür 2008). Our findings illustrate the importance of taking into account the effects of the institutions of the international trade regime on the nature and modes of interest representation in domestic settings (Goldstein and Martin 2000).

Fourth, while we complement existing studies that show how the institutional set up of global trade governance has affected business–government relations (Shaffer 2003, 2006; Woll and Artigas 2007), we highlight some potential future developments in the patterns of interest representation in global trade governance. The decline of the WTO as a forum for negotiated trade liberalisation, epitomised by the inability of the Doha Round to achieve substantive trade liberalisation commitments, has been accompanied by the continued resilience of the organisation's judicial arm. We thus expect that the current structure of interest representation at the WTO as characterised by the co-existence of sector-wide and product-specific lobbying will become more imbalanced over time, towards a structure in which narrower interests primarily determine the content of WTO commitments. Adding this development to the other impediments to trade cooperation at the WTO, the capacity of negotiators to deliver public goods in the form of liberalisation and/or trade rules within the WTO looks bleak. We should thus also expect a rise in bilateral free trade negotiations that take place outside the WTO framework

We proceed with our analysis in several steps. We first explore the strength of existing explanations regarding the character of interest mobilisation on international trade. We then develop our argument of the multilateral trade regime's effect on interest mobilisation. We first show the plausibility of our argument through a combination of quantitative and qualitative evidence from US and EU trade policy lobbying. It consists of general illustrative evidence on interest mobilisation for EU and US dispute settlement cases at the WTO as well as specific evidence on mobilisation by economic actors from the EU and the US during multilateral trade rounds. We then delve deeper into how judicialisation in the WTO has engendered institutional change in its members and affected interest mobilisation. We do so through an in-depth case study of institutional adaptation in the EU and an analysis of how judicial trade politics has changed the mobilisation and organisation of EU business associations in relation to multilateral trade issues.

Sector-wide and product-specific interest mobilisation

It is well established that domestic as well as international institutions affect state behaviour regarding international trade. Domestic institutions have been shown to affect a state's propensity to pursue protectionism or liberalisation (Rogowski 1989; Gilligan 1997a; Verdier 1994; Kono 2009), its compliance rates with GATT/WTO rules (Rickard 2010), its willingness to commit to preferential trading arrangements (Mansfield et al. 2007), the likelihood of it changing its trade policy (Henisz and Mansfield 2006), and its lobbying style at international negotiations (Woll 2008). International institutions also have been shown to affect the domestic politics of trade in that issue-linkage increases the likelihood of liberalisation (Davis 2004), the rising importance of the judicial arm of the WTO affects the balance between exporters and import-competing groups in the domestic political arena (Goldstein and Steinberg 2009; Ehlermann 2005), and the strength of the WTO's enforcement capacity is a critical factor that influences a state's propensity both to subject itself to further commitments and to comply with already agreed rules (Goldstein and Martin 2000, Goldstein and Steinberg 2008).

The existing literature on international trade politics has thus shed significant light on how institutions can affect international trade politics. Yet the answers to the question of how the institutions of the international trade regime influence patterns of interest mobilisation remain unsatisfactory. Existing explanations for the aggregation and representation of interests in trade politics have traditionally been sought by looking at domestic political cleavages along factors of production, sectors of industry, or specific product lines (Hiscox 2001; Rogowski 1989; Gilligan 1997a, 1997b). Within this literature, it has been argued that trade politics is characterised much more by product-specific lobbying than sector-wide and cross-sector lobbying. This has been attributed to the growing importance of intra-industry trade (Gilligan 1997b; Verdier 1998; Kono 2009; Kim 2013).

Discussions on interest representation in trade policy lobbying have often focused on why economic sectors or producers of particular products organise collectively. Two models from these discussions require further consideration here:

the sector model and the intra-industry model. Although originally these models were designed to predict the effects of international trade policies on economic welfare, they also make predictions regarding political cleavages and patterns in political representation (Frieden and Rogowski 1996).[1] Yet, as we will presently see, both models fail to fully account for the co-existence of the sector-wide and product-specific interest mobilisation that currently characterises the multilateral trading system.

Economic actors engaging in international trade or feeling the disruptive potential of trade liberalisation and/or trade regulation often mobilise politically at the level of the sector. Particularly well suited to explain this historical regularity as well as its occurrence in contemporary trade politics is the sector model, originally developed by Ricardo and Viner. The model assumes that production factors such as labour, capital, and possibly land, are sector-specific – as opposed to the assumption that they are freely mobile across sectors. Within this model of trade politics, trade liberalisation increases the returns from the abundant factors used within a sector, while it reduces returns from the scarce factors used within a sector (Alt and Gilligan 1994). Under such circumstances, firms are likely to organise in sector-wide trade associations to defend their interests on international trade.

Empirically, however, interest mobilisation on trade issues also takes the form of product-specific collective action. A well-known and convincing explanation for this phenomenon is provided by the intra-industry model. This model comes from strategic trade theory and assumes economies of scale and imperfect competition. If firms benefit from increasing returns to scale, barriers to entry for new firms go up, and established firms find themselves in a situation of imperfect competition. This results in intra-industry trade, that is, trade of different varieties of the same product between countries with similar factor endowments (Krugman 1981). Due to extensive product differentiation and specialisation, intra-industry trade turns firms or agglomerations of firms into the dominant actors in their market niche. Observing that intra-industry trade reduces the costs of trade *relative* to inter-industry trade, a number of analyses have argued that intra-industry trade lowers the incentives for more collective forms of representation (and may even make trade liberalisation politically easier to achieve) (Gowa and Mansfield 2004; Lipson 1982; Milner 1999; Verdier 1998).

Other authors have, however, pointed out that strategic trade theory tends to overlook *how* intra-industry trade affects incentives for collective action (Gilligan 1997b). While the costs of adjusting to intra-industry trade are probably less severe

---

1. We do not explicitly consider the factor model, which predicts political cleavages along factoral lines (Rogowski 1989). While this provides a powerful explanation for the politics of trade in the nineteenth and early twentieth centuries as characterised by political party mobilisation along class lines, it has been convincingly shown that the gradual and sustained downward trend in inter-industry worker mobility since the interwar period due to the growing complementarity between labour skills and technology has produced a marked shift from class-based trade policy coalitions to sector-based ones in major developed economies (Hiscox 2001). Since our analysis focuses on the period following the creation of the GATT in 1947, we do not discuss the factor model and its implications.

than with inter-industry, comparative advantage trade, they are not concentrated in one single social class or a single industry. Rather, a small set of hyper-specialised producers, or even a single firm, will face the burden. Because firms consider the expected benefits and costs of lobbying, as well as the likelihood that their individual and joint efforts will have an impact on policy outcomes (Olson 1965), intra-industry trade is expected to ease political mobilisation. The decreasing number of firms in markets with intra-industry trade increases the impact one single firm may have on policy outcomes and lowers the coordination costs for collective action (Kono 2009; Kim 2013). Gilligan (1997b) went so far as to state that the high concentration of benefits and the low coordination costs might turn lobbying over intra-industry trade into a private, rather than a public, good for the firms active in that product category within a country. Because intra-industry trade leads firms to act more individually or in small groups (rather than collectively within or across sectors), trade policy lobbying will take the shape of highly specialised and brand-specific associations dominated by a small number of firms.

The above reasoning suggests that an increase of intra-industry trade over time should be accompanied by a concomitant increase in the amount of product-specific trade policy lobbying. Conversely, a decrease in intra-industry trade should lead to a decrease in product-specific lobbying. Moreover, the implicit corollary of the intra-industry trade approach is that any increase (or decrease) of product-specific lobbying should be accompanied by a concomitant decrease (or increase) of sector-wide lobbying.

Figure 6.1 shows how intra-industry trade as a percentage of total trade has evolved over time in both the US and the EU, with inter-industry and intra-industry trade each making up about half of total trade of both the EU and the US in the late 1990s. [2]

In line with the intra-industry model, product-specific lobbying should have increased in both political systems between the mid-1970s and the late 1990s, the period when intra-industry trade grew at a rapid pace, while it should have

---

2. For both the EU and the US, we calculate the total proportion of intra-industry trade using the index proposed by Grubel and Lloyd (1975). For a given country a, trading commodities from N different industries with B different partners, the year's total proportion of intra-industry trade is expressed as:

$$IIT_a = \sum_{b=1}^{B} \left[1 - \frac{\sum_{i=1}^{N} \left| X_{ab,i} - M_{ab,i} \right|}{\sum_{i=1}^{N} \left(X_{ab,i} + M_{ab,i} \right)} \right]$$

where $X_{ab,i}$ represents a's exports to trading partner b in industry i, and $M_{ab,i}$ represents a's imports from b in industry i. This measure takes a value between 0 and 1, and is increasing in the share of intra-industry trade. To calculate intra-industry trade for the EU, we aggregated across all EU member states, excluding intra-EU trade. We calculated intra-industry trade for the EU and the US using two different data sets: the World Trade Flows dataset from Feenstra and colleagues (2005) contains all commodity-level bilateral trade flows between 1962 and 2000, while the UN COMTRADE dataset employed by Baccini and colleagues (2012) provides data on commodity-level bilateral trade from 1989 to 2009. To ensure compatibility between the two data sets, we aggregated the data from the World Trade Flows dataset to the two-digit SITC code format.

Figure 6.1: Intra-industry trade of EU-15 and US between 1962 and 2008 (per cent of total trade)

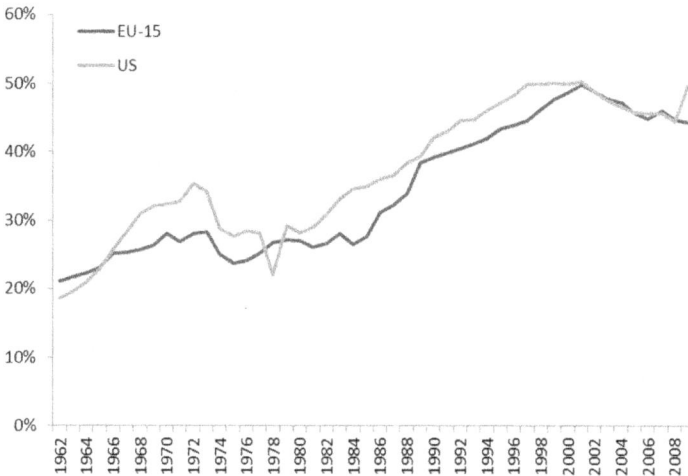

Source: (De Bièvre *et al.* 2016)

stabilised or even decreased after the mid-1990s. In addition, these changes should be expected to have caused concomitant changes in the amount of sector-wide lobbying. Yet, as we show in the remainder of the chapter, the patterns of interest mobilisation in the EU and the US do not follow these trends. First, product-specific lobbying did not decrease in line with the relative decline of intra-industry trade in the EU and the US in the mid-1990s. Second, the increase of product-specific lobbying over the last decades has not been accompanied by a decrease in sector-specific lobbying.

The inability of previous research to fully account for these observations stems from the fact that the research design and evidence used in these studies do not allow us to grasp the effects of institutional determinants of interest mobilisation. Although the DSM of the WTO underwent a significant reform in 1995, the existing studies on the effect of intra-industry trade on the character of trade policy lobbying neglect the impact of this important potential source of variation. For instance, Gilligan (1997b) considers evidence on trade complaints lodged at the US International Trade Commission by American interest groups in the 1988–1994 period, and Kim (2013) offers evidence on trade policy lobbying based on the reports that became available only after the adoption of the *Lobbying Disclosure Act* in 1995. Yet, both studies do not control for how changes in the institutional set-up of the WTO affect trade policy lobbying. Moreover, the increase of product specific lobbying at these venues does not necessarily affect sector-wide lobbying at other institutional venues.

An explanation for the increase in product-specific lobbying over time, and the co-existence of different types of interest group mobilisation within the international trade regime requires an appreciation of how the bifurcated structure of this regime, with both a judicial and a negotiation venue, creates different political opportunity structures for trade policy lobbying.

Judicialisation and interest mobilisation in the WTO

Both the sector model and the intra-industry model for interest mobilisation in trade policy are based on the assumption that political mobilisation is dependent on the type of trade countries engage in. Yet, for the question at hand, namely how to explain the representation and aggregation of interests in trade policy, the institutional environment and the governance of the international trade regime itself *could*, and, we submit, *should*, also be regarded as an important component of the explanation.

In formulating our hypotheses on the effects of the institutions of the multilateral trade regime on interest mobilisation within its members, we conceive of them as a political opportunity structure. While some institutions are structured in a way that means they deal with broad and encompassing sets of issues, other institutions, by design, deal with highly specific issues and consider each issue on its own merits. This institutional distinctiveness affects the organisational form of interest aggregation and representation.

The different institutional contexts of rule generation and law making on the one hand, and of rule application and enforcement on the other hand, have been shown to call for different forms of interest representation in the domestic realm. In the former institutional context, interests tend to be represented through encompassing organisations, while in the latter context special and narrow interests, and sometimes also individuals or individual firms, dominate the scene (Alter 1998; Bouwen and McCown 2007; Burley and Mattli 1993; Shapiro and Stone Sweet 2002).

We expect a similar logic to play out in the WTO as it has both a legislative and a judicial venue. The existing literature on the relationship between institutions and political mobilisation in trade policy has hitherto focused only on differences across *domestic* institutions (Kono 2009; Rickard 2010, 2012). Incentives to lobby, however, do not only vary in this way across domestic political institutions. Varying political opportunity structures within *international* institutions can also provide distinct incentive structures that shape interest aggregation. The judicial venue of the WTO sets different kinds of incentives for interest mobilisation by economic actors from those of the WTO's negotiating branch. Below, we set out a set of theoretical expectations about the likely effects of these institutions on interest mobilisation within WTO members.

Traditionally, the negotiating venue was the predominant aspect of the multilateral trading regime. As explained in the previous chapters, although the GATT did have an important dispute settlement mechanism, this was also a political–diplomatic venue rather than a judicial one. When acting in the negotiating venue of the trade regime, executive officials purposely engage in issue linkages. The more they are able to broaden the stakes of ongoing negotiations, the more market access they can obtain from foreign trading partners and the more they can counteract domestic obstacles to liberalisation (Davis 2004; Sebenius 1983; Steinberg 2002). Also, as there is a heterogeneity of capabilities and preference intensities among WTO members and a unanimity rule for decision-making, issue linkage enhances the chances for cooperation (Martin 1994).

The need for issue linkage in trade negotiations generates a demand for encompassing and aggregated interest representation. When negotiators assemble package deals on multiple issues, the credibility of their liberalisation demands, as well as of their offers of concessions, depends on their domestic support. To put it in two-level game language, the size of a negotiator's win-set decreases and their bargaining power increases when exporters and import-dependent firms express strong liberalisation demands and import-competing sectors draw clear red lines (Putnam 1988). Negotiators wanting to bring home an agreement thus have an incentive to enlarge their win-set by offering concessions in other domains through linking issues. To be successful in this exercise, negotiators rely on key interlocutors from key trade-related economic interests that are able to deliver stable and credible positions.

Hence, if business representatives want to obtain liberalisation benefits or to protect their domestic market by opposing particular concessions, they need coordinated positions. Umbrella associations constitute the best organisational form within which economic sectors can aggregate their preferences, with positions likely to be determined by the preferences of their largest members or those with the strongest preferences over issues; these preferences are then transmitted to their government representatives and negotiators (Dür 2008; Eising 2007a, 2007b). Trade-related economic actors, in other words, have an incentive to aggregate interests in order to weigh credibly in this negotiation process characterised by institutionalised issue linkage (Davis 2004). The need for these complex institutionalised issue linkages make product-specific or firm-level lobbying less effective. Sector-wide and cross-sector trade associations are better equipped to follow all parts of the negotiations, provide aggregated policy positions for negotiators, and can weigh more decisively in negotiation outcomes. Moreover, since trade negotiators face constraints on time, resources, and agenda space (Jones and Baumgartner 2005), and since there are transaction costs associated with interactions with interest groups, societal interests are likely to aggregate their interests at the level of entire sectors of industry.

With the creation of the WTO in 1995, a highly judicialised venue was also incorporated into the multilateral trade regime, creating different incentives for interest mobilisation. As the judicial institutions of the WTO de-link issues, they give incentives for product-specific interest mobilisation. Since WTO litigation is a bilateral, single issue interaction between states (Davis 2012), it incentivises exporters active in a particular product niche to organise interest representation at the product level, to push their public authorities to investigate their issue-specific demands, and to address issues through the WTO DSM.

The case-specific nature of the WTO dispute settlement process thus makes it attractive for product-specific types of complaints, which stimulates interest mobilisation at the product level. In the consultation stage of the dispute settlement process, the complainant usually advances multiple legal claims about a particular trade barrier within the defendant's borders. Generally, fewer legal claims actually end up being considered by panels and the AB. Irrespective of the number of legal claims, however, WTO disputes deal with one particular issue at a time, namely a trade barrier in a defendant that allegedly is harmful to the complainant. At the same time, the WTO DSM remains an inter-state process, unlike domestic courts where firms have direct access, can file cases on their own, and very often have no reason to engage in any form of collective action at all. Therefore, WTO dispute settlement sets incentives for narrow product-specific interest mobilisation, not in the form of individual action by firms, but in the form of collective action among firms at the level of specific product categories.

Strategic issue linkages, which are the bread and butter of negotiations, are near-excluded and difficult in this judicial context for a number of reasons. First, government representatives are generally not granted the authority to make commitments on issues other than the one under dispute. Second, the MFN obligation under WTO law makes issue linkages particularly costly, because any concession beyond the disputed issue would have to be automatically extended in a non-discriminatory way to all other WTO members.[3] And third, traditionally global trade diplomacy avoids compensating for losses in the form of direct cash payments. All these features make it difficult to engage in issue linkage within a WTO dispute (Guzmann and Simmons 2002).[4]

The de-linkage of issues thus brought about by the judicialised environment of WTO litigation decreases the need for firms to lobby through sector-wide or cross-sector associations, and stimulates them to lobby through product-specific associations. Since working through large encompassing organisations will not increase the probability that an individual firm's lobbying is going to contribute to a successful outcome, exporting firms seeking trade benefits are more likely to lobby only on the issues of importance to their companies, independently from other producers or sectors.

---

3.   Note that the core principle of non-discrimination in the WTO has important implications for the nature of the 'good' that can be obtained. It means that the nature of the good to be obtained by the removal of a WTO-incompatible measure through a WTO Dispute Settlement Body ruling is non-excludable and public. This is so because the benefits of the removal of these trade barriers might also accrue to all exporting firms or firms from WTO members other than the complainant in DSM proceedings.

4.   An important exception to this line of argument concerns potential retaliation by a complainant, whenever the defendant does not implement WTO panel and/or AB rulings, and the WTO has authorised such retaliatory measures. Indeed, in such cases, issue linkages become possible in the framework of WTO dispute settlement proceedings in the decision over whether retaliation takes place in the same product category, within the same sector, or across sectors (as is the case with so-called cross-retaliation, or in the US even 'carousel' retaliation). This of course can create incentives for interest aggregation at the sector or even at the cross-sector level. However, out of a total number of 402 WTO disputes between 1995 and 2009, Pauwelyn (2010) reports that retaliatory measures were only implemented for 8 disputes. Moreover, we are interested in gauging the underlying lobbying that triggers dispute initiation, not the lobbying reaction to retaliation.

Three further characteristics of international judicial institutions create disincentives to use sector-wide organisations. First, panel decisions and AB reports are not formally binding in the sense of the common law doctrine of precedent (Eckersley 2004: 37). In the absence of formally binding legal precedent, the benefits stemming from a WTO ruling can only be appropriated by the firms active in the product category affected by the dispute.[5] If instead there were consistently formally binding legal precedent, firms active in different product markets or sectors not directly affected by a dispute, but potentially affected by future disputes concerning the same WTO rule, could have incentives to engage in anticipatory collective action beyond their particular product category. Second, product-specific trade associations do not need to balance diverging membership interests, but can fully concentrate on compiling detailed, product-specific information and frame this in a highly specialised legal language that resonates well in a judicial venue. Third, the removal or the maintenance of trade barriers has direct effects on the economic success of specific firms, as one year without access to large consumer markets often has immediate consequences for the balance sheet. In order to maximise the effectiveness of lobbying efforts, such firms prefer to avoid lengthy sector-wide or cross-sector policy coordination, if the institutional route to do so is available.

In short, the WTO provides two incentive structures for interest mobilisation. The judicial institutions of the DSM trigger product-specific interest mobilisation, in contrast to the negotiation forum of the MCs, which creates incentives for sector-wide or cross-sector interest representation. If trade policy lobbying were only affected by changes in the composition of a country's trade, one would expect an increase in the amount of intra-industry trade to lead to an increase in product-specific interest representation at the expense of sector-level interest representation, and vice versa. Our institutionalist perspective suggests instead that the bifurcated institutional structure of the WTO creates two different opportunity structures, which attract different types of trade policy lobbying. Different types of trade policy lobbying may thus very well coexist, rather than exist as substitutes for each other. If these conjectures are correct, the judicialisation of the multilateral trade regime has contributed in its own right to the specialisation of interest mobilisation and lobbying in its members.

Interest mobilisation in the WTO: empirical evidence

We analyse the empirical accuracy of our theoretical expectations about WTO judicialisation and interest mobilisation by relying on different types of qualitative

---

5. The absence of formally binding legal precedent does not mean that there has never been a *de facto* legal precedent in some rulings. For instance, the panels and the AB have consistently condemned US zeroing in antidumping with an explicit reference to preceding rulings. However, the AB has also reversed its previous decisions, such as in the case of its different interpretations of environmental exemption provisions of the GATT in the Tuna–Dolphin and the Shrimp–Turtle cases. The point here is that only in the presence of a systematic and formal application of the legal precedent can actors be expected to engage in anticipatory collective action.

and quantitative evidence about the lobbying practices of EU and US economic actors, as well as by an in-depth case study on institutional adaptation and interest mobilisation in the EU. We focus on interest mobilisation in the EU and the US for several reasons. First, they are two pivotal players in international trade relations (Steinberg 2002), as they account for roughly 40 per cent of world trade (WTO 2012) and are the most frequent users of the WTO dispute settlement system (Horn *et al.* 2011). Second, the strong involvement of both the US and the EU in intra-industry trade makes us confident that we do not design our research in favour of our own expectations. Third, it is generally recognised that the EU and the US differ significantly in their domestic institutions and that this has resulted in different predominant modes of interest representation on each side of the Atlantic (Baumgartner and Mahoney 2008; Woll 2012). While the prevailing consensus-oriented decision making institutions in the EU coincide with the corporatist modes of interest representation that are seen in the domestic politics of many of its member states, the majoritarian institutions in the US are characterised by a pluralist and competitive interest group environment. These strong domestic differences should give extra leverage to our findings.

By conducting an in-depth case study on the EU, we have selected a WTO member with a very consensual political system with a high number of veto points – a property EU scholars have long considered as a prime cause for the EU's broad-based, corporatist style of interest mobilisation. In the wake of the judicialisation of the WTO, however, the EU made numerous changes to its institutional framework for EU trade policymaking and we show that these internal institutional changes triggered a significant specialisation of trade policy lobbying. In the final section, we show how these developments have had broader implications for the landscape of European associations, which have had to adapt to this new institutional environment by acting more as agents of powerful and often specialised members than as representatives of entire economic sectors.

WTO negotiations and lobbying in the EU and the US

In order to explore our conjecture about interest mobilisation during multilateral trade negotiations, we investigate the role sector-wide business associations have had during past GATT and WTO Rounds, as well as the level of interest aggregation that was predominant among interest groups which attended (or at least were eligible to attend) various sessions of the WTO MC.[6] Since interest groups

---

6. The data we present covers 1,968 organisations registered by the WTO Secretariat as eligible to attend one of the seven sessions of the WTO MC between 1996 and 2012 (see Hanegraaff *et al.* 2015 and De Bièvre *et al.* 2016). From this, all EU and US organisations were filtered, producing a total of 437 interest organisations, 215 of which originated from the US and 222 of which originated from the EU. Using web-based coding we added measures such as geographical origin, areas of interest, and organisational characteristics, as well as a measure of the level of interest aggregation of lobbying organisations using the ISIC classification system. See: http://unstats.un.org/unsd/cr/registry/isic-4.asp for an overview of this classification system. We used the classification system in order to ensure comparability between our product scope coding of dispute settlement cases and interest group presence at sessions of the WTO MC.

consider attending sessions of the WTO MC as one of the relevant ingredients of their lobbying strategy in relation to trade policies (Hanegraaff *et al.* 2011), looking at the presence or absence of product-specific sector-wide and cross-sector interest groups at WTO MCs constitutes an important source of information on interest mobilisation during multilateral negotiations in the WTO. Since this leaves out lobbying in national capitals (as much as it leaves out lobbying behind closed doors) and since interest group presence during GATT rounds was limited and not formalised, we rely on the existing literature about interest group lobbying during those GATT Rounds, especially about the Kennedy and Uruguay Rounds.

Existing evidence on interest mobilisation during GATT negotiation rounds corroborates the expectation that the institutional setting of multilateral trade negotiations based on issue linkages sets incentives for sector-wide interest mobilisation. Over the course of decades, the GATT negotiation Rounds led to reciprocal liberalisation in a host of economic sectors, such as the machinery, chemicals, pharmaceuticals, and agricultural sectors. Throughout the first five GATT Rounds, countries negotiated with an item-by-item, request–offer approach, and linked these in packages that seemed balanced to all (Stewart 1993; Hoekman 1989). The exact form of this basic structure of reciprocal liberalisation commitments, also called exchanges of concessions, was changed somewhat after these first five rounds. Whereas the first five rounds focused on tariff reductions, the Kennedy Round (1963–7) focused on linear tariff cuts, and a harmonisation approach was taken in the Tokyo Round (1973–9) reducing tariff peaks further, with some sectors excepted (such as agricultural and textile). Next to the exchange of tariff concessions, negotiations covered rules governing the conduct of domestic antidumping investigations, the desirability of rules on foreign direct investment, the institutional design of the DSM, intellectual property protection, technical barriers to trade, and so on. The gradual worldwide lowering of tariff barriers corresponded with the increasing importance of non-tariff trade barriers or so-called behind-the-border issues during negotiations.

This basic structure of an exchange of packages of concessions decisively affected the way economic interests were aggregated and organised during these rounds. During the Kennedy Round, sector-wide agricultural organisations from the US insisted on the inclusion of agriculture in the Round, whereas the European agricultural sector insisted, successfully, on keeping this sector outside the liberalisation package (Stewart 1993). Also, sector-wide trade associations for aluminium, ceramics, coal, electrical and glass products, as well as producers in the car industry and mechanical manufacturing, textiles, agriculture, chemicals, and commercial services sectors actively mobilised in favour of increased market access to the American market (Dür 2010).

During the Uruguay Round, sector-wide trade associations were the main interlocutors for governments in the sectors of agriculture and manufactured goods (Paarlberg 1997; Moyer 1993; Milner 1988). In the European Community, sector-wide trade associations formulated positions and communicated these to the European Commission's negotiators; these included the European chemical industry council (CEFIC), the European federation of pharmaceutical industries and associations, and the European Automobile Manufacturers' Association. Also cross-sector encompassing trade associations, such as the Union of industrial and employers' confederations of Europe (UNICE, now called BusinessEurope), the European roundtable of industrialists, and the American chamber of commerce in Brussels, formulated and communicated positions to European Commission negotiators (Dür 2010; Cowles 1996). The European Commission even actively summoned economic sectors to bring to bear their demands through sector-wide and cross-sector groups, in order to have a representative overview of the demands and a common thread running through them, which could be brought to the negotiation table.[7] It was also the sector-wide CEFIC that, together with its American and Japanese counterparts, initiated the zero-for-zero tariff proposal that negotiators incorporated into the overall package of the Uruguay Round, which reduced tariffs on chemicals to zero on both sides of the Atlantic (Quick 2007). In the textiles sector, sector-wide trade associations were crucial in securing the agreement on textiles and clothing as one of the major building blocks of the overall package of the Uruguay Round (Steinberg 2002). The European sector-wide trade association COMITEXTIL, now called EURATEX, served as the central interlocutor for European Commission negotiators.[8] Negotiators were hesitant, or even refused, to interact with representatives of more specialised, product-specific organisations, as taking less aggregated demands into account would have hindered their potential to bring weight and credibility to their negotiation positions.

On the American side, the large sector-wide trade associations, rather than the more specialised, product-specific representatives from American industry, were the most frequent and prominent to give testimony in hearings before the House Committee on Ways and Means. Those arguing in favour of increased foreign market access included the American Electronics Association, the Semiconductor Industry Association, the Motor and Equipment Manufacturers Association, and the Motion Picture Association of America, whereas those defending the status quo of existing levels of protection actually worked through cross-sector trade associations such as the Labor-industry coalition for international trade and the Trade reform action coalition (Dür 2010). Both European and American sector-wide, as well as cross-sector, organisations thus played a key role in constructing the package deals of the Uruguay Round of multilateral trade negotiations (Davis 2004; Meyerson 2003).

---

7. Interview with European Commission chief and Uruguay Round negotiator Ambassador Hugo Paemen, Brussels, Autumn 1999.

8. Interviews with the following Brussels-based trade policy-makers, conducted in the winter of 1999–2000: Camille Blum, former director-general of the COMITEXTIL; Ambassador Hugo Paemen, European Commission chief Uruguay Round negotiator; Monique Julien, former Director of the External Relations Department at the UNICE; Adrian van den Hoven, international relations staff member at UNICE (Winter 2006); Reinhard Quick, director of the Brussels Liaison Office of the VCI, the Verband der Chemischen Industrie. See also Bouwen 2004, Eising 2007b and De Bièvre 2003.

During the WTO period, sector-wide and cross-sector lobbying has also been the dominant mode in the institutional context of multilateral trade negotiations (Dür 2008). Throughout the Doha Round, the European farmers and agro-cooperatives organisation (COPA-COGECA), for example, has aggregated demands and preferences from the agricultural sector and relayed them to the European Commission. The same has been seen with regards to other sector-wide trade associations such as the ESF, the CEFIC, and the European pharmaceuticals trade association EFPIA (Blustein 2009; CEFIC 1999; Conceicao-Heldt 2011; EFPIA 2001; De Bièvre 2002; Woolcock 2005).

Interest mobilisation during multilateral trade rounds in the pre-1995 and post-1995 periods have thus predominantly taken the form of sector-wide and cross-sector trade associations acting centre stage. Existing evidence on interest group attendance at WTO MCs for the post-1995 period also lends support to this claim. In Figures 6.2 and 6.3, we reproduce the findings of a recent study that offers an overview of how the relative share of product-specific and sector-level associations attending sessions of the WTO MC has evolved over time (De Bièvre *et al.* 2016).

The figures illustrate the relative dominance of sector-wide interest organisations over product-specific ones within multilateral trade negotiations – with some slight, but noteworthy, differences between the EU and the US. The share of product-level interest groups that attended these negotiations never exceeded 40 per cent (at Seattle) in the case of the EU, while the average share of product-specific US interest groups present at sessions of the MC was 44 per cent, arguably a consequence of the more pluralist character of the US system of interest representation.

WTO dispute settlement and lobbying in the EU and the US

We now turn to the effect of the institutional structure of the WTO's judicial arm on interest mobilisation, by looking at the product coverage of all GATT/WTO

Figure 6.2: EU interest groups at WTO MCs by level of interest mobilisation (per cent, 1995–2012)

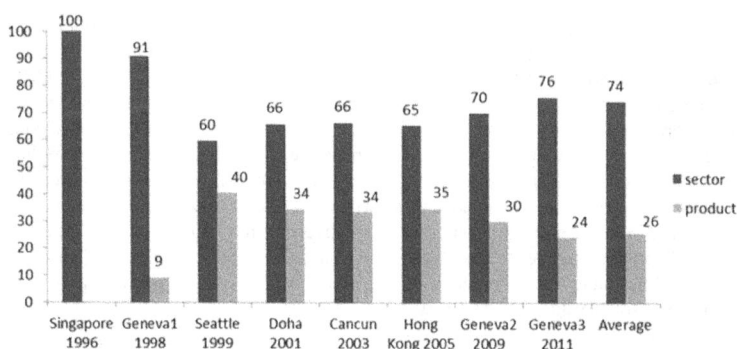

Source: (De Bièvre *et al.* 2016)

Figure 6.3: US interest groups at WTO MCs by level of interest mobilisation (per cent, 1995–2012)

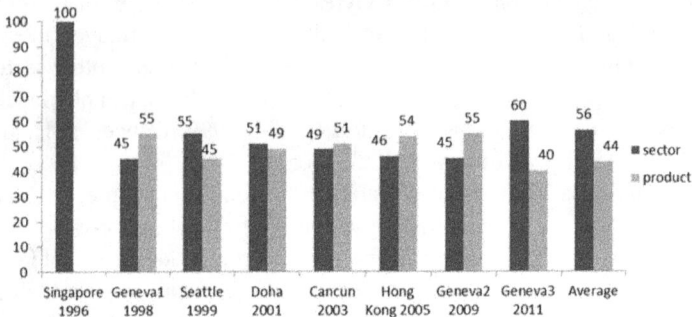

Source: (De Bièvre *et al.* 2016)

dispute settlement cases lodged by the EU and the US. Product coverage of EU- and US-initiated WTO complaints is a good indicator of interest mobilisation for WTO litigation (Davis 2012), as it is eminently plausible to assume that changes in the types of case that are filed reflect changes in underlying patterns of political mobilisation.[9] Our approach aligns with research on interest group communities that uses sector-related proxies as indirect measures for the mobilisation of interest groups in the absence of more direct evidence (Lowery and Gray 1995; Mahoney 2008; Leech *et al.* 2005).

To measure the product scope of disputes at both the GATT and the WTO, we coded all US and EU disputes (282 cases) according to the International Standard Industrial Classification of All Economic Activities (ISIC) classification system. This means that we coded disputes on agriculture (ISIC code 1) and the manufacturing of food products (ISIC code 2) as sector wide (or possibly cross sector), and disputes regarding issues such as animal production (ISIC code 3) and the manufacturing of wines (ISIC code 4) as product specific. We coded all EU and US initiated GATT and WTO disputes according to this simple rule.[10]

9.   Various scholars have investigated the nature and size of US trade policy coalitions by looking at official data on interest group testimonies to the Senate finance committee (Verdier 1994), trade complaints lodged at the International Trade Commission (Gilligan 1997), trade lobbying expenditures from the US Senate Office of Public Records (Bombardini and Trebbi 2012), and congressional votes on trade policy bills (Hiscox 2002). Similar and therefore comparable sources on trade policy lobbying in the EU context are not readily available, one of the reasons being that data on interest group spending are not systematically collected, and direct campaign contributions by firms are forbidden in most EU member states. Second, while numerous US- and EU-initiated WTO dispute settlement cases respectively stem from US Section 301 and EU Trade Barriers Regulation market access investigations, this evidence only consists of cases that were brought publicly, and leaves out the large majority of WTO dispute settlement cases where firms and interest groups value confidentiality.

10. For GATT disputes, we rely on Hudec 1992; for WTO disputes, on Horn and Mavroidis 2011. We recoded the Horn and Mavroidis database from the Harmonised system to ISIC codes to ensure comparability with our data on interest aggregation during negotiation Rounds.

Whenever the US or the EU were both complainants in a dispute, we treated them as distinct cases, as we are interested in capturing the type of lobbying that triggered the public authorities to file a complaint in each political system. In order to cross-validate our proxy-measure for interest mobilisation, we double-checked the coding of the product scope of disputes with the actual lobbying origin of these dispute settlement cases, whenever we had such information at our disposal. To this purpose, we based ourselves on information from interest groups requesting US Section 301 and EU Trade Barriers Regulation market investigations (which often lead to WTO cases) as well as on secondary sources (Poletti *et al.* 2016).

We start our analysis of how judicialised adjudication in the trade regime has affected the share of product-specific interest aggregation by showing the distribution of dispute settlement cases during the GATT and WTO periods. Since a possible explanation for product-specific interest mobilisation may well be the rise of intra-industry trade, we also display evidence concerning the evolution of intra-industry trade between 1962 and 2009. Figures 6.4 and 6.5 show the development of product level cases filed as a share of all cases during the GATT and the WTO period by the EU and the US, as well as the evolution of intra-industry trade as a percentage of total trade.[11]

The share of product-level cases filed at the WTO does not move in line with the changing composition of EU and US trade. While in the pre-1995 period product-level lobbying and intra-industry trade seem to go fairly hand in hand, they diverge in the subsequent period for both the EU and the US.

In the case of EU trade with the rest of the world, the share of intra-industry trade increased from around 30 per cent in the early 1980s to nearly 50 per cent in the mid and late 1990s. The average percentage of product-level dispute settlement cases filed by the EU also grows in this period at a rather consistent rate (that is, from around 35 per cent in the early 1980s to about 55 per cent in the mid 1990s). However, in the period after the creation of the WTO, the share of intra-industry trade as a percentage of total trade actually decreased over time, whereas the share of product-level dispute settlement cases increased considerably. In the late 2000s, the average share of product-level cases exceeded 80 per cent of all the WTO dispute settlement cases filed by the EU, while the share of intra-industry trade had dropped to less than 45 per cent of total EU trade in the same period.

The US displays a very similar pattern. As portrayed in Figure 6.5, the share of product-level dispute settlement cases filed and the share of intra-industry trade increased rather consistently during the GATT period, whereas this is not the case for the period after the creation of the WTO. Between 1980 and 1995, US intra-industry trade grew from a share of 28 to almost 50 per cent of total US trade. Likewise, the average share of product level dispute settlement cases increased from less than 40 per cent to almost 60 per cent. After the creation of the WTO, however, the share of product-level cases rose to almost 80 per cent of all WTO dispute settlement cases filed by the US, whereas the level of intra-industry trade

---

11. With regard to the dispute settlement cases, due to the low number of cases in some periods, especially in the 1960s and 1970s, we used a moving average of cases over a period of ten years.

Figure 6.4: Product-level dispute settlement cases and intra-industry trade in the EU (1962–2008)

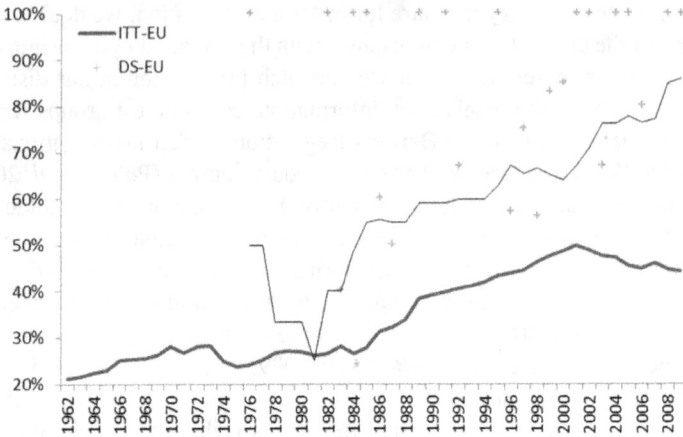

Source: (De Bièvre *et al.* 2016)

actually dropped by a few percentage points, from around 50 per cent to close to 45 per cent of total US trade in the mid and late 2000s.

The contrast is even starker when we compare the entire GATT period with the WTO period, in line with our argument that, as soon as the multilateral dispute settlement system became highly judicialised, the incentives it set for the

Figure 6.5: Product-level dispute settlement cases and intra-industry trade in the US (1962–2008)

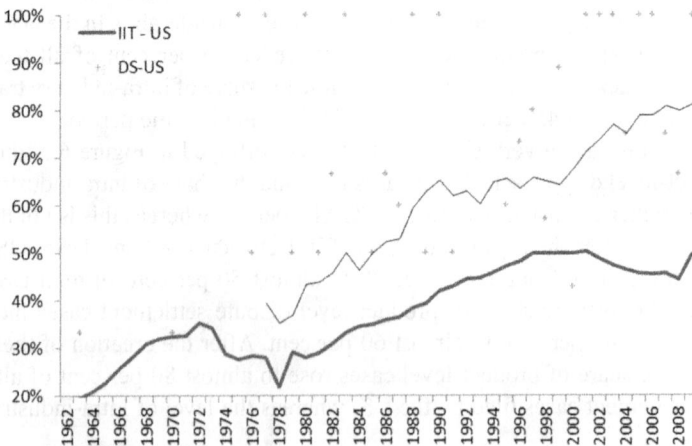

Source: (De Bièvre *et al.* 2016)

activation of particular economic interests also changed (see Table 6.1). If we look at the average shares of product and sector level cases filed in both periods, we see that the average share of product-level cases increased from 53 per cent of all dispute settlement cases in the GATT period to 79 per cent in the WTO period. For the EU, product-specific dispute settlement cases increased from an average share of 56 per cent in the GATT period, to no less than 82 per cent in the WTO period. In the US, the share of product-specific complaints increased from an average of 51 per cent in the GATT period, to an average of 76 per cent in the WTO period. Given that the share of intra-industry trade in both the EU and the US did not increase in the WTO period, and even decreased a bit, it is clear that intra-industry trade (alone) cannot account for the increase of product level dispute settlement cases since the WTO came into existence.

The judicial arm of the WTO thus provides incentives for lobbying specialisation. While the institutional environment of issue-linkage based negotiations mainly attracts sector-wide lobbying, or even across-sector coordination, WTO litigation mainly attracts product-specific interest mobilisation. Figures 6.6 and 6.7 give a comparative overview of the shares of sector-wide and product-specific interest mobilisation in the EU and the US for WTO dispute settlements and sessions of the WTO MC.

Despite the institutional differences between the EU and the US, litigation attracts much more product-specific interests, whereas negotiations create more incentives for sector-wide interest aggregation. This is most profoundly seen with the EU. Between 1995 and 2011, on average, 82 per cent of the EU cases filed within the judicialised WTO dispute settlement context were product specific, while at each of the sessions of the WTO MC, on average, only 24 per cent of the EU interest groups represented such narrow interests. For interest organisations from the US, the difference is somewhat smaller, but the same pattern is exhibited. Between 1995 and 2011, more product-specific interest groups mobilised for international trade dispute settlements than sector-wide groups (on average 76 to

Table 6.1: Sector and product-level EU- and US-initiated GATT and WTO dispute settlement cases

	Product	**Sector**	**Cramer's V**
Overall			
GATT (N=115)	53%	47%	0.272
WTO (N=170)	79%	21%	(p=0.000)
European Union			
GATT (N=41)	56%	43%	0.275
WTO (N=83)	82%	18%	(p=0.002)
United States			
GATT (N=74)	51%	49%	0.255
WTO (N=87)	76%	24%	(p=0.001)

Source: (De Bièvre *et al*. 2016)

Figure 6.6: EU product-specific mobilisation, product-specific DS cases, and intra-industry trade

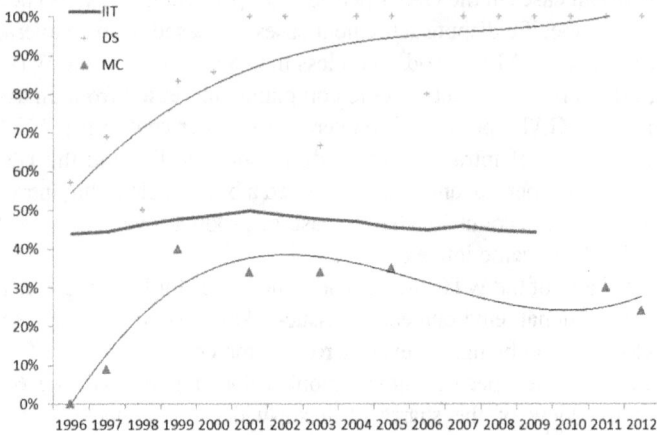

Source: (De Bièvre *et al.* 2016)

Figure 6.7: US product-specific mobilisation, product-specific DS cases, and intra-industry trade

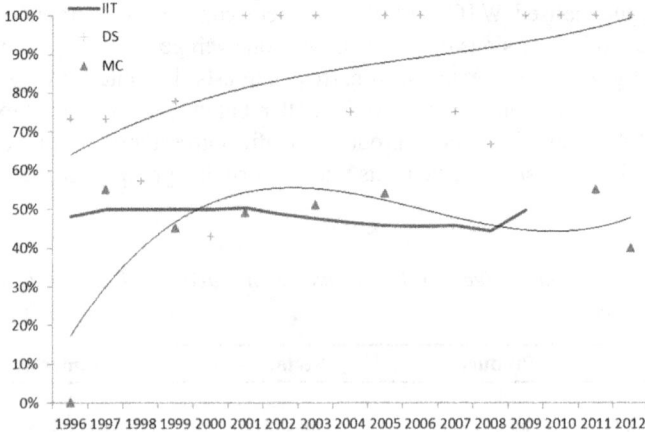

Source: (De Bièvre *et al.* 2016)

24 per cent), while at the sessions of the MC, US sector-wide mobilisation was more pronounced than product-specific mobilisation (on average 44 to 56 per cent). While differences between WTO members suggest additional effects from domestic characteristics, such as domestic patterns of interest intermediation and political institutions, the evidence we have presented so far confirms that judicialisation in the WTO has contributed to the specialisation of interest

mobilisation, while the organisation's negotiation venue has mainly continued to attract broad-based, sector-wide or across-sector interest mobilisation.

The impact of WTO judicial politics on the EU: a case study

The judicialisation of the world trade regime has not been without consequences for the institutions of its members. Indeed, several members made institutional reforms right after the creation of the WTO DSM in order to reap the benefits of the opportunity for legal recourse. Some scholars have already highlighted how the judicialisation of the WTO dispute settlement system has led to the replacement of traditional forms of interaction between public officials and economic interests with public–private partnerships characterised by horizontal, network-like exchanges based on expertise, learning and information give-and-take (Shaffer 2003, 2006; Woll and Artigas 2007). We complement these studies by showing that judicialisation has also affected the character and form of interest mobilisation in the EU, more specifically the level at which these interests tend to get aggregated. By means of an in-depth case study, we analyse how this institutional adaptation to the international institutional environment came about in the EU, and show how it has shifted the balance between product-specific and broad sector-wide interest mobilisation. By looking at the effects of judicialisation in three economic sectors – chemicals, pharmaceuticals and steel – we illustrate the broader implications it has had for the landscape of European associations, which now more often act as agents of powerful and frequently specialised members than as representatives of entire economic sectors.

Delving into the empirics of the EU's internal structure, as well as the patterns of interest mobilisation observed within the EU, has the potential to be particularly revealing about the systematic effects that the judicialised WTO has had on the policymakers and trade-related economic interests of its member states. The EU is probably the most notable example of a consensual political system (Lijphart 1999; Hix and Goetz 2000; Heisenberg 2005; Mahoney 2008; Scharpf 1988). In such democratic political systems, power is dispersed among multiple actors, and decisions are not adopted through simple majority voting, but through a process in which all major actors have a decisive say in the shape of the final decision. The EU takes most of its decisions by consensus among its member states under the shadow of qualified majority voting in the Council of Ministers. Even when supranational institutions have formal policy authority, such as in trade policy, a wide range of informal mechanisms exist to ensure that member states retain control over policy outputs (De Bièvre and Dür 2005; Woll 2012: 208; Dür 2008).

Scholars have widely documented how the particular institutional set-up of the EU affects processes of interest intermediation. EU lobbying practices closely resemble corporatist models of interest intermediation, in which interest groups coordinate their positions and create stable and institutionalised patterns of interaction and cooperation. As a result, interest groups formulate their demands in terms of pan-European goals and principles, and endeavour to channel these demands efficiently to policymakers through the complex multi-level institutional structure of the EU. In order to coordinate and aggregate the different interests within and across entire industry sectors, as well as across national boundaries, these interest groups have to be spread out across the EU (Broscheid and Coen 2003; Coen 1998; Greenwood 2002; Eising 2004; Woll 2006; Mahoney 2007a and 2008; Mahoney and Baumgartner 2008). Since failure to reach EU-wide consensus can easily lead to blockage, firms, industries and producers at large have to take a constructive approach and coordinate and aggregate their demands if they want to weigh in on the EU trade policymaking process (Broscheid and Coen 2003). Furthermore, lobbyists need to adopt a multi-level approach to press for their causes as multi-level representation is necessary on virtually all policy issues dealt with by EU institutions (Eising 2004). Hence, trade associations have a much more central standing in the EU's political system than in the American one (Woll 2012; Mahoney 2007).

The EU trade policymaking process has been no exception with respect to this general observation. Indeed, the rules for defining the position of the EU in trade negotiations, are still based on a de facto consensus procedure despite various institutional changes throughout time. Although the Amsterdam, Nice and Lisbon treaties streamlined rules governing the formation of EU trade policies, extending the scope of EU exclusive competences (De Bièvre and Dür 2005; Woolcock 2010), unanimity still applies to politically sensitive sectors (i.e. cultural, audio-visual, social, educational and health services), the consent of the European Parliament is still required for the adoption of trade agreements, and any trade agreement that has been approved at the negotiation stage can still be vetoed by a member state at the ratification stage. Because the consensus principle has continued to operate so strongly in EU trade policy, the incentives for forming broad trade associations rather than specialised interest groups are still strong (Dür 2008).

Nevertheless, despite these generally strong institutional incentives for broad sector-wide interest mobilisation in EU politics, the judicialisation of the WTO has led EU policymakers to adapt EU trade policymaking institutions, which has increased the importance of specialised interest groups relative to sector trade associations. These special interests often choose to lobby through associations rather than to increase their own lobbying efforts, which relates precisely to the institutional set-up of the EU. Business associations are often the first contact point for policymakers, and they are also more active than firms when it comes to lobbying (Berkhout et al. 2014). Since relations between business associations and EU policymakers are well established and based on mutual trust (Greenwood 2002), special product-specific interests have an interest in working through them rather than engaging in their own lobbying efforts directly.

So far, we have argued that WTO judicialisation has led to institutional changes in EU trade policymaking, which has increased incentives for product-specific and specialised lobbying. While it is important to analytically distinguish these two causal pathways brought about by the EU's embeddedness in the WTO, the twin dynamics engendered by the judicialisation of the WTO feed into each other, reinforcing the tendency towards greater specialisation in EU trade-policy lobbying.

The institutional adaptation enacted by the EU immediately after the judicialisation of the WTO has created domestic institutions that ease the flow of information between decision makers and private parties regarding multilateral trade dispute settlement. This has strengthened the incentives for firms to mobilise on a product-specific basis, creating even more pressure for specialised lobbying. As we will show, the domestic institutional mechanisms put into place by the EU were geared towards channelling demands of individual or small groups of firms seeking the removal of WTO incompatible trade barriers and are characterised by the absence of issue-linkages and by an exclusive focus on single issues. In addition, by providing an additional access point through which demands by societal groups can be channelled, these institutions for market access investigations have increased the potential for these groups to attain their desired trade policy outcomes (Ehrlich 2007). This in turn has led business associations to even further focus on a few and highly specialised members.

Institutional adaptation in EU trade policy

The judicialisation of the world trade regime prompted the EU to create information gathering and market access investigation procedures in order to ease the processing of private industry complaints about foreign trade barriers with the WTO.

Before the creation of the WTO, the European Commission had already put a New Commercial Policy Instrument (NCPI) in place in 1984 (Tassy 1997). This procedure was somewhat similar to the US Section 301 procedure to process complaints about alleged 'unfair trade' with the US Trade Representative (Bayard and Elliott 1994). The NCPI, however, was almost never used by European exporters, because it lacked juridical teeth and did not provide for an administrative structure to collect and centralise systematic data on export possibilities to third countries or on their lack of conformity with bilateral or multilateral trade agreements (Mavroidis *et al.* 1998). It was thus uncertain that the procedure would lead to a GATT dispute settlement case, which also had uncertain chances of success.

In the beginning of the 1990s, however, when the major trading partners reached an agreement to reform the GATT dispute settlement system during the Uruguay Round and to create the WTO (Hudec 2000), the European Commission faced compelling incentives to engineer a significant reform of its own trade policymaking institutions. This reform process started in 1994 and led to the adoption of the so-called market access strategy (European Commission 1996), which introduced three mutually complementary institutional components.

The first component of this institutional reform was the creation of the *Trade Barriers Regulation* (TBR) (Council of Ministers Regulation 3286/94), which became operational in the course of 1996. The TBR was created to improve the formal complaint procedure for industry associations, single enterprises and member states to inform the Commission of foreign trade barriers that appeared to violate EC and/or GATT/WTO rules (Bronckers and McNelis 2001).

The TBR streamlined the procedures and functioning of European market access investigations in two important ways.

First, the TBR allowed single firms as well as associations to file complaints, whereas the NCPI had only allowed complaints that represented a major portion of the relevant Community industry (Rydelski and Zonnekeyn 1997). Second, the TBR procedure lowered the decision threshold for an industry complaint to be acceptable to a mere qualified minority of member states in a specially created TBR committee in the Council. The European Commission from now on *had* to investigate an industry complaint, unless a qualified majority in the TBR committee opposed doing so. This for the first time permitted industry to avoid the more political route of approaching the EU trade policy committee (formerly called the art. 133 committee), the Council of Ministers' standing committee on external trade matters. Up until the creation of the TBR, firms or associations had to gather the support of a qualified majority in the trade policy committee for the Commission to start an NCPI investigation or to file a GATT/WTO complaint.[12] As of 1996, an association or firm only needs to convince a qualified *minority* of member states to support a market access investigation.[13]

The TBR unit is an administrative unit that was created to conduct market access investigations. It was created with the explicit aim of allowing exporting firms confronted with a trade barrier to concentrate their energies on establishing their rights under existing WTO rules rather than also having to completely carry the burden of an investigation. The TBR unit investigates without having to enter into tit-for-tat reciprocal negotiations with the partner country.[14]

In order to take advantage of the strengthened multilateral architecture of the WTO dispute settlement system, the European Commission also introduced a second key institutional reform by installing its market access unit in 1996. The unit was entrusted with the task of systematically gathering and processing information about foreign trade barriers in order to co-ordinate all efforts to 'go on the offensive' and use EU trade powers 'forcefully but legitimately to open new markets around the world' (WTO Director, Commission General Press conference, as quoted in Shaffer 2001). An extensive system was put in place to ease the flow of information between exporters and the market access unit, with the goal of encouraging private industry to provide information on trade barriers, especially on non-compliance with WTO rules.[15] The unit thus functions as the *antechamber* for formal proceedings, such as bilateral consultations between the EU and a third country, a TBR complaint, or a request for WTO dispute settlement. By far the most important responsibility of the market access unit is the management of

---

12. Both the administrative apparatus and the functioning of the TBR were reformed in the course of 2010 to 2013. This institutional change followed an internal Commission review, and the entry into force of the Lisbon Treaty.

13. Interview R. M. Petriccione, Head of Unit, DG Trade.

14. Interview P. Sourmelis, trade barriers unit, DG Trade and N.A. Zaïmis, trade barriers unit, DG Trade.

15. Interview with J.-P. De Laet and C. Keijzer, market access unit, DG Trade.

the so-called market access database, an online available computer database on export formalities, WTO-bound tariff levels and existing barriers to trade. Since its creation, the database has served as the informational backbone to EU litigation in the WTO, a systematic and centralised source of information on market access difficulties encountered by EU industry that, until its creation, had been dispersed among different services of the Commission (Shaffer 2003).

The last component of the EU market access strategy launched in the wake of the creation of the WTO DSM, is the DG on Trade's *WTO Division*. In charge of all WTO matters, the division takes care of the EU's position among the standing WTO committees. The division was created to prepare the files for ongoing negotiations or an upcoming round and, more importantly, to handle all WTO dispute settlement cases in which the EU is involved as a complainant or a defendant.[16] Once the decision to file a trade complaint in Geneva is taken, the information gathered by the market access unit and/or the TBR unit, with the assistance of the EU trade policy committee, ends up on the desks of the WTO Division (European Commission 1999). Furthermore, the WTO Division is responsible for the follow-up of all other WTO dispute settlement cases where the EU is involved as an observing third party.

In short, the replacement of the GATT's system of political–diplomatic settlement of disputes with the quasi-judicial system of dispute resolution of the WTO led to substantial changes in the institutional set-up of the EU. These developments increased incentives for specialised types of interests to become politically active and have had important implications for the major sector business associations.

The transformation of European trade interest mobilisation in three sectors

In this section, we analyse for three sectors how the organisational form of key sector-wide trade associations has been deeply affected by the judicialisation of the WTO DSM and the subsequent institutional reform within the DG for Trade.

The institutional changes in EU trade policy that occurred in the wake of the judicialisation of the WTO and the subsequent increase in product-specific lobbying indeed has not been without consequences for the internal organisation of European sector-wide trade associations. In the last two decades, some key sector-wide associations in Europe have reshuffled their memberships to accommodate product-specific interests. To be sure, the idea of sector-wide representation has not gone out of business entirely among these organisations. Most have maintained encompassing representation and still retain the political clout in order to decisively influence international trade negotiations. Yet, they have certainly given more weight and leeway to product-specific interests in the wake of WTO judicialisation and the enhancement of EU market access investigation channels.

---

16. Interviews with B. van Barlingen and A. Bensch, WTO Division, DG Trade.

We focus on three sectors of European industry: chemicals, pharmaceuticals, and steel. This selection allows for greater depth, while at the same time keeping constant a couple of important characteristics that otherwise would make these cases difficult to compare. All three sectors are highly trade dependent, have equally high levels of international competitiveness (although in some of its sub-segments, somewhat less so for the steel sector), and have high levels of intra-industry trade with non-EU trading partners. More importantly, all three sectors have for a long time been characterised by a very high degree of consolidation, meaning that they consist of a relatively low number of firms and/or are dominated by a small set of very large firms (De Bièvre and Eckhardt 2011). This aspect is important as we can thus exclude the possibility that industry consolidation has been the prime cause of lobbying specialisation during the period under investigation, rather than changes to the institutional environment within which these actors operate.

The European chemical industry council

The European chemical industry is arguably one of the best-organised sectors of industry in Europe. Its trade association CEFIC is a large 'carrier' of collective action with several decades of experience in lobbying European institutions in several fields of public policy.

One of the most important activities carried out by the CEFIC as a sector-wide trade association was, and still is, to provide the Commission with information necessary to conduct reciprocal trade negotiations with third countries. In the course of its history, the CEFIC has been a key partner for the Commission in assessing whether it is obtaining enough market access concessions from trading partners and in determining the importance of different concessions in negotiations. The CEFIC has played a key coordinating role in the framework of international trade negotiations during the GATT/WTO Rounds and in other free trade negotiations.

At the same time, the judicialisation of the WTO and the subsequent changes in the EU administrative apparatus gave the CEFIC incentives to reshuffle and change its organisational format in order to allow for political mobilisation at a more specialised level. Founded in 1972, the CEFIC had long been a Euro-Confederation of national chemical industry federations. In the 1990s, however, the CEFIC reorganised its membership structure twice. In 1990, 39 large companies became direct members of the CEFIC, transforming the organisation into a two-fold structure that included both national federations and company members. This membership change took place in light of the creation of the EC internal market, with its expansion of EU regulatory competences, as well as the concurrent conclusion of the Uruguay Round, which sanctioned the move to a more binding system of international trade rules.[17]

Firms active in particular chemical product niches faced with trade barriers outside the EU realised very well in 1995 that the liberalisation commitments

---

17. Interview with R. van Sloten, CEFIC, Brussels.

entered into by WTO member states could now be more credibly enforced due to the WTO DSM. In 1998, a total of 108 product-specific trade associations were included as full members of the CEFIC.[18] Of course, the membership of these product-specific associations was also triggered by firm-level changes, such as the creation of business units within chemical companies. Yet these product-related associations were especially interested in becoming well anchored in the Brussels sector-wide interest representation body to pursue offensive, market access strategies outside the EU.[19] Their newly found status within the organisation made them more fit to follow important developments in trade policymaking, not only in the area of anti dumping (as before), but also with regard to EU foreign market access investigations and WTO dispute settlement (CEFIC 1999).[20] This membership change was no trivial matter for the CEFIC. It realised full well that the easier access private industry had to the DG for Trade through the TBR had made it possible for their members to bypass it. Indeed, in 1998, without the involvement of the CEFIC, Cerestar and Federchimica had filed a TBR complaint on Brazilian import restrictions on sorbitol and CMC products, leading to an EU-initiated WTO complaint in October 1999 (DG Trade and WTO websites).

Hence, the creation of the WTO DSM and the subsequent EU institutional reforms which eased access to EU market access investigations gave the CEFIC incentives to adapt its internal structure in order to be geared towards a more product-specific manner of engaging in trade policy lobbying.

The European federation of pharmaceutical industries and associations

A similar shift towards product-specific membership took place in the pharmaceutical industry. During its first twenty years of existence, the European Federation of Pharmaceutical Industries and Associations (EFPIA), founded in 1978, had been a typical European confederation with a membership composed exclusively of national pharmaceutical federations. The organisation proved rather successful with promoting a number of issues within the internal EC market during this period. It had helped realise the harmonisation of marketing authorisations in the EC and defended the industry's monopoly on information about medicines. It had also successfully coordinated national association positions on tariff levels and the rules of the international trading system for international negotiations during the GATT Rounds.

In 1998, just after the creation of the WTO, the introduction of a fully operational DSM, and the coming into operation of the EU market access strategy, forty large individual pharmaceutical producers in Europe asked the EFPIA to change its organisational format in order to take advantage of the new opportunities within

---

18. Interviews with R. van Sloten, CEFIC, Brussels, and Reinhard Quick, German Verband der Chemischen Industrie, member of CEFIC; Paul Launoye, Federation of the Belgian Chemical Industry.

19. Interview with Paul Launoye, Federation of the Belgian Chemical Industry.

20. Interview with R. van Sloten, CEFIC, Brussels.

the WTO for enforcing market access and intellectual property commitments. The companies became direct members of the association, allowing them to bypass their own national federations.[21]

These large companies joined the trade association under the explicit condition that the association would develop a new case-by-base mechanism to monitor foreign compliance with international trading rules, especially the rules on the protection of intellectual property rights contained in the WTO Agreement on TRIPS.[22] Thus, from then on, in addition to the traditional tasks of monitoring and coordinating positions in international trade negotiations, the EFPIA was also to monitor third country markets, to lodge TBR complaints, to feed the market access database, to ask for WTO complaints with the European Commission, and to manage an 'early warning' system on market access problems (EFPIA 2001).[23] Evidence for the importance of this new role was seen shortly after. The EFPIA lobbied the DG for Trade to file a WTO complaint against Canadian intellectual property law in 1997, and also filed two TBR complaints against Turkish and Korean barriers to trade in pharmaceuticals in 1999 and 2003 (WTO and DG for Trade websites). Three years after the fully fledged institutionalisation of the WTO DSM, the association had thus re-organised with the explicit aims of being able to channel issue- and product-specific information about barriers to trade in pharmaceutical products to the relevant institutions and to gather the economic and legal information needed for WTO cases.

The European confederation of iron and steel industries

Founded as a state-sponsored cartel in 1977, the European confederation of iron and steel industries (EUROFER) long functioned as a traditional Euro-confederation of national steel federations. Activities carried out by the EUROFER in this period consisted of the promotion of a mix of domestic and external trade measures. On the domestic side they were responsible for acquiring state subsidies, outright nationalisations, and the imposition of production quota. On the foreign trade side, they helped organise anti dumping investigations and push through large sector-wide exceptions to the principles of non-discriminatory trade of the GATT (Mény and Wright 1987).

After the conclusion of the Uruguay Round agreements and the setting up of the WTO, EUROFER had to adapt to a world in which the negotiation of sector-wide production and import quotas within and outside the EC was no longer the order of the day. Instead negotiations increasingly involved the provision of detailed, legalistically justified and often product-specific information for antidumping (as in the past), but now ever more on TBR market access investigations, the market

---

21. Interview with François Bouvy, manager economic and social affairs, EFPIA, Brussels.

22. Interview with Eric Noehrenberg, director intellectual property and trade issues, International Federation of Pharmaceutical Manufacturers Associations IFPMA, Genève; and François Bouvy, manager economic and social affairs, EFPIA, Brussels.

23. Interview with François Bouvy, manager economic and social affairs, EFPIA, Brussels.

access database, or WTO dispute settlements.[24] In response to these changes to the process and content of trade policymaking, the organisation was transformed at the end of 1997 to include company members directly[25] The organisation's membership now includes both national federations and large companies.[26]

In the field of trade policy, the EUROFER has initiated several TBR investigations and it provides the DG for Trade with information necessary for initiating WTO complaints. For instance, at the request of firms exporting steel products to the US that were suffering from a particular way the US imposed antidumping duties, the association filed a TBR complaint against US antidumping legislation in 1997, which lead the DG for Trade to file a WTO complaint on the matter in 1998. Similarly, firms exporting stainless steel to Brazil had the EUROFER file a TBR complaint on a particular trade barrier, leading Brazil to remove it. The EUROFER has also provided key information to the DG for Trade with regard to numerous WTO dispute settlement cases contesting the legality of countervailing and antidumping duties and safeguards imposed by the US, Argentina and China

The WTO DSM and the subsequent EU institutional reforms thus profoundly co-shaped the nature of the EUROFER from a confederation of national steel associations into a sector association that also includes direct company membership.

Concluding remarks

In previous chapters, we have looked into the question of how the judicialisation of the WTO has changed the incentives for trade-related interests and policymakers to engage in further cooperation in the form of multilateral negotiations. In this chapter, we have analysed *which* type of interest is incentivised to mobilise in a judicialised multilateral trading regime, namely broad or specialised interests. This question is important, as more broadly shaped interests help to deliver the public goods of international trade liberalisation and/or regulatory agreements with potential benefits for all members, while specialised preferences are more likely only to generate benefits to a select group. We have therefore looked into how the judicialisation of the WTO has affected the way economic interests are aggregated.

Our argument has been that, while trade negotiations foster broad sector-wide or even across-sector interest mobilisation, judicial institutions incentivise firms to engage in more specialised, product-specific interest mobilisation. We attributed this to the fact that negotiations are characterised by issue linkages, which create a demand for the broad aggregation of interests, whereas the judicial institution of

---

24. Interview with Christian Mari, EUROFER, Brussels; and M. Alois, former Director General of European Independent Steelworks Association.

25. Interview with Robert Joos, former Director General of Groupement de la Sidérurgie/ Staalindustrie Verbond, Belgium.

26. Interview with Paul Verstraeten, former secretary general of SIDMAR, ARBED-Group (now part of Arcelor Mittal).

the WTO de-links issues, which creates demand for specific inputs into the policy process. Qualitative and quantitative evidence on patterns of mobilisation in EU and US trade policy lobbying in the negotiation and judicial branch of the WTO corroborated our argument.

Our institutional perspective on the phenomenon complements the economic explanation for the rise of specialisation in interest mobilisation over trade matters, namely that it has been due to a rise in intra-industry trade. While the increase in intra-industry trade, at the expense of inter-industry trade based on comparative advantages between countries, has certainly been an important driver for more firm-specific and/or product-specific forms of interest representation, it cannot fully account for the increase in product-specific lobbying in recent decades. Since the early 2000s, the share of intra-industry trade has even slightly decreased in both the US and the EU, while dispute settlement cases have only become far more product-specific since the creation of the WTO dispute settlement system. What is more, interest mobilisation during trade rounds has continuously been marked by sector-wide interest mobilisation. Hence, product-specific interest mobilisation is in no way a substitute for sector-wide interest mobilisation, and vice versa. Both types of political mobilisation complement each other, each targeting distinct institutional venues.

Even though there are good reasons to assume that these causal mechanisms are at work in other advanced industrialised members of the WTO, it may be interesting to explore whether these mechanisms play out in exactly the same way. For instance, it might be revealing to investigate the effect the judicialisation of WTO politics has had in countries that either do not significantly weigh in on negotiations and/or make little use of the WTO DSM. These may include, for example, least developed countries (LDCs) and non-democracies which have largely state-driven systems of interest intermediation.

Our finding that judicialisation favours specialisation in interest mobilisation may well have implications for the relative balance between the WTO's negotiation and judicial branches. For some time, it seemed reasonable to assume that the fragmenting effect of judicial trade policymaking on trade policy lobbying would be countered by the increased importance of negotiated trade-related regulatory agreements for many, if not all economic sectors within the WTO framework. Yet, the multilateral negotiating track is vastly diminishing in importance, and has only yielded very small partial agreements in recent years. The Bali 2013 agreement on trade facilitation was only possible by separating it from the overall package of the Doha Round, and at the great cost of granting India immunity for its highly inefficient domestic farm subsidies that drive down prices for African producers (Rushford Report 2014). Also the 2015 expansion of the tariff-free product list of the WTO information technology agreement took place outside any greater package deal. If these trends continue, the members of sector-wide trade associations may become less interested in seeking to influence WTO negotiations. At the same time, the judicial arm of the WTO has been, and continues to be, the most active part of the organisation, and its rulings are largely respected and considered authoritative.

If the increase in specialised interest mobilisation for WTO matters continues, the capacity of sector-wide trade associations to influence trade issues could also begin to fade. The more sector-wide trade associations function as vessels of special interests, the less they are able to perform the function of representing encompassing groups with a broad set of economic interests in the WTO. This would change the picture that we have portrayed in this book to one in which product-specific interests dominate the WTO governance system.

In our case study on the EU we have found evidence that such a transformation may well be occurring. The system of interest intermediation in the EU has long been regarded as a political system less dominated by special interests (Greenwood and Dreger 2013; Mahoney 2008; Woll 2012), and many scholars have characterised it as corporatist system in which interest groups coordinate their positions and create stable and institutionalised patterns of interaction and cooperation by means of encompassing interest organisations (Broscheid and Coen 2003; Coen 1998; Greenwood 2002; Eising 2004; Woll 2006; Mahoney 2007, 2007a, and 2008; Mahoney and Baumgartner 2008). Yet, this line of research may well have to come to terms with the fact that such consensual politics may become more and more disaggregated into ever more specialised lobbying, hampering the coordination between producers within broad economic sectors.

While we have come to these conclusions about the effects of the judicialisation of the world trade regime on domestic interest mobilisation, our argument and findings do not need to mean the end of sector-wide interest mobilisation overall. Partially as a result of the WTO deadlock, contemporary international trade governance has increasingly shifted to bilateral, regional, and plurilateral deal making. If our postulation that the need for broad issue-linkage packages favours sector-wide coordination by economic interests is accurate, then the negotiation of such agreements may just as well keep eliciting such sector-wide articulation of interests, especially in the framework of those agreements or ongoing negotiations which cover a wide range of issues, such as the trans-pacific partnership and the negotiations on a transatlantic trade and investment partnership between the EU and the US. Future research will tell whether this is the case. If it is, the co-existence of product-specific and sector-wide lobbying may well turn out to remain a continuing general feature of patterns of interest mobilisation in international trade governance.

Conclusion

The most important message we wanted to convey with this book is that the strengthening of the enforcement mechanisms of the multilateral trade regime brought about by the creation of the WTO in 1995 has had systematic consequences for the politics of legislative trade liberalisation. The main aim of the reform was to create stronger institutional incentives for members of the multilateral trade regime to comply with mutually agreed commitments and rules. Yet, its consequences have extended far beyond merely incentivising compliance with existing rules. The judicialisation of the WTO has also crucially affected the propensity of its members to deepen and/or widen existing commitments.

We wanted to show in particular how the judicialisation of the WTO has affected the preferences, the strategies, and the patterns of political mobilisation of the relevant domestic actors involved in the politics of multilateral legislative trade liberalisation in systematic ways. While this basic argument should be quite intuitive, it has largely been overlooked so far both by scholars and practitioners. The analysis of the politics of the WTO in the last two decades has focused on the influence of many important factors in negotiations such as, amongst others, the increasing heterogeneity of preferences among negotiating parties due to the broadening of WTO membership, the inclusion of China in the multilateral trading system, the assertiveness and coalitional strategies of emerging economies, and the extension of the multilateral trade agenda to a broad set of regulatory issues, as well as the impact of the rise of preferential trade agreements. All these elements have certainly played an important role in shaping the politics of negotiated multilateral trade liberalisation in the past two decades. Yet, analyses that only focus on these factors overlook the important fact that all these changes have taken place under the incentives and constraints brought about by the judicialisation of the multilateral trade regime and thus might even partly be endogenous to this important institutional transformation.

Another important general message we wanted to communicate with this book is that any analysis of how the judicialisation of the WTO has affected the politics of negotiated multilateral trade liberalisation needs to investigate the causal influences this has had on the domestic politics of trade among WTO members. Trade policy, as any other policy, generates distributive consequences that pit some organised groups seeking to influence policymakers against others within society. Understanding the politics of trade policymaking thus requires untangling the dynamics that underlie the political conflicts between these groups and how these affect the set of political choices available to policymakers.

Attempts to develop statements with some degree of generalisability in this context require delving into two questions. First, one needs to develop propositions on the conditions under which some groups will prefer trade liberalisation, *in casu* multilateral trade liberalisation. Second, it is crucial to learn about the groups that want a particular trade policy outcome and whether they will be able to effectively mobilise to make their voice heard and thus to weigh in on the trade policymaking process. Throughout the book we have thus sought to move beyond the perspective that considers states as unitary actors. Instead, we have investigated how judicialisation has affected patterns of legislative trade liberalisation by looking at how the greater enforceability of prospective rules has affected the preferences and patterns of political mobilisation of trade-related domestic interests in WTO members.

While our analysis clearly shows that the judicial politics and legislative politics of the WTO are connected in systematic ways, the arguments we have developed in this book show that the effects of judicialisation on cooperation are conditional. At first glance, identifying the content of a causal relationship between judicial and legislative politics would seem an easy task. If it is true that judicialisation has affected the politics of multilateral trade liberalisation, then, given that the WTO became unable to perform its legislative functions precisely as it equipped itself with strengthened enforcement mechanisms, it would seem plausible to argue that judicialisation has *caused* the stalemate in multilateral trade deal making.

This statement is in line with one of the few important studies that delved into the question addressed in this book. One year before the Doha Round was launched with great fanfare in 2001, Goldstein and Martin (2000) warned us that the legalisation (or judicialisation) of the multilateral trade regime might eventually interfere with the pursuit of progressive liberalisation of multilateral trade. These authors argued that this institutional innovation would ultimately empower protectionists relative to free-traders in the domestic trade policymaking process and make policymakers more reluctant to tie their hands. The more this constellation of domestic interests contributed to the deadlock of legislative liberalisation, the more the adjudicators within the dispute settlement process might even be inclined to turn to judicial rule making rather than negotiated rule making.

While we concur with conceiving of WTO judicialisation as a key factor to understanding how processes of deal making have unfolded in the post-1995 period in the trade regime, the arguments we have developed in this book provide a more nuanced view on the nature of this causal relationship. Our analyses show that judicialisation can indeed sometimes act as an impediment on the road towards cooperation, but that under certain conditions it can also incentivise domestic interests to commit to new multilateral trade rules and commitments. We showed that judicialisation, far from only acting as a systematic impediment to cooperation by increasing protectionist preferences across the WTO membership, was also responsible for increasing the probability of agreements in important instances of the Doha Round. Thus, at the very least, the reasoning we have developed throughout this book and the empirical findings we have presented suggest that two statements cannot be maintained: that judicialisation makes cooperation less likely consistently across issue areas, as well as across WTO members.

This all suggests that the explanation for the failure of the Doha Round to deliver on its ambitious agenda based on a pessimist assessment of the effects of judicialisation on processes of deal making in the WTO does not seem to be correct. As we showed in Chapter Three, in the case of some pivotal international trade players such as the EU, judicialisation acted as a systematic trigger for the emergence of a domestic coalition composed of traditional exporters and importers, which began tilting the EU towards a marked pro-trade liberalisation direction even before the start of the Doha Round. Furthermore, in Chapter Four, we showed that policymakers and trade-related interests with a preference for high degrees of enforceability have been incentivised to seek further regulatory agreements in new issue areas within the framework of the WTO. Finally, in Chapter Five we illustrated that, in the absence of the effects generated by the 'shadow of WTO law,' the likelihood of an acceptable agreement on the liberalisation of agricultural trade would have been even slimmer. A closer look at how judicialisation has affected the domestic politics of negotiated trade liberalisation in WTO members thus reveals that other factors might have pushed negotiations towards a stalemate, despite the positive influence judicialisation has had on the odds of cooperation in many important ways in critical areas of negotiations.

Throughout this book, we have found that a useful way to organise different arguments about the effects of judicialisation on multilateral negotiated trade liberalisation is to distinguish between how such effects play out in the context of the two broad types of issues in which the contemporary multilateral trade agenda can be categorised. For one, the multilateral trade agenda is still largely about eliminating traditional barriers to trade such as tariffs, quotas and export subsidies. The analyses we developed in Chapters Three and Five suggest that, when it comes to the processes of negotiated trade liberalisation concerning these issues, the pessimist view about the effects of WTO judicialisation is by no means warranted.

First, given that judicialisation tends to advantage the relatively less mobilised, exporters seeking greater market access and importers seeking cheaper imports seem to have been empowered relative to the traditionally influential import-competing groups. Furthermore, judicialisation seems to have significantly defused the opposition to trade liberalisation from key import-competing groups due to the effects of legal vulnerability. Indeed, as we showed in Chapter Five, the greater ability of WTO members to target WTO-incompatible trade barriers of other members seems to have increased the odds of cooperation in sensitive areas such as agricultural trade.

Looking at the empirical evidence on the domestic trade politics in the EU that we presented in Chapters Three and Five, we should appreciate how judicialisation simultaneously seems to have led to a greater political mobilisation of pro-trade groups, such as services exporters and importers, and defused the opposition of traditionally influential groups such as farmers. This double movement of greater mobilisation and decreasing opposition by import-competing groups in a pivotal developed international trade player has certainly contributed to increasing the odds of success in the Doha Round. The opening up of this political space has so far proved insufficient for the Doha Round to come to a successful conclusion, at least given its initial ambitions.

However, the Doha Round has only partly, even if largely, been about traditional trade liberalisation. Beginning in the 1980s, the international trade agenda has increasingly expanded to tackle existing differences in regulatory practices among WTO members. As we showed in Chapters Four and Five, when it comes to regulatory issues, judicialisation can indeed be expected to act as an impediment to cooperation. While judicialisation has made the WTO an attractive location to negotiate regulatory issues for WTO members with high levels of domestic regulation, it has created sustained opposition to an expansion of the WTO's regulatory reach by members with lower levels of domestic regulation and may even have created incentives for these trade partners to bring regulatory flexibility back in through the back door. Moreover, given the often 'all-or-nothing' character of regulatory issues, the opposition to such cooperation cannot even be defused by legal vulnerability, as such a possibility crucially depends on the divisibility of the issue at stake. We think that the difference between traditional trade liberalisation and regulatory trade liberalisation is quite fundamental, and therefore one of the keys to understanding why, despite the positive dynamics of cooperation engendered by judicialisation in the field of traditional liberalisation, legislative trade liberalisation has not materialised in the form of a successful conclusion of the Doha Round.

Unless we overlooked other crucial determinants of cooperation within the world trading regime, the WTO is likely to remain a viable and attractive forum for negotiations on traditional trade barriers. Indeed, negotiators seem to be salvaging exactly those types of agenda item from the wreck of the Doha Round. For one, they have concluded a deal on trade facilitation. Moreover, key trading partners are pushing negotiations on trade in environmental goods. They have thereby gradually but inexorably steered away from any issue linkage in such negotiations between traditional barriers to trade and regulatory issues.

It is plausible to assume that those members of the multilateral trading system that do wish to conclude regulatory agreements are likely to continue doing so, not in the multilateral framework, but in the institutional framework of bilateral preferential trade agreements, or perhaps plurilateral agreements. This development would not need to spell the end of the WTO, as some Cassandras have wanted us to believe, but would rather consist of a division of labour between the WTO and these bilateral and plurilateral frameworks. If this is so, then the increasing specialisation of interest mobilisation on trade issues that we have traced back to the judicialisation of the WTO is likely to continue to be countered to some extent by the enduring relevance that broad sector-wide and cross-sector interest mobilisation will have in the framework of civil society consultations for bilateral and plurilateral negotiations.

Bibliography

Abbott, K. W., Keohane, R. O., Moravcsik, A., Slaughter, A-M. and Snidal, D. (2000) 'The concept of legalization', *International Organization*, 54(3): 401–19.

Ackrill, R. and Kay, A. (2009) 'Historical learning in the design of WTO rules: The EC Sugar Case', *The World Economy*, 32(5): 754–71.

Allee, T. 'The hidden impact of the World Trade Organization on the reduction of trade conflict', paper presented at the Midwest Political Science Association Conference, Chicago, Illinois, April 2005.

Allee, T. and Elsig, M. (2014) 'Dispute settlement provisions in PTAs: new data and new concepts', in A. Dür and M. Elsig (eds) *Trade Cooperation: the Purpose, design and effects of preferential trade agreements*, Cambridge: Cambridge University Press.

Alt, J. and Gilligan, M. (1994) 'The political economy of trading states: factor specificity collective action problems and political institutions', *Journal of Political Philosophy*, 2(2): 165–92.

Alter, K. (1998) 'Who are the masters of the Treaty? European governments and the European Court of Justice', *International Organization*, 52(1): 121–47.

— (2012) 'Global spread of European-style international courts', *West European Politics*, 35(10): 135–54.

Alter, K. J. and Meunier, S. (2009) 'The politics of international regime complexity', *Perspectives on Politics*, 7(1): 13–24.

Anania, G. and Bureau J. C. (2005) 'The negotiations on agriculture in the Doha Development Agenda Round: current status and future prospects', *European Review of Agricultural Economics*, 32(4): 539–74.

Ando, M. and Kimura, F. (2005) 'The formation of international production and distribution networks in East Asia', in T. Ito and A. Rose (eds) *International Trade in East Asia*, Chicago: University of Chicago Press.

Axelrod, R. and Keohane R. (1985) 'Achieving cooperation under anarchy: strategies and institutions', *World Politics*, 38(1): 226–54.

Baccini, L. and Kim, S. Y. (2012) 'Preventing protectionism: international institutions and trade policy', *Review of International Organizations*, 7(4): 369–98.

Baccini, L., Dür, A. and Elsig, M. 'The politics of trade agreement design: the obligation–flexibility tradeoff', paper presented at the ECPR Joint Sessions of Workshops, Antwerp, April 2012.

Bagwell, K. and Staiger, R. (2002) *The Economics of the World Trading System*, Cambridge, MA: MIT Press.

Baldwin, R. (2011) '21st century regionalism: filling the gap between 21st century trade and 20th century trade rules', Centre for Economic Policy Research Policy, Insight No. 56.

Baumgartner, F. R. and Jones, B. (1993) *Agendas and Instability in American Politics*, Chicago: University of Chicago Press.

Baumgartner, F. R. and Leech, B. L. (1998) *Basic Interests: The Importance of Groups in Politics and in Political Science*, Princeton, NJ: Princeton University Press.

—— (2001) 'Interest niches and policy bandwagons: patterns of interest group involvement in national politics', *Journal of Politics*, 63(4): 1191–213.

Baumgartner, F. R. and Mahoney, C. (2008) 'The two faces of framing: individual-level framing and collective issue-definition in the EU', *European Union Politics* 9(3): 435–49.

Bayard, T. and Elliott, K. (1994) *Reciprocity and Retaliation in US Trade Policy*, Washington DC: Institute for International Economics.

Bechtel, M. M. and Sattler, T. (2015) 'What is litigation in the World Trade Organization worth?', *International Organization*, 69(02): 375–403.

Berkhout, J., Braun, C., Beyers, J., Hanegraaff, M. C. and Lowery, D. 'Making inference across mobilization and influence research: comparing top-down and bottom-up mapping of interest systems', paper presented at the ECPR General Conference, Glasgow, September 2014.

Bernauer, T. and Sattler, T. (2011) 'Gravitation or discrimination? Determinants of litigation in the World Trade Organization', *European Journal of Political Research*, 50(2): 143–67.

Bernauer, T., Elsig, M. and Pauwelyn, J. (2014) 'Dispute settlement mechanism: analysis and problems', in M. Daunton, A. Narlikar and R. M. Stern (eds) *The Oxford Handbook on The World Trade Organization*, Oxford: Oxford University Press.

Blustein, P. (2009) *Misadventures of the Most Favored Nations: Clashing egos, inflated ambitions, and the great shambles of the world trade system*, New York: Public Affairs.

Bombardini, M. and Trebbi, F. (2012) 'Competition and political organization: together or alone in lobbying for trade policy?', *Journal of International Economics*, 87(1): 18–26.

Bouwen, P. (2004) 'Exchanging access goods for access: a comparative study of business lobbying in the EU Institutions', *European Journal of Political Research*, 43(3): 337–69.

Bouwen, P. and McCown, M. (2007) 'Lobbying versus litigation: political and legal strategies of interest representation in the European Union', *Journal of European Public Policy*, 14(3): 422–43.

Bown, C. (2004) 'On the economic success of GATT/WTO dispute settlement', *The Review of Economics and Statistics*, 86(3): 811–23.

—— (2005) 'Participation in WTO dispute settlement: complainants, interested parties and free riders', *World Bank Economic Review*, 19(1): 287–310.

Boyle, J. (2004) 'A manifesto on WIPO and the future of intellectual property', *Duke Law & Technology Review*, 9: 1–12.

Brittan, L. *The Next WTO Negotiations on Agriculture: A European view*, Speech delivered at the 53rd Oxford Farming Conference, January 1999.

Bronckers, M. and McNelis, N. (2001) 'The EU trade barriers regulation comes of age', *Journal of World Trade*, 35(4): 427–82.

Broscheid, A. and Coen, D. (2003) 'Insider and outsider lobbying in the European Commission', *European Union Politics*, 4(2): 165–89.

Burch, D. and Lawrence, G. (2005) 'Supermarket own brands, supply chains and the transformation of the agri-food system', *International Journal of Sociology of Agriculture and Food*, 13(1): 1–18.

Burley, A. and Mattli, W. (1993) 'Europe before the Court: a political theory of legal integration', *International Organization*, 47(1): 41–76.

Busch, L. M. (2000) 'Democracy, consultation, and the paneling of disputes under GATT', *Journal of Conflict Resolution*, 44(4): 425–46.

— (2007) 'Overlapping institutions, forum shopping, and dispute settlement in international trade', *International Organization*, 61(4): 735–61.

Busch, L. M. and Pelc, K. (2010) 'The politics of judicial economy at the World Trade Organization', *International Organization*, 64(2): 257–9.

Busch, L. M. and Reinhardt, E. (2000) 'Bargaining in the shadow of the law: early settlement in GATT/WTO disputes', *Fordham International Law Journal*, 24(1–2): 158–72.

— (2003) 'Transatlantic trade conflicts and GATT/WTO dispute settlement', in E. U. Petersmann and M. A. Pollack (eds) *Transatlantic Economic Disputes: the EU, The US and the WTO*, Oxford: Oxford University Press.

— (2006) 'Three's a crowd: third parties and WTO dispute settlement', *World Politics*, 58(3): 446–77.

Busch, L. M., Reinhardt, E. and Shaffer, G. (2009) 'Does legal capacity matter? A survey of WTO members', *World Trade Review*, 8(4): 559–77.

Cairns Group (2000) *Cairns Group negotiating proposal on export competition*, G/AG/NG/W/11, June.

— (2000a) *Cairns Group negotiating proposal on domestic support*, G/AG/NG/W/35, September.

— (2000b) *Cairns Group negotiating proposal on market access*, G/AG/NG/W/54, November.

— (2005) *Communiqué*, Hong Kong, December.

— (2006) *Communiqué*, Cairns, September.

— (2007) *Communiqué*, Lahore, April.

Cairns Group Farm Leaders (1998) *Communiqué*, Sydney, March.

— (1999) *Proposal of Cairns Group Farm Leaders to the next WTO round of negotiations on agriculture*, Buenos Aires, August.

— (1999a) *Proposal of Cairns Group Farm Leaders to the next WTO round of negotiations on agriculture*, Seattle, November.

— (2000) *Cairns Farm Leaders presentation to Cairns Ministers*, Alberta, October.

— (2001) *Cairns Group Farm Leaders' statement to Cairns Group Ministers*, Punta del Este, September.

Camargo, P. (2005) 'An end to antidumping through domestic agricultural support', *Bridges*, 9(8): 3–4.

— (2008) 'Cotton in the Doha Round: a lost opportunity?', Available at: http://blog.gmfus.org/2008/09/23/cotton-in-the-doha-round-a-lost-opportunity/.

CEFIC (1999) *CEFIC Comments on a New Multilateral Trade Round*, European Chemical Industry Council, Brussels.

Coen, D. (1998) 'The European business interest and the nation state: large-firm lobbying in the European Union and member states', *Journal of Public Policy*, 18(1): 75–100.

Conceição-Heldt, E. (2011) *Negotiating Trade Liberalization at the WTO: Domestic politics and bargaining dynamics*, Basingstoke: Palgrave Macmillan.

COPA-COGECA (1998) *A revision of the Commission's Agenda 2000 CAP Reform proposals*, Brussels, September.

— (1999a) *COPA-COGECA Statement on the WTO Ministerial Conference in Seattle on behalf of farmers in the European Union*, WTO(99)22-1, November.

— (1999b) *COPA and COGECA present the key elements for the EU's approach to agriculture in the forthcoming WTO Round*, CdP(99)47-1, November.

— (2000) *Position of COPA and COGECA on the use of gene technology in agriculture*, January.

Correa, C. M. (2000) *Intellectual Property Rights, the WTO and Developing Countries: The TRIPS agreement and policy options*, London: Zed Books.

— (2001) *Traditional Knowledge and Intellectual Property: Issues and options surrounding the protection of traditional knowledge. A discussion paper*, Geneva: Quaker United Nations Office.

Cotta, F. 'Presentation at the Forum Permanente de Negociacoes Agricolas Internacionais', Buenos Aires, May 2001: www.iadb.org/intal/aplicaciones/uploads/ponencias/Foro_INTAL_2001_02_cotta.pdf (accessed 1 March 2016).

Cowles, M. G. (1996) 'The EU Committee of AmCham: the powerful voice of American firms in Brussels', *Journal of European Public Policy*, 3(3): 339–58.

Croome, J. (1999) *Reshaping the World Trading System: A history of the Uruguay Round*, The Hague: Kluwer Law International.

Da Motta, V. P. (2005) 'Brazil and the G20 Group of Developing Countries', in P. Gallagher, P. Low and A. L. Stoler (eds), *Managing the Challenges of WTO Participation: 45 Case Studies*, Cambridge: Cambridge University Press.

Daugbjerg, C. and Swinbank, A. (2008) 'Curbing agricultural exceptionalism: the EU's response to external challenge', *The World Economy*, 31(5): 631–52.

— (2009) 'Ideational change in the WTO and its impact on EU agricultural policy institutions and CAP', *Journal of European Integration*, 31(3): 311–27.

Davey, W. (2005) 'The WTO Dispute Settlement System: the first ten years', *Journal of International Economic Law*, 8(1): 17–50.

Davis, C. L. (2004) 'International institutions and issue linkage: building support for agricultural trade liberalization', *American Political Science Review*, 98(1): 153–69.

Davis, C. L. (2008) 'The Effectiveness of WTO Dispute Settlement: An Evaluation of Negotiations versus Adjudication Strategies', paper presented at the Annual Meeting of the Political Science Association, Boston.

— (2012) *Why Adjudicate? Enforcing trade rules in the WTO*, Princeton, NJ: Princeton University Press.

Davis, C. L. and Blodgett Bermeo, S. (2009) 'Who files? Developing country participation in WTO adjudication', *Journal of Politics*, 71(3): 1033–49.

Davis, C. L. and Pelc, K. (forthcoming) 'Cooperation in hard times: self-restraint of trade protection', *Journal of Conflict Resolution*.

Davis, C. L. and Shirato, Y. (2007) 'Firms, governments, and WTO adjudication: Japan's selection of WTO disputes', *World Politics*, 59(2): 274–313.

De Bièvre, D. (2002) *The WTO and domestic coalitions: the effects of negotiations and enforcement in the European Union*, PhD Dissertation, Department of Social and Political Sciences, European University Institute.

De Bièvre, D. (2002a) 'Redesigning the virtuous circle: two proposals for WTO reform. Resolving and preventing US-EU, and other trade disputes', *Journal of World Trade*, 36(5): 1005–1013.

— (2003) 'International institutions and domestic coalitions: the differential effects of negotiations and judicialisation in European trade policy', *EUI Working Paper SPS* 2003(17).

— (2004) *Governance in international trade: judicialisation and positive integration in the WTO*, Preprint 2004/7, Bonn: Max Planck Project Group on Collective Goods.

— (2006) 'The EU regulatory trade agenda and the quest for WTO enforcement', *Journal of European Public Policy*, 13(6): 105–29.

— (2006a) 'Legislative and judicial decision making in the World Trade Organization', in M. Koenig-Archibugi and M. Zürn (eds) *New Modes of Governance in the Global System: Exploring publicness, delegation and inclusiveness*, Houndmills, Basingstoke: Palgrave Macmillan pp. 31–51.

De Bièvre, D. (2014) 'A glass quite empty: issue groups' influence in the global trade regime', *Global Policy*, 5(2): 222–228.

De Bièvre, D. (2015) 'Directorate-General for Trade of the European Commission', in E. Drieskens, A. K. Aarstad, K. E. Jørgensen, K. Laatikainen and B. Tonra (eds), *SAGE Handbook on EU Foreign Policy*, London: SAGE.

De Bièvre, D. and Dür, A. (2005) 'Constituency interests and delegation in European and American trade policy', *Comparative Political Studies*, 38(10): 1271–96.

De Bièvre, D. and Eckhardt, E. (2011) 'Interest groups and EU anti-dumping policy', *Journal of European Public Policy*, 18(3): 339–60.

De Bièvre, D. and Hanegraaff, M. (2011) 'Non-state Actors in Multilateral Trade Governance' in B. Reinalda (ed), *Ashgate Companion to Non-state Actors*, Aldershot: Ashgate.

De Bièvre, D. and Poletti, A. (2014) 'The EU in EU Trade Policy: From regime shaper to status quo power', in G. Falkner and P. Müller (eds) *EU Policies in a Global Perspective*, London: Routledge pp. 20–37.

—— (2015) 'Judicial politics in international trade relations: an introduction', *World Trade Review*, 14(S1): 1–21.

De Bièvre, D., Poletti, A. and Thomann, L. (2014) 'To enforce or not to enforce? Judicialization, venue shopping and global regulatory harmonization', *Regulation & Governance*, 8(3): 269–286.

De Bièvre, D., Hanegraaff, M., Poletti, A. and Beyers, J. (2016) 'International institutions and interest mobilization: the WTO and lobbying in EU and US trade policy', *Journal of World Trade* (in press).

Deere, C. (2005) *International trade technical assistance and capacity building*, Occasional Paper, UNDP http://hdr.undp.org/en/content/international-trade-technical-assistance-and-capacity-building (accessed 1 March 2016).

DeSombre, E. (2000) *Domestic Sources of International Environmental Policy*, Cambridge, MA: MIT Press.

Destler, I. M. and Odell, J. S. (1987) *Anti-Protection: Changing Forces in United States Trade Politics*, Washington, DC: Institute For International Economics

Downs, G. and Rocke, D. (1995) *Optimal Imperfection? Domestic uncertainty and institutions in international relations*, Princeton, NJ: Princeton University Press.

Downs, G., Rocke, D. and Barsoom, P. (1996) 'Is the good news about compliance good news about cooperation?', *International Organization*, 50(3): 379–406.

Dür, A. (2008) 'Bringing economic interests back into the study of EU trade policy-making', *British Journal of Politics and International Relations*, 10(1): 27–45.

—— (2010), *Protection for Exporters: Power and discrimination in transatlantic trade relations, 1930–2010*, Ithaca, NY: Cornell University Press.

Dür, A. and De Bièvre, D. (2007) 'Inclusion without influence? NGOs in European trade policy', *Journal of Public Policy*, 27(1): 79–101.

Eckersley, R. (2004) 'The big chill: the WTO and multilateral environmental agreements', *Global Environmental Politics*, 4(2): 24–50.

Eckhardt, J. (2011) 'Firm lobbying and EU trade policy making: reflections on the anti-dumping case against Chinese and Vietnamese shoes (2005–2011)', *Journal of World Trade*, 45(5): 965–91.

—— (2013) 'EU unilateral trade policy-making: what role for import-dependent firms?', *Journal of Common Market Studies*, 51(6): 989–1005.

—   (2015) *Business Lobbying and Trade Governance: The case of EU–China relations*, Basingstoke: Palgrave Macmillan.

Eckhardt, J. and Poletti, A. (2015) 'The politics of global value chains: import-dependent firms and EU–Asia trade agreements', *Journal of European Public Policy*, DOI:10.1080/13501763.2015.1085073.

Eckstein, H. (1975) 'Case studies and theory in political science', in F. Greenstein and N. Polsby (eds) *Handbook of Political Science*, Reading, MA: Addison-Wesley pp. 79–138.

EFPIA (2001) *Communication of the Commission to the Council and the European Parliament on accelerated action targeted at major communicable diseases within the context of poverty reduction*, Brussels: European Federation of Pharmaceutical Industries and Associations: http://efpia.org/Objects/1/Files/povertyreduc.pdf (accessed 8 June 2012).

Ehlermann, C.-D. (2002) 'Tensions between the dispute settlement process and the diplomatic and treaty-making activities of the WTO', *World Trade Review*, 1(3): 301–308.

Ehrlich, S. (2007) 'Access to protection: domestic institutions and trade policy in democracies', *International Organization*, 61(3): 571–605.

Eising, R. (2004) 'Multilevel governance and business interests in the European Union', *Governance*, 17(2): 211–46.

—   (2007) 'The access of business interests to EU institutions: towards elite pluralism?', *Journal of European Public Policy*, 14(3): 384–403.

—   (2007a) 'Institutional context, organizational resources and strategic choices: Explaining interest group access in the European Union', *European Union Politics*, 8(3): 329–62.

Elsig, M. (2007) 'The EU's choice of regulatory venues for trade negotiations: a tale of agency power', *Journal of Common Market Studies*, 45(4): 927–48.

—   (2013) 'The EU as an effective trade power? Strategic choice of judicial candidates in the context of the World Trade Organization', *International Relations*, 27(3): 325–40.

Elsig, M. and Eckhardt, J. (2015) 'The creation of the multilateral trade court: design and experiential learning', *World Trade Review*, 14(S1): 13–32.

Elsig, M. and Pollack, M. A. (2014) 'Agents, trustees, and international courts: the politics of judicial appointment at the World Trade Organization', *European Journal of International Relations*, 20(2): 391–415.

ESF (1999) *Declaration of the European services industries for the third WTO ministerial conference towards the Millennium Round*, 25 October.

—   (2001) *Declaration of the European services industries towards the launch of a new WTO round in Qatar*, September.

—   (2003) *New ESF priorities for the DDA*, 5 November.

—   (2005) *The importance of the services negotiations in the WTO Ministerial in Hong Kong*, Letter to the prime ministers of all EU member states, 21 November.

Eurochambres (2003) *The WTO ministerial conference in Cancun*, position paper, September.

— (2006) *Chambers of commerce and industry worldwide support trade facilitation*, statement, July.

— (2007) *Save the Doha Round now*, statement, 25 January.

— (2009) *The seventh WTO ministerial conference*, position paper.

Eurocommerce (2003) *The Stake of European Commerce in the WTO Negotiations on Trade in Distributive Services*, Speech by Ralph Kanphoner at the WTO Symposium 'Challenges Ahead on the Road to Cancun', Geneva, 18 June.

— (2005) *True liberalizaiton, more development, simpler procedures and better rules: priorities for the 6th WTO ministerial conference*, position paper, December.

— (2009) *WTO Geneva Ministerial: conclude the Doha Round – companies need results*, position paper, 26 November.

— (2013) *Eurocommerce joins forces for a successful outcome of WTO negotiations*, press release.

Eurocommerce and FTA (1999) *Statement of Eurocommerce and FTA on the forthcoming WTO ministerial conference in Seattle on the new negotiation round*, position paper received by WTO Secretariat, 23 November https://www.wto.org/english/forums_e/ngo_e/posp10_e.htm (accessed 1 March 2016).

European Commission (1996) *The global challenge of international trade: a market access strategy for the European Union*, COM(96)53.

— (1999) *Communication from the Commission to the Council and to the European Parliament: the EU approach to the Millennium Round*, COM (99) 331 final, Brussels: CEC.

— (2002) *Communication from the Commission to the Council and the European Parliament. Mid-term review of the Common Agricultural Policy*, COM (2002) 394, Brussels: CEC.

— (2004) *The EU and the WTO: EU ready to go extra miles in three key areas of the talks*, 10 May.

Falkner, R. (2007) 'The political economy of "normative power" Europe: EU environmental leadership in international biotechnology regulation', *Journal of European Public Policy*, 14(4): 507–26.

Fearon, J. (1998) 'Bargaining, enforcement, and international cooperation', *International Organization*, 52(2): 269–306.

Feenstra, R. (1998) 'Integration of trade and disintegration of production in the global economy', *Journal of Economic Perspectives*, 12: 31–50.

Feenstra, R., Lipsey, R. E., Deng, H., Ma, A. and Mo, H. (2005) *World trade flows 1962–2000*, NBER Working Paper no. 11040.

Finger, M. (1991) 'The GATT as an International Discipline over Trade Restrictions: A public choice approach', in R. Vaubel and T. Willett (eds) *The Political Economy of International Organizations: A public choice approach*, Boulder: Westview Press.

Finnemore, M. and Toope, S. J. (2001) 'Alternatives to legalization: a richer view of law and politics', *International Organization*, 55(3): 743–58.

Fischler, F. (2003) 'The new, reformed agricultural policy', final press conference after the decision of the Council of Agriculture, Speech 03/326, Luxembourg, 26 June.

Frieden, J. (1991) 'Invested interests: the politics of national economic policies in a world of global finance', *International Organization*, 45(4): 425–51.

Frieden, J. and Rogowski, R. (1996) 'The impact of the international economy on national policies: an analytical overview', in R. Keohane and H. V. Milner (eds) *Internationalization and Domestic Politics*, New York: Cambridge University Press.

Friends of Earth (1999) *Free trade at what cost? The World Trade Organization and the environment*, 19 October.

FTA (2002) *Editorial* FTA Bulletin, 2(1).

— (2003) *The Doha development agenda: interim results of current WTO world trade Round.*

FTA (2003a) *FTA Position Regarding the WTO Investment Agreement*, Brussels.

— (2004) *FTA position: reviving the DDA after Cancun*, Brussels, March.

— (2006) *FTA position: for a successful conclusion of the Doha development agenda*, Brussels, April.

— (2011) *European trade calls for progress and a clear timeline of the WTO Doha Round*, Press Release, 14 December.

— (2011a) *European commerce sees light and shadow after WTO Ministerial in Geneva*, Press Release, 20 December.

— (2013) *Bali and beyond: for a palpable progress of WTO negotiations*, position paper, Brussels, November.

— (2014) *Joint statement by business organizations on WTO trade facilitation agreement*, Press Release, 15 October.

G20 (2005) *G20 proposal on domestic support and G20 proposal on market access*, 12 October: http://www.twn.my/title2/twninfo272.htm (accessed 1 March 2016).

GATT (1990) 'Improvements to the GATT dispute settlement rules and procedures, decision of 12 April 1989 (L/6489)', in the contracting parties to the GATT *Basic Instruments and Selected Documents, Thirty-sixth Supplement. Protocols, Decisions, Reports 1988–1989 and Forty-fifth Session*, Geneva: GATT.

George, A. and Bennett, A. (2005) *Case Studies and Theory Development in the Social Sciences*, Cambridge, MA: MIT Press.

Gereffi, G. (1999) 'International trade and industrial upgrading in the apparel commodity chain', *Journal of International Economics*, 48(1): 37–70

Gereffi G., Humphrey, J. and Sturgeon, T. (2005) 'The governance of global value chains', *Review of International Political Economy*, 12(1): 78–104.

Gilligan, M. (1997) 'Lobbying as a private good with intra-industry trade', *International Studies Quarterly*, 41(3): 455–74.

—   (1997a) *Empowering Exporters: Reciprocity, delegation, and collective action in American trade policy*, Ann Arbor, MI: University of Michigan Press.

Goldberg, A. R., Lawrence R. and Milligan, K. (2004) 'Brazil's cotton case: negotiation through litigation', *Harvard Business School Case 905-405*.

Goldstein J. (1988) 'Ideas, institutions and American trade policy', *International Organization*, 42(1): 179–217.

Goldstein, J. and Martin, L. (2000) 'Legalization, trade liberalization and domestic politics: a cautionary note', *International Organization*, 54(3), 603–32.

Goldstein, J. and Steinberg, R. (2008) 'Negotiate or litigate? Effects of WTO judicial delegation on US trade politics', *Law and Contemporary Problems*, 71: 257–82.

—   (2009) 'Regulatory Shift: The rise of judicial liberalization at the WTO', in W. Mattli and N. Woods (eds) *The Politics of Global Regulation*, Princeton, NJ: Princeton University Press.

Goldstein, J., Kahler, M., Keohane, R. and Slaughter, A-M. (2000) 'Introduction: legalization and world politics', *International Organization*, 54(3): 385–99.

Goldstein, J., Kahler, M., Keohane R. and Slaughter, A-M. (eds) (2001) *Legalization and World Politics*, Cambridge, MA: MIT Press, reprint of *International Organization* 2000 special issue 54(3).

Gowa, J. and Kim, S. Y. (2005) 'An exclusive country club: the effects of the GATT on trade, 1950–94', *World Politics*, 57(4): 453–78.

Gowa, J. and Mansfield, E. D. (2004) 'Alliances, imperfect markets, and major-power trade', *International Organization*, 58(4): 775–805.

Greenwood, J. (2002) *Inside the EU Business Associations*, Basingstoke: Palgrave.

Greenwood, J. (2011) 'The lobby regulation element of the European Transparency Initiative: Between liberal and deliberative models of democracy', *Comparative European Politics*, 9 (3): 317–343.

Greenwood, J. and Dreger, J. (2013) 'The transparency register: a European vanguard of strong lobby regulation?', *Interest Groups & Advocacy*, 2(2): 139–162.

Grossman, G. M. and Helpman, E. (1994) 'Protection for sale', *The American Economic Review*, 84(4): 833–50.

—   (1996) 'Electoral competition and special interest politics', *The Review of Economic Studies*, 63(2): 265–86.

—   (2001) *Special Interest Politics*, Cambridge, MA: MIT Press.

Grubel, H. G. and Lloyd, P. J. (1975) *Intra-industry Trade: The theory and measurement of international trade in differentiated products*, New York: Wiley.

Gschwend, T. and Schimmelfennig, F. (2007) *Research Design in Political Science: How to practice what they preach*, Basingstoke: Palgrave Macmillan.

Gurry, F. (1999) 'The dispute resolution services of the World Intellectual Property Organization', *Journal of International Economic Law*, 2: 385–98.

Guzman, A. and Simmons, B. (2002) 'To settle or empanel? An empirical analysis of litigation and settlement at the WTO', *Journal of Legal Studies*, 31(1): 205–27.

— (2005) 'Power plays and capacity constraints: the selection of defendants in World Trade Organization disputes', *Journal of Legal Studies*, 34(2): 557–98.

Hanegraaff, M. (forthcoming) 'Interest groups at transnational negotiation conferences: goals, strategies, interactions, and influence', *Global Governance*.

Hanegraaff, M., Beyers, J. and Braun, C. (2011) 'Open the door to more of the same? The development of interest group representation at the WTO', *World Trade Review*, 10(4): 447–72.

Hanegraaff, M., Braun, C., De Bièvre, D. and Beyers, J. (2015) 'The domestic and global origins of transnational advocacy: explaining lobbying presence during WTO ministerial conferences', *Comparative Political Studies*, 48(12): 1591–621.

Heisenberg, D. (2005) 'The institution of "consensus" in the European Union: formal versus informal decision-making in the Council', *European Journal of Political Research*, 44(1): 65–90.

Helfer, L. (2004) *Intellectual property rights in plant varieties: International legal regimes and policy options for national governments*, FAO Legislative Study 85, Rome.

— (2004a) 'Regime shifting: the TRIPs agreement and new dynamics of international intellectual property lawmaking', *Yale Journal of International Law*, 29: 1–81.

Henisz, W. J. and Mansfield, E. D. (2006) 'Votes and vetoes: the political determinants of commercial openness', *International Studies Quarterly*, 50(1): 189–212.

Hiscox, M. J. (1999) 'The magic bullet? The RTAA, institutional reform and trade liberalization', *International Organization*, 53(4): 669–98.

— (2001) 'Class versus industry cleavages: inter-industry factor mobility and the politics of trade', *International Organization*, 55(1): 1–46.

— (2002) 'Commerce, coalitions, and factor mobility: evidence from congressional votes on trade legislation', *American Political Science Review*, 96(3): 593–608.

Hix, S. and Goetz, K. H. (2000) 'Introduction: European integration and national political systems', *West European Politics*, 23(4): 1–26.

Hoekman, B. M. (1989) 'Determining the need for issue linkages in multilateral trade negotiations', *International Organization*, 43(4): 693–714.

Hoekman, B. M. and Kostecki, M. (2009) *The political economy of the world trading system*, Oxford: Oxford University Press.

Hoekman, B. M. and Mavroidis, P. C. (2000) 'WTO dispute settlement, transparency and surveillance', *World Economy*, 23(4): 527–42.

Hoekman, B. M., Matoo, A. and Sapir, A. (2007) 'The political economy of services trade liberalization: a case for international regulatory cooperation?', *Oxford Review of Economic Policy*, 23(3): 367–91.

Hojnacki, B. M., Kimball, D. C., Baumgartner, F. R., Berry, J. M. and Leech, B. L. (2012) 'Studying organizational advocacy and influence: reexamining interest group research', *Annual Review of Political Science*, 15: 379–99.

Hooghe, L. and Marks, G. (2014) 'Delegation and pooling in international organizations', *The Review of International Organizations*, 10(3): 305–28.

Hooghe, L., Bezuijen, J. and Derderyan, S. 'Designing dispute settlement bodies in international organizations', paper presented at the workshop on design and effects of international institutions, 2013 ECPR Joint Sessions, Mainz, March 2013.

Horn, H. and Mavroidis, P. C. (2011) 'The WTO dispute settlement database', Version 2.0, World Bank, Washington: http://go.worldbank.org/X5EZPHXJY0 (accessed 25 January 2013).

Horn, H., Johannesson, L. and Mavroidis, P. C. (2011) 'The WTO dispute settlement system 1995–2010: some descriptive statistics', *Journal of World Trade*, 45(6): 1107–38.

Horn, H., Mavroidis, P. C and Nordstrom, H. (1999) *Is the use of the WTO dispute settlement system biased?*, Discussion Paper 2340, Center for Economic Policy Research.

Hudec, R. E. (1993) *Enforcing International Trade Law: The evolution of the modern GATT legal system*. Salem, NH: Butterworth.

—   (2000) 'Broadening the scope of remedies in the WTO dispute settlement', in W. Friedl (ed.) *Improving WTO Dispute Settlement Procedures: Issues and lessons from the practice of other international courts and tribunals*, London: Cameron.

Hummels, D., Jun, I. and Kei-Mu, Y. (2001) 'The nature and growth of vertical specialization in world trade', *Journal of International Economics*, 54: 75–96.

Irwin, D. A. and Mavroidis, P. C. (2008) 'The WTO's difficulties in light of the GATT's history', *Vox*.

Jackson, J. H. (1998) *The World Trading System: The law and policy of international economic relations*, Cambridge, MA: MIT Press.

Johns, L. and Pelc, K. (2014) 'Who gets to be in the room? Manipulating participation in WTO disputes', *International Organization*, 68(3): 663–99.

Joint Statement by Business Associations (2013), *Business calls for a deal on trade facilitation in Bali*, 21 January: https://www.wto.org/english/thewto_e/minist_e/mc9_e/buisiness_calls.pdf (accessed 1 March 2016).

Jones, B. D. and Baumgartner, F. (2005) *The Politics of Attention: How government prioritizes problems*, Chicago: Chicago University Press.

Josling, T. (1998) 'The Uruguay Round: a forward looking assessment', paper prepared for the seminar of the Organization for Economic Cooperation and Development, Paris, 26–27 October.

Josling, T., Zhao, L., Carcelen, J. and Arha, K. (2006) 'Implications of WTO litigation for the WTO agricultural negotiations', *Issue Brief 19*, Washington DC: International Food and Agricultural Trade Policy Council.

Jupille, J., Mattli, W. and Snidal, D. (2013) *Institutional Choice and Global Commerce*, Cambridge: Cambridge University Press.

Kahneman, D. and Tversky, A. (1979) 'Prospect theory: an analysis of decision under risk', *Econometrica*, 47(2): 263–91.

Kelemen, D. (2001) 'The limits of judicial power: trade–environment disputes in the GATT/WTO and the EU', *Comparative Political Studies*, 34(6): 622–50.

—— (2010) 'Globalizing European Union environmental policy', *Journal of European Public Policy*, 17(3): 335–49.

Kelemen, D. and Vogel, D. (2010) 'Trading places: the role of the United States and the European Union in international environmental politics', *Comparative Political Studies*, 43(4): 427–56.

Kennedy, K. (2008) 'The Doha Round negotiations on agricultural subsidies', *Denver Journal of International Law and Policy*, 36: 335–43.

Keohane, R. (1984) *After Hegemony: Cooperation and discord in the world political economy*, Princeton, NJ: Princeton University Press.

Kerremans, B. (2004) 'What went wrong in Cancun? A principal–agent view on the EU's rationale towards the Doha Development Round', *European Foreign Affairs Review*, 9(3): 363–93.

Kim, I. S. (2013) 'Political cleavages within industry: firm-level lobbying for trade liberalization', paper presented at the IPES 2013 conference: http://www.princeton.edu/~insong/research/exporters.pdf (accessed 1 March 2016).

Kim, M. (2008) 'Costly procedures: diverging effects of legalization in the GATT/ WTO dispute settlement process', *International Studies Quarterly*, 52(3): 657–86.

Kim, S. Y. (2015) 'Regionalization in search of regionalism: production networks and deep integration commitments in Asia's PTAs', in A. Dür and M. Elsig (eds) *The Purpose, Design, and Effects of Preferential Trade Agreements*, Cambridge: Cambridge University Press.

Kono, D. Y. (2009) 'Market structure, electoral institutions, and trade policy', *International Studies Quarterly*, 53(4): 885–906.

Koremenos, B., Lipson, C. and Snidal, D. (2001) 'The rational design of international institutions', *International Organization*, 55(4): 761–99.

Krugman, P. (1981) 'Intraindustry specialization and the gains from trade', *Journal of Political Economy*, 89: 959–73.

Kucik, J. and Pelc, K. (forthcoming) 'Measuring the cost of privacy: a look at the distributional effects of private bargaining', *British Journal of Political Science*.

Lamy, P. (2004), *The Emergence of Collective Preferences in International Trade: Implications for regulating globalisation*: available at http://trade. ec.europa.eu/doclib/docs/2004/september/tradoc_118929.pdf (accessed 1 March 2016).

Lanz, R. and Miroudot, S. (2011) *Intra-firm trade: patterns, determinants and policy implications*, OECD Trade Policy Papers, No.114, OECD Publishing.

Leech, B. L., Baumgartner, F., La Pira, T. M. and Semanko, N. A. (2005) 'Drawing lobbyists to Washington: government activity and the demand for advocacy', *Political Research Quarterly*, 58(1): 19–30.

Levy, J. S. (1992) 'An introduction to prospect theory', *Political Psychology*, 13(2): 171–86.

Levy, J. S. (1997) 'Prospect Theory, Rational Choice, and International Relations', *International Studies Quarterly*, 41 (1): 87–112.

— (2008) 'Case studies: type, designs and logics of inference', *Conflict Management and Peace Science*, 25(1): 1–18.

Lijphart, A. (1999) *Patterns of Democracy*, New Haven, CT: Yale University Press.

Lipson, C. (1982) 'The transformation of trade: the sources and effects of regime change', *International Organization*, 36(2): 417–55.

Lowery, D. and Gray, V. (1995) 'The population ecology of Gucci Gulch, or the natural regulation of interest group numbers in the American states', *American Journal of Political Science*, 39(1): 1–29.

— (1997) 'How some rules just don't matter: the regulation of lobbyists', *Public Choice*, 91(2): 139–47.

Lowery, D., Gray, V., Anderson, J. and Newmark, J. (2004) 'Collective action and the mobilization of institutions', *Journal of Politics*, 66(3): 684–705.

Magee, S., Brock W. and Young L. (1989) *Black Hole Tariff and Endogenous Policy Theory*, Cambridge: Cambridge University Press.

Mahoney, C. (2007) 'Networking vs allying: the decision of interest groups to join coalitions in the US and the EU', *Journal of European Public Policy*, 14(2): 366–83.

— (2007a) 'Lobbying success in the United States and the European Union', *Journal of Public Policy*, 27(2): 35–56

— (2008) *Brussels versus the Beltway: Advocacy in the United States and the European Union*, Washington DC: Georgetown University Press.

Mahoney, C. and Baumgartner, F. (2008) 'Converging perspectives on interest group research in Europe and America', *West European Politics*, 31(6): 1253–73.

Majone, G. (1996) *Regulating Europe*, London: Routledge.

Manger, M. (2009) *Investing in Protection: The politics of preferential trade agreements between North and South*, Cambridge: Cambridge University Press.

— (2012) 'Vertical trade specialization and the formation of North–South PTAs', *World Politics*, 64(4): 622–58.

Mansfield, E. D., Milner, H. V. and Pevehouse, J. C. (2007) 'Vetoing co-operation: the impact of veto players on preferential trading arrangements', *British Journal of Political Science*, 37(3): 403–32.

Martin, L. (1992) 'Interests, power, and multilateralism', *International Organization*, 46(4): 765–92.

— (1994) 'Heterogeneity, linkage and commons problems', *Journal of Theoretical Politics*, 6(4): 473–93.

Maskus, K. E. (2002) 'Regulatory standards in the WTO: comparing intellectual property rights with competition policy, environmental protection, and core labor standards', *World Trade Review*, 1(2): 135–52.

Mattli, W. and Woods, N. (2009) 'Introduction', in W. Mattli and N. Woods (eds) *The Politics of Global Regulation*, Princeton, NJ: Princeton University Press.

Mavroidis, P. C. (2012) *On compliance in the WTO: enforcement among unequal disputants*, Briefing Paper No. 4, CUTS International 2.

— (2015) 'Dealing with PTAs in the WTO: falling through the cracks between judicialization and legalization', *World Trade Review*, 14 (S1): 107–21.

Mavroidis, P. C., Cottier, T., Davey, W. J., Fox, E. M., Horlick, G. N., Komuro, N. and Rosenthal, D. E. (1998) 'Is the WTO dispute settlement mechanism responsive to the needs of the traders? Would a system of direct action by private parties yield better results?', *Journal of World Trade*, 32(2): 147–65.

Mayer, W. (1981) 'Theoretical considerations on negotiated tariff adjustments', *Oxford Economic Papers*, 33(1): 125–53.

McAdam, D., McCarthy, J. and Zald, M. (eds) (1996) *Comparative Perspectives on Social Movements: Political opportunities, mobilizing structures, and cultural framings*, Cambridge: Cambridge University Press.

McCall Smith, J. (2000) 'The Politics of Dispute Settlement Design: Explaining Legalism in Regional Trade Pacts', *International Organization* 54(1): 137–180.

Mény, Y. and Wright, V. (1987) *The Politics of Steel: Western Europe and the steel industry in the crisis years*, New York: Walter de Gruyter.

Meunier, S. (2005) *Trading Voices: The European Union in international commercial negotiations*, Princeton, NJ: Princeton University Press.

Meunier, S. and Nicolaïdis, K. (2006) 'The European Union as a conflicted trade power', *Journal of European Public Policy*, 13(6): 906–25.

Meyerson, C. C. (2003) *Domestic Politics and International relations in US–Japan Trade Policymaking: The GATT Uruguay Round agriculture negotiations*, Basingstoke: Palgrave Macmillan.

Milner, H. V. (1988) *Resisting Protectionism: Global industries and the politics of international trade*, Princeton, NJ: Princeton University Press.

— (1999) 'The political economy of international trade', *Annual Review of Political Science*, 2: 91–114.

Molyneux, C. T. G. (2001) *Domestic Structures and International Trade: The unfair trade instruments of the United States and the European Union*, Oxford and Portland, Oregon: Hart Publishing.

Moravcsik, A. (1993) 'Preferences and power in the European Community: a liberal intergovernmentalist approach', *Journal of Common Market Studies*, 31(4): 473–524.

— (1998) *The Choice for Europe: Social purpose and state power from Messina to Maastricht*, Ithaca, NY: Cornell University Press.

Moyer, H. W. (1993) 'The European Community and the GATT Uruguay Round: preserving the Common Agriculture Policy at all costs', in W. P. Avery (ed.) *World Agriculture and the GATT*, Boulder, CO: Lynne Rienner Publishers pp. 95–119.

Odell, J. (1993) 'International threats and internal politics: Brazil, the European Community, and the United States, 1985–1987', in P. Evans, H. Jacobson, and R. Putnam (eds) *Double-Edged Diplomacy: International bargaining and domestic politics*, Berkeley, CA: University of California Press, pp. 233–64.

OECD (2005) *OECD Review of Agricultural Policies: Brazil*, Paris: OECD Publishing.

Olson, M. (1965) *The Logic of Collective Action: Public goods and the theory of groups*, Cambridge, MA: Harvard University Press.

— (1982) *The Rise and Decline of Nations: Economic growth, stagflation, and social rigidities*, New Haven, CT: Yale University Press.

Oye, K. (1985) 'Explaining cooperation under anarchy: hypotheses and strategies', *World Politics*, 38(1): 1–24.

Paarlberg, R. (1997) 'Agricultural policy reform and the Uruguay Round: synergistic linkage in a two-level game?', *International Organization*, 51(3): 413–44.

Paemen, H. and Bensch, A (1995) *From the GATT to the WTO: The European community in the Uruguay Round*, Leuven: Leuven University Press.

Pauwelyn, J. (2010) 'The calculation and design of trade retaliation in context: what is the goal of suspending WTO obligations?', in C. Bown and J. Pauwelyn (eds) *The Law, Economics and Politics of Retaliation in WTO Dispute Settlement*, Cambridge: Cambridge University Press pp. 34–65.

Pelc, K. (2009) 'Seeking escape: the use of escape clauses in international trade agreements', *International Studies Quarterly*, 53(2): 349–68.

— (2010) 'Eluding efficiency: why do we not see more efficient breach at the WTO?', *World Trade Review*, 9(4): 629–42.

Poletti, A. (2010) 'Drowning protection in the multilateral bath: WTO judicialisation and European agriculture in the Doha Round', *British Journal of Politics and International Relations*, 12(4): 615–33.

— (2011) 'WTO judicialisation and preference convergence in EU trade policy: making the agent's life easier', *Journal of European Public Policy*, 18(3): 361–82.

—   (2012) *The European Union and Multilateral Trade Governance: The politics of the Doha Round*, London, Routledge.

Poletti, A. and De Bièvre, D. (2014) 'On the effects of the design of international institutions: judicialization and cooperation in the WTO', *Rivista Italiana di Scienza Politica / Italian Political Science Review*, 2014(1): 3–28.

—   (2014) 'Political mobilization, veto players, and WTO litigation: explaining European Union responses in trade disputes', *Journal of European Public Policy*, 21(8): 1181–98.

—   (2015) 'Judicial politics in international trade relations: an introduction', *World Trade Review*, 14 (S1): 1–21.

Poletti, A. and Sicurelli, D. (2012) 'The European Union as a promoter of environmental rules in the Doha Round', *West European Politics*, 35(4): 911–32.

—   (2015) 'The European Union, preferential trade agreements, and the international regulation of sustainable biofuels', *Journal of Common Market Studies*, available at DOI: 10.1111/jcms.12293.

Poletti, A., De Bièvre, D. and Chatagnier, T. (2015) 'Cooperation in the shadow of WTO law: why litigate when you can negotiate', *World Trade Review*, 14(S1): 33–58.

Poletti, A., De Bièvre, D. and Hanegraaff, M. (2016) 'WTO judicial politics and EU trade policy: business associations as vessels of special interest?', *The British Journal of Politics & International Relations* (in press).

Pollack, M. and Shaffer, G. (2009) *When Cooperation Fails: The international law and politics of genetically modified foods*, New York: Oxford University Press.

Porterfield, M. (2006) 'US farm subsidies and the expiration of the peace clause', *University of Pennsylvania Journal of International Economic Law*, 27(4): 1002–42.

Posner, E. A. and Yoo, J. (2005) 'Judicial independence in international tribunals', *California Law Review*, 93(1): 1–74.

Princen, S. (2002) *EU Regulation and Transatlantic Trade*, The Hague: Kluwer Law International.

Princen, S. and Kerremans, B. (2008) 'Opportunity structures in the EU multi-level system', *West European Politics*, 31(6): 1129–41.

Prusa, T. and Vermulst, E. (2011) 'United States – continued existence and application of zeroing methodology: the end of zeroing?', *World Trade Review*, 10(1): 45–61.

Putnam, R. (1988) 'Diplomacy and domestic politics: the logic of two-level games', *International Organization*, 42(3): 427–60.

Quick, R. (2007) 'Business in economic diplomacy', in N. N. Bayne and S. Woolcock (eds) *The New Economic Diplomacy: Decision-making and negotiation in international economic relations*, Aldershot: Ashgate pp. 105–21.

Raghavan, C. (2001) *Agri-Talks Mark Time: For end of peace clause or new Round?* Geneva, 25 July: http://www.twn.my/title/agri.htm (accessed 1 March 2016).

Raustiala, K. (1997) 'Domestic institutions and international regulatory cooperation: comparative responses to the convention on biological biodiversity', *World Politics*, 49(4): 482–509.

Raustiala, K. and Victor, D. (2004) 'The regime complex for plant genetic resources', *International Organization*, 58(2): 277–309.

Reinhardt, E. (2001) 'Adjudication without Enforcement in GATT Disputes', *Journal of Conflict Resolution*, 45 (2): 174–195.

Rickard, S. (2010) 'Democratic differences: electoral institutions and compliance with GATT/WTO agreements', *European Journal of International Relations*, 16(4): 711–29.

— (2012) 'A non-tariff protectionist bias in majoritarian politics: government subsidies and electoral institutions', *International Studies Quarterly*, 56(4): 777–85.

Rogowski, R. (1987) 'Trade and the variety of democratic institutions', *International Organization*, 41(2): 203–23.

— (1989) *Commerce and Coalitions: How trade affects domestic alignments*, Princeton, NJ: Princeton University Press.

Rosendorff, P. (2005) 'Stability and rigidity: politics and the design of the WTO's dispute resolution procedure', *American Political Science Review*, 99(3): 389–400.

Rosendorff, P. and Milner, H. V. (2001) 'The optimal design of international trade institutions: uncertainty and escape', *International Organization*, 55(4): 829–57.

Rydelski, M. and Zonnekeyn, G. (1997) 'The EC trade barriers regulation – the EC's move towards a more aggressive market access strategy', *Journal of World Trade*, 31(5): 147–66.

Scharpf, F. (1988) 'The joint-decision trap: lessons from German federalism and European integration', *Public Administration*, 66(3): 239–78.

Schattsneider, E. (1935) *Politics, Pressure and the Tariff*, New York: Prentice Hall.

Schnepf, R. (2011) *Brazil's WTO case against the US cotton program*, Washington DC: Congressional Research Service, Report RL32571,

Schnepf, R. and Womach, J. (2007) *Potential challenges to US farm subsidies in the WTO*, Washington DC: Congressional Research Service Report to Congress.

Schwartz, W. F. and Sykes, A. O. (2002) 'The economic structure of renegotiations and dispute resolution in the World Trade Organization', *Journal of Legal Studies*, 31: 179–204

Sebenius, J. K. (1983) 'Negotiation arithmetic: adding and subtracting issues and parties', *International Organization*, 37(2): 281–316.

Sell, S. K. (2003) *Private Power, Public Law: The globalization of intellectual property rights*, Cambridge: Cambridge University Press.

Shaffer, G. (2001) 'The blurring of the intergovernmental: Public–private partnerships in the bringing of US and EC trade claims', in M. Pollack and G. Shaffer (eds) *Transatlantic Governance in the Global Economy*, Lanham, MD: Rowman & Littlefield.

— (2003) *Defending Interests: Public–private partnerships in WTO Litigation*, Washington DC: Brookings Institution Press.

— (2006) 'What's new in EU trade dispute settlement? Judicialization, public–private networks, and the WTO legal order', *Journal of European Public Policy*, 13(6): 832–50.

Shaffer, G. C. and Melendez-Ortiz, R. (2010) *Dispute Settlement at the WTO: The Developing countries experience*, Cambridge: Cambridge University Press.

Shapiro, M. and Stone Sweet, A. (2002) *On Law, Politics and Judicialization*, Oxford: Oxford University Press.

Skogstad, G. (2003) 'Legitimacy and/or policy effectiveness? Network governance and GMO regulation in the European Union', *Journal of European Public Policy*, 10(3): 321–38.

Snidal, D. (1985) 'Coordination versus prisoners' dilemma: implications for international cooperation and regimes', *American Political Science Review*, 79(4): 923–42.

Staiger, R. (1995) 'International rules and institutions for trade policy', in G. Grossman and K. Rogoff (eds) *Handbook of International Econmics*, Amsterdam: North Holland, pp. 1497–551.

Stasavage, D. (2004) 'Open Door or Closed Door? Transparency in Domestic and International Bargaining', *International Organization*, 58(4): 667–704.

Steinberg, R. (2002) 'In the shadow of law or power? Consensus-based bargaining and outcomes in the GATT/WTO', *International Organization*, 56(2): 339–74.

Steinberg, R. and Josling, T. (2003) 'When the peace ends: the vulnerability of EC and US agricultural subsidies to WTO legal challenge', *Journal of International Economic Law*, 6(2): 369–417.

Stewart, T. P. (1993) *The GATT Uruguay Round: A negotiating history (1986–1992)*, Den Haag: Kluwer Law International.

Stone Sweet, A. (1997) 'The New GATT: Dispute resolution and the judicialisation of the trade regime', in M. L. Volcansek (ed) *Law Above Nations: Supranational courts and the legalization of politics*, Gainesville, FL: University Press of Florida pp. 118–41.

— (1999) 'Judicialization and the construction of governance', *Comparative Political Studies*, 32(2): 147–84.

Sumner, A. D. (2005) 'Boxed in: conflicts between US farm policies and WTO obligations', *Trade Policy Analysis 32*, Washington DC: Cato Institute.

Swinbank, A. (1999) 'EU agriculture, Agenda 2000 and the WTO commitments', *The World Economy*, 22(1): 42–54.

Swinnen, J. (2008) *The Perfect Storm: The political economy of the Fischler reforms of the Common Agricultural Policy*, Brussels: Centre for European Policy Studies.

Tallberg, J. and McCall Smith, J. (2014) 'Dispute settlement in world politics: states, supranational prosecutors, and compliance', *European Journal of International Relations*, 20(1): 118–44.

Tallberg, J., Sommerer, T., Squatrito, T. and Jonsson, C. (2014) 'Explaining the transnational design of international organizations, *International Organization*, 68(4): 741–74.

Tangermann, S. (1999) 'Europe's agricultural policies and the Millennium Round', *The World Economy*, 22(9): 1155–78.

Tassy, A. (1997) *Enforcement of International Trade Rules: The European complaint procedure*, Copenhagen: Copenhagen Business School.

Third World Network (2010) *Members discuss implementation of TRIPS 'Para 6' solution*. TWN Info Service on WTO and Trade Issues, 22 February 2010: http://www.twnside.org.sg/title2/wto.info/2010/twninfo100212.htm (accessed 10 September 2012).

Thompson, A. (2009) 'The rational enforcement of international law: solving the sanctioners' dilemma', *International Theory*, 1(2): 307–21.

Tiberghien, Y. (2009) 'Competitive governance and the quest for legitimacy in the EU: the battle over the regulation of GMOs since the mid-1990s', *Journal of European Integration*, 31 (3): 389–407.

Tsebelis, G. (2002) *Veto Players: How political institutions work*, Princeton, NJ: Princeton University Press.

UNCTAD-ICTSD (2005) *Resource Book on TRIPs and Development*, Cambridge: Cambridge University Press.

UNICE (2000) *UNICE strategy on services negotiations*, speech by Guide Vaucleroy at the ESF Conference, the GATS 2000 negotiations, 27 November.

— (2001) *Why launch a new round of multilateral trade negotiations?* address by Baron Georges Jacobs, President of UNICE, at the conference organised by "Confrontations", 27 September.

— (2003) Letter from Philippe de Buck to Commissioner Lamy on the European Commission consultations with civil society on services negotiations at the WTO, 30 January.

USTR (2005) 'US proposal for bold reform in global agricultural trade' *Doha development agenda policy brief*, Washington DC: Office of the United States Trade Representative.

— *US, Brazil agree on framework regarding WTO cotton dispute*, Washington, DC: Office of the United States Trade Representative.

Van den Hoven, A. (2002) 'Interest group influence on trade policy in a multilevel polity: analysing the EU position at the Doha WTO ministerial conference', *EUI Working Papers* 2002/67.

— (2004) 'Assuming leadership in multilateral economic institutions: the EU's development round discourse and strategy', *West European Politics*, 27(2): 256–83.

Verdier, D. (1994) *Democracy and International Trade: Britain, France and the United States, 1860–1990*, Princeton, NJ: Princeton University Press.

— (1998) 'Democratic convergence and free trade', *International Studies Quarterly*, 42(1): 1–24.

Vermulst, E. and Ikenson, D. (2007) 'Zeroing under the WTO anti-dumping agreement: where do we stand?', *Global Trade and Customs Journal*, 2(6): 231–42.

Vogel, D. (1995) *Trading Up: Consumer and environmental regulation in the global economy*, Cambridge, MA: Harvard University Press.

Walter, A. (2001) 'Unravelling the Faustian bargain: non-state actors and the multilateral agreement on investment', in D. Josselin and W. Wallace (eds) *Non-state Actors in World Politics*, Houndmills: Palgrave, pp. 150–68.

Wilson, J. Q. (1973) *Political Organizations*, New York: Basic Books.

Wissen, M. (2003) 'TRIPs, TRIPs-plus und WIPO. Konflikte um die Eigentumsrechte an genetischen Ressourcen'. in U. Brand and C. Görg *Postfordistische Naturverhältnisse. Konflikte um genetische Ressourcen und die Internationalisierung des Staates*, Münster: Verlag Westfälisches Dampfboot 128–55.

Woll, C. (2006) *Trade Policy Lobbying in the European Union: Who captures whom?*, MIfG Working Paper 06/7, October 2006, Köln: Max-Institut für Gesellschaftsforschung: http://www.mpifg.de/pu/workpap/wp06-7/wp06-7.html (accessed 1 March 2016).

Woll, C. (2006a) 'Lobbying in the European Union: from sui generis to a comparative perspective', *Journal of European Public Policy*, 13(3): 456–70.

— (2008) *Firm Interests: How governments shape business lobbying on global trade*, Ithaca, NY: Cornell University Press.

— (2012) 'The brash and the soft-spoken: lobbying styles in a transatlantic comparison', *Interest Groups and Advocacy*, 1(2): 193–214.

Woll, C. and Artigas, A. (2007) 'When trade liberalization turns into regulatory reform: The impact on business–government relations in international trade politics', *Regulation and Governance*, 1(2): 121–38.

Woolcock, S. (2005) 'European Union trade policy: domestic institutions and systemic factors', in D. Kelly and W. Grant (eds) *The Politics of International Trade in the Twenty-first Century: Actors, issues and regional dynamics*, Basingstoke: Palgrave, pp. 234–52.

— (2010) *The Treaty of Lisbon and the European Union as an Actor in International Trade*, ECIPE Working Paper, No. 1/2010, Brussels: European Centre for International Political Economy.

WTO (1995) *The Legal Texts: The results of the Uruguay Round of multilateral trade negotiations*, Cambridge: Cambridge University Press.

— (2000) *Resolving the relationship between WTO rules and MEAs.* Submission by the European Community, WT/CTE/W/170.

— (2001) *Ministerial declaration,* WT/MIN(01)/DEC/1, 20 November.

— (2002) *European Communities – export subsidies on sugar – request for consultations by Brazil,* WT/DS266/1.

— (2002a) *United States – subsidies on upland cotton – request for consultations by Brazil,* WT/DS267/1.

WTO (2003) *A proposal for modalities in the WTO agriculture negotiations, specific drafting input by the EC,* JOB(03)/12, 5 February. http://trade.ec.europa.eu/doclib/html/111446.htm

WTO (2003a) *Specific Drafting Input by the EC,* JOB(03)/12.

— (2004) *European Communities – export subsidies on sugar – complaint by Brazil – report of the panel,* WT/DS266/R.

— (2004a) *Decision adopted by the General Council,* WT/L/579.

— (2004b) *United States – subsidies on upland cotton – complaint by Brazil – report of the panel,* WT/DS267/R.

— (2004c) *Handbook on the WTO Dispute Settlement System,* Cambridge: Cambridge University Press.

— (2005) *European Communities– export subsidies on sugar – AB-2005-2 – report of the appellate body,* WT/DS283/AB/R.

— (2005a) *United States – subsidies on upland cotton – AB-2004-5 – report of the appellate body,* WT/DS267/AB/R.

— (2005b) *Doha work programme – draft ministerial declaration,* WT/MIN(05)/W/3/Rev.2. Available at: https://www.wto.org/english/thewto_e/minist.../min05.../final_text_e.htm

— (2008) *Revised draft modalities for agriculture,* TN/AG/W/4/Rev.4.

— (2009) *WTO disputes reach 400 mark,* Press Release N. 578, 6 November. (accessed 1 March 2016).

— (2012) *World Trade Report 2012,* Geneva: WTO Publications.

WWF (1999) *WWF urges urgent WTO reform,* 11 March: http://wwf.panda.org/wwf_news/?1923/WWF-Urges-Urgent-WTO-Reform (last accessed 1 March 2016).

— (2001) *Can the World Trade Organization live up to the challenges of a globalizing world?,* Position statement, October.

Young, A. (2003) 'Political transfer and trading up? Transatlantic trade in genetically modified food and US politics', *World Politics,* 55: 457–84.

— (2004) 'The incidental fortress: the single market and world trade', *Journal of Common Market Studies,* 2(2): 393–414.

Young, A. and Peterson, J. (2006) 'The EU and the new trade politics', *Journal of European Public Policy,* 13(6): 795–814.

— (2014) *Parochial Global Europe: 21st Century Trade Politics,* Oxford: Oxford University Press.

Zangl, B. (2008) 'Judicialization matters! A comparison of dispute settlement under GATT and the WTO', *International Studies Quarterly*, 52(4): 825–54.

Zangl, B., Helmedach, A., Mondré, A., Kocks, A., Beubauer, G. and Blome, K. (2012) 'Between law and politics: explaining international dispute settlement behavior', *European Journal of International Relations*, 18(2): 369–401.

Zerbe, N. (2007) 'Contesting privatization: NGOs and farmers' rights in the African model law', *Global Environmental Politics*, 7(1): 97–119.

Index

italics – material in Figures and Tables

agricultural trade
  Doha Rounds (WTO) on 69, 81, 82,
    83, 84, 113
  EU-US negotiations 9, 69, 81, 84
  export subsidies dispute 81, 82–5
    Cairns Group position 83, 85 n.9
    EU additional concessions in
      85–6
    EU legal vulnerability in 82–3
    peace clause expiry, effect of 84,
      85
    see also under Brazil; European
      Union
  G20 group, influence in 84–5, 86
  genetic resources regulation in
    59–62
    International Treaty (IT/PGRFA
      2001) 62
  Uruguay Round Agreement
    (URAA) 69, 81–2, 83, 87
    impact of 81
    'peace clause' in 81–2, 83, 84,
      87, 96
  see also biotechnology; under
    Brazil
antidumping rules 81, 93–5, 111, 125,
  126–7
  EUROFER, role in 126–7
  WTO disputes 81, 93–5, 109 n.5,
    127
Argentina 127
Australia 83

biotechnology 59–62, 93
  Convention on Biological Diversity
    (CBD) 58, 60, 61, 62
  GATT Uruguay Round 60–1
  patents safeguards in 59–62

and developing countries 59–60,
    61, 62
  FAO International Undertaking
    60, 61, 62
  for genetic resources 58, 59–62
  harmonisation in 59, 62
  International Treaty (2001) 62
  UPOV Convention (1961) 58, 60,
    61
    1991 revision of 60
  WTO judicialisation, effectiveness
    of 59, 61, 62
  Cartagena Protocol 62
  Doha Round review 61
  and TRIPS agreement 61–2
  see also intellectual property rights
    (IPR)
Brazil
  agricultural trade negotiations 9, 41,
    81, 82–7, 88–90, 93, 96
    bargaining power in 84, 85–7,
      89–90, 96
    and EU subsidies challenge 82–7
    US cotton subsidies challenge
      87–8, 89–90, 93
    WTO DSM use in 84, 86, 87, 90
  economic power of 4, 97
  and steel trade policy 127
BusinessEurope (UNICE) 112

Camargo, P. 88
CEFIC (chemical association) 111,
  112, 113, 124–5
  EU role of 124
  trade negotiations, role in 124
  WTO judicialisation, effect on 124
chemical industry 111, 112, 124–5
  in EU 119, 124–5